Rescaling the state

DEVOLUTION series
series editor Charlie Jeffery

Devolution has established new political institutions in Scotland, Wales, Northern Ireland, London and the other English regions since 1997. These devolution reforms have far-reaching implications for the politics, policy and society of the UK. Radical institutional change, combined with a fuller capacity to express the UK's distinctive territorial identities, is reshaping the way the UK is governed and opening up new directions of public policy. These are the biggest changes to UK politics for at least 150 years.

The *Devolution* series brings together the best research in the UK on devolution and its implications. It draws together the best analysis from the Economic and Social Research Council's research programme on Devolution and Constitutional Change. The series has three central themes, all of which are vital components in understanding the changes devolution has set in train.

1 **Delivering public policy after devolution: diverging from Westminster**: Does devolution result in the provision of different standards of public service in health or education, or in widening economic disparities from one part of the UK to another? If so, does it matter?

2 **The political institutions of devolution**: How well do the new devolved institutions work? How effectively are devolved and UK-level matters coordinated? How have political organisations which have traditionally operated UK-wide – political parties, interest groups – responded to multi-level politics?

3 **Public attitudes, devolution and national identity**: How do people in different parts of the UK assess the performance of the new devolved institutions? Do people identify themselves differently as a result of devolution? Does a common sense of Britishness still unite people from different parts of the UK?

already published

Devolution and constitutional change in Northern Ireland
Paul Carmichael, Colin Knox and Bob Osborne (eds)

Beyond devolution and decentralisation
Alistair Cole

Between two Unions
Europeanisation and Scottish devolution
Paolo Dardanelli

Territorial politics and health policy
UK health policy in comparative perspective
Scott L. Greer

The English Question
Robert Hazell

Using Europe: territorial strategies in a multi-level system
Eve Hepburn

Devolution and electoral politics
Dan Hough and Charlie Jeffery (eds)

Devolution and the governance of Northern Ireland
Colin Knox

The Northern Veto
Mark Sandford (ed.)

Towards a regional political class?
Professional politicians and regional institutions in Catalonia and Scotland
Klaus Stolz

Debating nationhood and government in Britain, 1885–1939
Perspectives from the 'four nations'
Duncan Tanner, Chris Williams, Wil Griffith and Andrew Edwards (eds)

Devolution and power in the United Kingdom
Alan Trench

Rescaling the state

Devolution and the geographies of economic governance

Mark Goodwin, Martin Jones and Rhys Jones

Manchester University Press

Copyright © Manchester University Press 2012

While copyright in the volume as a whole is vested in Manchester University Press, copyright in individual chapters belongs to their respective authors, and no chapter may be reproduced wholly or in part without the express permission in writing of both author and publisher.

Published by Manchester University Press
Altrincham Street, Manchester M1 7JA, UK
www.manchesteruniversitypress.co.uk

British Library Cataloguing-in-Publication Data is available

ISBN 978 0 7190 7637 4 *hardback*
ISBN 978 1 5261 1699 4 *paperback*

First published by Manchester University Press in hardback 2012

This edition first published 2017

The publisher has no responsibility for the persistence or accuracy of URLs for any external or third-party internet websites referred to in this book, and does not guarantee that any content on such websites is, or will remain, accurate or appropriate.

Printed by CPI Group (UK) Ltd, Croydon CR0 4YY

Contents

List of figures and maps	*page* vii
Preface to the first edition	ix
Preface to the paperback edition	xi
Acknowledgements	xix
List of abbreviations	xxi

1	Introduction: Devolution and the geographies of economic governance	1
2	The theoretical challenge of devolution and constitutional change	12
3	New politics/new institutions/new strategies	26
4	Territories and scales of economic governance	65
5	Peopling a devolved UK state	88
6	The political geographies of filling in: the case of Northern Ireland	119
7	Conclusions: devolution in retrospect	148
	References	162
	Index	181

Figures and maps

Figures

3.1 Structures of economic governance in Northern Ireland in 2005	*page* 35
3.2 Structures of economic governance in Wales in 2005	41
3.3 Structures of economic governance in Scotland in 2005	45
3.4 Structures of economic governance in England in 2005	50
4.1 EMRA's Integrated Regional Strategy	79

Maps

4.1 Map of English RDAa	75
5.1 Wales's four regions in 2005	104

Preface to the first edition

This book has emerged out of an eighteen-month project that was funded as part of the ESRC's Devolution and Constitutional Change Research Programme. Our aim in the project was to examine the geographies of economic governance in each of the four territories of the UK – England, Scotland, Wales and Northern Ireland – and the way in which these had changed as a result of the process of devolution. Out of thirty-five projects that were funded as part of the Programme, ours was the only one that was solely directed by geographers and we sought to use this geographical perspective as a way of understanding the different complexions of the devolution settlement in each of the four territories. The notion of economic governance seemed a particularly apposite theme to study in this respect. At one level, economic development had been touted as one of the key drivers for the whole devolution process, since regions and territories at scales smaller than the nation state were viewed as being the most appropriate political units with which to develop and embed economies. At the same time, economic development was one of the key policy areas that had been devolved to each of the four territories of the UK and, as such, it was a perfect test case to examine the differential impact of devolution in the different territories. Two research assistants were employed for eighteen months and the official period of data collection for the project took place between 2001 and 2003. A vast amount of documentary research was undertaken, as well as ninety-nine interviews with key figures in economic governance in each of the four territories. Additional documentary data was also collected in the period after 2003.

What follows in the pages of the book is a somewhat retrospective view of devolution and economic governance in the UK. We believe that this approach possesses at least two significant advantages. First, the period that we studied most closely – the period between 1999 and approximately 2006 – represesented in many ways the period of most intensive activity with regard to the formation of new organisations of economic governance. It was during this period, for instance, that Regional Development Agencies were created in England, Education and Learning Wales was formed and disbanded in Wales, Local Economic Forums were created in Scotland, and Invest Northern Ireland and the Economic Development Forum were formed in Northern Ireland. The period between 2005/6 and 2010 was far more stable in terms of the development or reorganisation of organisations of economic governance within each of the four territories. Admittedly, circumstances have changed somewhat recently as a result of the economic downturn and its impacts on public spending. Indeed, we may now be witnessing a second period in which organisations of economic governance are being reformed or discontinued, largely on cost grounds. This is a theme that we take up further in the conclusion to the book where we seek to bring up to date some of the empirical changes to forms of economic governance in each of the UK territories since 2007.

The second advantage that derives from having what might be termed a historico-political view of devolution is that it has enabled us to develop a far more measured interpretation of the significance of some of the key changes that took place to organisations of economic governance in the period between 1999 and 2006. It is only by looking back – with some measure of distance – that one is able to appreciate what were, in fact, the key changes to forms of economic governance and what turned out to be, in many ways, minor distractions in the overall patterns of economic governance in the four territories. Rather than writing in the midst of the 'white heat' of devolution, we have deliberately sought to take stock of the devolution project over the longer term. In doing so, we believe that we have been able to provide a comprehensive and detailed account of economic governance in the four territories, along with the impact that these new forms of economic governance have had on the devolution project as a whole.

Preface to the paperback edition

The 'devolution revolution' and new geographies of 'filling-in'

We welcome the 2017 paperback publication of *Rescaling the state: Devolution and the geographies of economic governance*. The original edition was published in September 2012, and this preface to the new paperback edition offers a timely opportunity to reflect on the strengths, relevance and refinement of our original conceptual arguments, and also to take stock of how these can be used to read more recent devo-developments, given that our fieldwork was conducted during the Labour administration (1997–2010) and the early years of the Conservative–Liberal Democrat coalition that followed (specifically 2010–2011).

Rescaling the state was written by three political geographers to capture the new institutional geographies of devolution and state restructuring that were occurring in the UK as part of, perhaps, as we said at the time, the biggest changes to the UK state since the Acts of Union. Focusing on economic governance, i.e. the governance of economic development and that interface between state intervention and the economy, we examined the changes taking place around the Scottish Parliament, elected Assemblies for Wales, Northern Ireland and London, and the Regional Development Agencies within England's regions. We offered an institutional-materialist lens through which to view this process, and extended Bob Jessop's strategic–relational approach to the state by arguing that it is no longer enough simply to refer to a multivariate 'hollowing-out' of the nation state, as Jessop and others had done by focusing on government and governance in an era of intense economic and political restructuring. Bringing into centre-stage a sharp analytical focus on geographical scales of governance, *Rescaling the state* suggested that devolution represented, for us at that time, a geographically uneven 'filling-in' of the state's institutional and scalar matrix, which was creating uneven capacities to act and an increasingly crowded institutional landscape, with overlapping roles, powers and responsibilities.

This theoretical extension of Jessop was well received by our geography and social science peers, who sought to engage with the nuances of our argument in the papers we published and in *Rescaling the state*. It is fair to say that we were indeed correct to go down this conceptual path, and those who have engaged with it have offered wider applications of 'filling-in'. Shaw and Mackinnon, for instance, applied a filling-in perspective to transport policy and suggested a need to think less in institutional-organizational terms and more relationally about scale to capture the stretched-out, diverse forms of state agency which they were witnessing in Scotland at the time. We appreciate this perspective, and in fact Chapter 7 of *Rescaling the state* acknowledges the need to bring those relational literatures into Jessop's and our thinking.

Jessop too has acknowledged the importance of filling-in, with his turn in recent years towards notions of 'collibration' (after the work of Dunsire) and the development and extension of regulation theory and cultural political economy to capture concerns with 'multispatial metagovernance'. By engaging with the critiques of multilevel governance, Jessop's recent work highlights the repeated efforts to improve the spatial balancing and coordination of governance arrangements, especially when they generate policy failures or prove inadequate in the face of crises – and there have been numerous failures and crises of economic governance since we wrote *Rescaling the state*. Like Shaw and Mackinnon, Jessop expresses a desire to think relationally and draws on other dimensions of spatiality, outside of scalar perspectives, to examine the sites of government and governance. Mobilizing a territory, place, scale, network (TPSN) schema to widen the envelope of filling-in, Jessop concurs that these socio-spatial relations of filling-in are objects and means of government and governance. They are not just sites where these practices occur. This necessitates empirical research on what Jessop calls 'spatio-temporal fixes' – attempts to build relative stability for economic competitiveness and social cohesion. We maintain that searches for stability are being regressively driven by the governance failures of previous rounds of state intervention, as opposed to progressive interventions to tackle new social cohesion and economic competiveness policy challenges emerging in the context of globalisation.

Following this, and by drawing on a mixture of mainly qualitative research strategies on the dynamics of devolution and those processes behind big events, *Rescaling the state* also attempted to make an original empirical intervention into economic governance studies. We concluded by questioning whether the new economic development institutions had the capacity to tackle the emerging economic tensions within and between different parts of the UK. Reflecting in 2017 on the changing institutional geographies of the British state, we would suggest that the capacity of such institutions has been weakened and that geographical tensions have increased. Devolution is not a coherent and relatively stable institutional fix that supports the neoliberal growth project, but instead, like other neoliberalisation projects, it should be seen as a state spatial strategy that is best regarded as mutable and involving variegated responses and uneven geographical outcomes. We would argue that since the writing of *Rescaling the state*, these variegated responses and their uneven geographical outcomes have increased. A 'Disunited Kingdom' is certainly in the making, and the discourse of the past year has been about spatial rebalancing, inclusive growth and the need to marry economic agglomeration with a more social devolution.

The notion of 'devolution revolution' is not ours: it comes from the Conservative government's 2016 Communities and Local Government Committee, which asserted that such a 'revolution' was evidenced by the transferring of opportunities and powers to localities across England through a series of formal 'devolution deals'. Although these are at an early stage and need time to bed in, as we write there are a set of complex institution-building projects and negotiations in train, which, we would argue, increasingly point to the relevance of filling-in as a means of looking at devolution.

The localities and regions of England have witnessed further rounds of hollowing-out and filling-in since we last conducted our empirical research. In 2012 the Local Enterprise Partnerships (LEPs) were embryonic and were not established players in local and regional economic development. Since then, LEPs have become an established element of England's institutional map and a central part of the Northern Powerhouse and Midlands Engine spatial imaginaries. However, LEP capacities to act have been weak on two counts.

First, like many similar projects before them, LEPs have struggled with issues of accountability, standing outside of parliamentary scrutiny procedures and receiving critiques from the National Audit Office and others. The partial solution to this has been to legislate for and implement Combined Authorities, where LEP reporting and strategic structures are combined with certain aspects of local government to provide a democracy segue. In recent years, LEPs and Combined Authorities have been recipients of 'city deals' and 'devolution deals', contingent on the election of metro mayors, but this has taken place without public consultation and has lacked rigour as to process. The November 2016 judicial review challenge made in the High Court by Derbyshire County Council against Barnsley, Doncaster and Sheffield Combined Authority, which ruled that their citizens were not properly consulted about whether to opt for full constituent status of the Sheffield City Region, is indicative of the Northern Powerhouse plans being somewhat ad hoc, ill-devised and lacking the consent of the people they affect.

Secondly, and indicative of the need to act strategically and think spatially (in the context of territories, places, scales and networks), LEPs in some localities have formed regional groupings, akin to the geographies of previous RDA boundaries, so as to be able to access resources for and be key players in spatial framework debates (planning, transport and housing). However, all this is occurring in the context of austerity: local authorities are at the sharp end of austerity-driven expenditure cuts, and are managing these as well as providing a critical voice in relation to increasing poverty and social inequalities. This said, metro mayors have been elected for six city-regions (Cambridgeshire and Peterborough, Greater Manchester, Liverpool, Tees Valley, West of England, and the West Midlands) and granted a 30-year investment fund.

Changes have also taken place in Wales since 2012, and in many respects Wales is moving much closer to England in adopting neoliberal models of economic agglomeration through city-region building endeavours. For Wales, a city-region approach is seen as improving the planning system, improving connectivity and driving investment through a stronger and more visible offering from an agglomerated wider region. Since we wrote *Rescaling the state*, two distinctive city-region projects have been implemented – South-East Wales (described initially as Cardiff for 'external promotion purposes', to distinguish Cardiff from neighbouring Newport, and later renamed the 'Cardiff Capital Region' to acknowledge both capital city status and the stretched-out variegated geography of city-region building) and Swansea Bay City Region – with support given to strengthening the cross-border Mersey–Dee Alliance, with the proviso that all this has to be about creating urban engines and powerhouses of growth by harnessing the benefits of transport, housing, inward investment and funding opportunities. As we noted previously, city-region boundaries in turn reflect fuzzy economic reality rather than political or administrative boundaries, which provides a challenge for engagement and meaningful collaboration across local authorities, as well as ceding power, funding and decision-making to a more regional level. These projects are experiencing problems exactly along these spatial dimensions of filling-in. The granting of a city deal to Cardiff in 2016, offered through the Whitehall state apparatus, cuts across and brings into question the role of the Cardiff City Region Transformation Board, which is a Welsh government-appointed entity. This raises the question of whose devolution is at work, a question which is echoed in the Welsh valleys, where issues regarding inclusive growth are being raised and the limits of improved connectivity via the South Wales Metro project are germane. Given the granting of a city deal also to Swansea in 2017, it raises the question too of the applicability of the 'filling-in' city-region model across non-urban parts of Wales, mirroring criticisms regarding the difficulty of extending the metro mayor model of devolution to non-conurbation areas of England.

We maintain the position that we adopted previously: changes to the forms of economic governance in the other two UK territories have certainly not been as far-reaching as those that are taking place in England and Wales. Scottish Enterprise and Highlands and Islands Enterprise remain the two strategic economic development bodies in Scotland (uniformly called 'enterprise bodies'), and celebrated their 25th birthdays in 2016. In recent years, to acknowledge the strategic importance of investing in and creating the (non-local) conditions for the knowledge-based economy, as we predicted in the original edition of *Rescaling the state*, the skills function of Scottish Enterprise has been moved out of the organization to Skills Development Scotland. The current emphasis here is on work-based learning and apprenticeships. Likewise, the functions of the Local Economic Forums (LEFs) have been fully consolidated into local authority structures and the business of economic development strategies therein. Set within the context of National Performance Frameworks (NPFs), this represents a filling-in which has moved more towards government than governance, and stands in stark contrast to the perpetual waves of institutional tinkering (TECs, LSCs, SSCs, LEPs) in similar sectors in England. In contrast to England, where the policing roles of the National Audit Office and select committees reveal governance tensions, the enterprise bodies' boards and chief executives (the accountable officers) regularly meet the minister to discuss issues such as performance and setting priorities. The local office structures for the Local Enterprise Companies (LECs) and LEFs also remain in some areas, and are used by local authorities to connect with businesses, which is indicative of the adaptability of state projects to different modes of intervention.

In Northern Ireland, the power-sharing agreement between the nationalist and unionist communities remains critical to the functioning of the Assembly. INI, now called Invest NI, remains as Northern Ireland's regional business development agency, with the remit of growing local economies by helping new and existing businesses to compete internationally and by attracting new investment to Northern Ireland. DETINI and DEL no longer exist, and Invest NI is now part of the Department for the Economy. We would argue that this singular nomenclature represents a consolidated form of filling-in, which is also evident across all the nine agencies of the Northern Irish Executive. In *Rescaling the state* we argued that such a 'Department of the Economy' would create a more holistic way of approaching economic development than has been achieved to date. The Department for the Economy's documentation seems to offer a more focused and pointed signal towards providing strong government support for business by effectively delivering the government's economic development strategies. Austerity, however, is biting deep. Delayed welfare reforms are being introduced in 2017 and the finance minister has unveiled a budget that aims to reduce public-sector employment by 20,000. Reducing Northern Ireland's dependence on the state is a bigger challenge, but with low costs and, unlike the rest of Britain, a land border with the eurozone, there are opportunities to attract more foreign investment: 50 new foreign direct investment projects were secured in 2014. The latest economic strategy, Economy 2030, is an ambitious, long-term vision to transform Northern Ireland into a globally competitive economy that works for everyone.

Despite this relative institutional stability of economic governance, far-reaching changes have been taking place with respect to the government dimensions of these two territories, which in the context of a permanent level of advantage and potential increases in devolution powers will certainly shift the geographies of economic development and capacities to act. The wider national, UK-wide and indeed international operation of economic governance matters and we must not lose sight of this in our studies of local and regional economic development.

The Scottish independence referendum of September 2014, by rejecting independence by 55% to 45%, triggered the concessionary Smith Commission and Scotland Act 2016, which granted more powers over certain parts of welfare, social security and taxation. As Brexit looms large across the UK following a 52% to 48% referendum vote in 2016 to leave the European Union and the triggering of article 50 in 2017, which commences this process, a second independence referendum has not been ruled out, though the immediate priority of the SNP is concerned with getting the best Brexit deal possible for Scotland.

This political dynamic can also be felt strongly in Northern Ireland. As part of the Stormont House Agreement 2015, new tax powers were devolved to the Assembly, which should allow Northern Ireland to set its own rate of corporation tax. Northern Ireland though has been without a functioning devolved government since January 2017, when the coalition led by the two biggest parties, the DUP and Sinn Féin, collapsed over a green energy ('cash for ash') scandal. At the time of writing, talks between politicians have failed to restore the power-sharing executive.

Specifically on economic governance, debates during 2016 and 2017 have been over whether the border between Northern Ireland and the Republic will be hard or soft as a result of Brexit, impacting in turn on trade and investment patterns. The winning of 10 of the 18 seats by the Democratic Unionist Party in Northern Ireland in the June 2017 General Election indicated a possible mood swing away from devolution and towards forms of unionism.

Following this General Election, the DUP agreed to support a Conservative minority government on a case-by-case basis on matters of mutual concern. Prime Minister Theresa May has signed a deal to give the Northern Ireland Executive £1 billon over two years in return for the support of the DUP in Parliament. The money will be spent on new road improvement schemes, digital infrastructure, enterprise zones and city deals. The financial scale of this deal is staggering and far outweighs the various 'devo deals' to the city-regions of England. The suspension of the Northern Ireland Assembly and Executive, however, raises questions over how this deal can be implemented.

The complexity of the interface by the UK state and the global economy is staggering and these are certainly interesting times for social scientists seeking to trace the devolved geographies of economic governance across the UK. In the words of Amyas Morse, Head of the National Audit Office (NAO), the UK is at risk of falling apart 'like a chocolate orange' (*The Observer*, 16th July) and, we would add, with the chocolate melting at the same time. We maintain that the concept of 'filling-in' remains a key way of understanding the particularities of the devolution settlements in each of the four territories, as new and alternative configurations of state–society relations continue to emerge.

Mark Goodwin, Martin Jones, Rhys Jones
Exeter, Yarnfield, Aberystwyth
July 2017

Acknowledgements

We have incurred many debts of gratitude in producing this book. First of all, we are grateful for financial support that we received from the ESRC (Grant number L219 25 2013), which enabled us to employ two research assistants for a period of eighteen months. The ESRC's support existed, however, in far more than financial terms. The fact that the project formed part of a larger programme of research on 'Devolution and Constitutional Change' created, from the very outset, an extended series of support networks, which helped to inform our project in many ways. Thank you to all the support and input that we received from the other programme participants. If our project existed within what we might term an 'extended family' of other research projects, then our thanks must also go to the family's patriarch, Charlie Jeffery, who, as Programme Director, provided considerable input and support for our project. His work as a Programme Director was admirable and helped to ensure that every project was embedded into the broader research programme in an effective way. He also succeeded in ensuring that project findings were communicated to policy-makers, thus ensuring that the research programme's projects possessed considerable 'impact', long before the term achieved such status – or notoriety – within academic research.

We wish to express our formal gratitude to our research assistants for the major contribution that they made to the project's success. Kevin Pett and Glenn Simpson collected the lion's share of the empirical data for the project and also contributed to the analysis of this material through their impressive grasp of qualitiative analysis packages! We are extremely grateful to them for their hard work and consistent input into the project.

The project also benefited in more intangible – though equally significant – ways from the contributions made by friends and colleagues over a number of years. The ESRC project, on which this book is based, was formulated and conducted in the Institute of Geography and Earth

Sciences (IGES) at Aberystwyth University. The high levels of collegiality and academic endeavour within IGES – and we believe that the connections between these two attributes are significant and distinctive – provided the three of us with an unparalleled working environment within which to conduct the project. Thanks also to Anthony Smith and Ian Gulley for producing the illustrations to a very high quality. Other friends and colleagues from outside IGES have provided much support for this project. They are too numerous to mention but our thanks go to you all for your patience and guidance. Thanks also to the various individuals who have provided us with feedback on the project in various conference and seminar presentations over the years.

Our thanks and gratitude also go the staff of Manchester University Press for their patience and forbearance in supporting this book. We greatly appreciate it. Thanks also to Charlie Jeffery for developing a series of books that could examine various aspects of devolution and consititutional change in the UK.

Finally, we would like to thank our families for their constant support for our endeavours. Writing a book like this can be a lonely, sometimes dispiriting and certainly time-consuming process. It would have been difficult – nigh-on impossible – for us to have completed this book without our families' constant support, and for this we are especially grateful.

It goes without saying that any mistakes, misrepresentations or omissions are all ours.

Abbreviations

General

BERR	Department of Business, Enterprise and Regulatory Reform
CBI	Confederation of British Industry
DCLG	Department of Communities and Local Government
DCSF	Department for Children, Schools and Families
DETR	Department of Environment, Transport and the Regions
DfEE	Department for Education and Employment
DfES	Department for Education and Skills
DIUS	Department for Innovation, Universities and Skills
DoT	Department of Transport
DTI	Department of Trade and Industry
DTLR	Department of Transport, Local Government and the Regions
DWP	Department for Work and Pensions
ESRC	Economic and Social Research Council
FDI	Foreign Direct Investment
GDP	Gross Domestic Product
HR	Human Resources
ICT	Information and Communication Technology
KWNS	Keynesian Welfare National State
LSC	Learning and Skills' Council
MLG	Multilevel governance
MP	Member of Parliament
ODPM	Office of the Deputy Prime Minister
R&D	Research and Development
RCU	Regional Coordination Unit
SRA	Strategic-relational approach
SWPR	Schumpeterian Workfare Post-National Regime
TEC	Training and Enterprise Council

England

EMDA	East Midlands Development Agency
EMRA	East Midlands Regional Assembly
FEFC	Further Education Funding Council for England
GO	Government Office for the Region
GOEM	Government Office for the East Midlands
IRS	East Midlands Integrated Regional Strategy
LEP	Local Enterprise Partnership
LSP	Local Strategic Partnership
RA	Regional Assembly
RDA	Regional Development Agency
RES	Regional Economic Strategy
SecSP	Sector Skills Partnership
SME	Small and Medium Enterprise
SSP	Sub-regional Strategic Partnership

Northern Ireland

CDP	Company Development Programme
DED	Department of Economic Development
DEL	Department for Employment and Learning
DETINI	Department for Enterprise, Trade and Investment (Northern Ireland)
EDF	Economic Development Forum
IDB	Industrial Development Board
INI	Invest Northern Ireland
IRTU	Insdustrial Research and Technology Unit
LEDU	Local Enterprise Development Unit
MTSP	Medium Term Strategic Priorities
NIA	Northern Ireland Assembly
NIEC	Northern Ireland Economic Council
NIO	Northern Ireland Office
RoI	Republic of Ireland
RSP	Regional Sales Proposition
T&EA	Training and Employment Agency

Scotland

ELLC	Enterprise and Lifelong Learning Committee
ELLD	Enterprise and Lifelong Learning Department
FEDS	*The Way Forward: Framework for Economic Development in Scotland*
HIDB	Highlands and Islands Development Board
HIE	Highlands and Islands Enterprise
JPT	Joint Performance Team
LEC	Local Enterprise Company
LEF	Local Economic Forum
MSP	Member of the Scottish Parliament
SDA	Scottish Development Agency
SE	Scottish Enterprise
SNP	Scottish National Party
SSS	*A Smart, Successful Scotland*

Wales

AGW	Auditor General for Wales
AM	Assembly Member
ASPB	Assembly Sponsored Public Body
CCET	Community Consortium for Education and Training
DBRW	Development Board for Rural Wales
ELWa	Education and Learning Wales
ETAG	Education and Training Action Group
ETAP	Education and Training Action Plan
LAW	Land Authority for Wales
NAfW	National Assembly for Wales
NEDS	National Economic Development Strategy
W:AVE	*Wales: A Vibrant Economy*
WAG	Welsh Assembly Government
WDA	Welsh Development Agency
WO	Welsh Office
WTB	Wales Tourist Board

1
Introduction: Devolution and the geographies of economic governance

Introduction

The number of people employed by the Assembly Government's civil service has more than doubled in the past 10 years – with 380 staff now employed in the human resources department alone. The startling rise is revealed in official figures released to the *Western Mail*. They show that before devolution began in 1999 there were 2,358 full-time equivalent employees in the Welsh Office. By March this year the total had risen to 6,186. Ian Price, the assistant director of CBI Wales, said: 'It is beyond me to understand how the figure can possibly be that high. It seems an unbelievable figure'. Wyn Pryce, secretary of the West Wales Business Initiative said: 'It is clear that the Assembly Government is vastly overstaffed'. Caren Fullerton, the Assembly Government's deputy director of human resources (business change) who sent us the figures, said in an accompanying letter: 'Since 1999, 2,368 staff have joined the Assembly Government through mergers with other bodies including the Welsh Development Agency, Wales Tourist Board and ELWa (Education and Learning Wales). The evolving role of the Assembly Government has resulted in additional responsibilities being assumed as functions have been transferred from other UK Government departments' ... Mr Pryce added that: 'The analysis by department reflects the organisation structures that were in place as at the date of the analysis. There have been changed to structures and responsibilities of departments in every year since 1999.' (Shipton, 2010: 1–2)

Welcome to the world of devolution! The passage above is taken from an article in the *Western Mail: National Newspaper of Wales* with the heading 'Revealed: shocking growth in the number of Welsh civil servants'. This story broke at the same time as this chapter was being written – a timely occurrence, as it highlights some of the main themes of this book, namely the link between devolution, economic development, new state structures, and the peopled geographies of implementation. The territories of Scotland, Wales, Northern Ireland and England – armed with a Parliament (Scotland), Elected Assemblies (Wales, Northern Ireland and London) and, at the time of writing, Regional Development Agencies (England) – provide the basis for doing things differently. Wales, in the example above, has taken a particular road, merging organisations into the National Assembly and governing through expanded central coordination accordingly; hence the 'revealed shocking' headline. Devolution has certainly been the biggest shake-up to the British and UK state apparatus in recent times. In the words of Vernon Bogdanor, we are witnessing 'the most radical constitutional change this country has seen since the Great Reform Act of 1832' (1999: 1). The Great Reform Act set in motion our modern democratic state. The Labour Party (1997–2010) saw devolution and constitutional change as *furthering* modernisation to safeguard the socio-economic and political future of this United Kingdom. In the words of Tony Blair, towards the end of Labour's first term of office:

> When we came to office, the Party of no change – the Conservatives – were left without any seats in Scotland or Wales. Forces for change were left with no alternative but status quo or separatism. Devolution at long last offered a *sensible modernisation* of the partnership in the UK. Let Scotland and Wales do what they do best locally. Let the UK do what it is right to do together. (Blair, 2000: 2, emphasis added)

This book examines the shifting institutional architectures of economic development in a post-devolution UK. It is unique, as it provides a comparative account of economic governance across all four devolved territories. It compares changes to the institutions and practices of economic development in England, Scotland, Wales and Northern Ireland. In doing so, as will become evident in Chapter 2, it builds on a range of academic and policy work that has argued that the securing of economic success within any given territory is not exclusively the result of narrow sets of economic factors, but instead is partly dependent upon a whole range of social, cultural and institutional forms and supports. The book, therefore, examines how the structures of economic governance have developed differently in each territory of the UK since devolution. What is clear, as illustrated above in reference to institutions in Wales, is that devolution has significantly altered these structures, has led to a rescaling of economic governance and has set in train changes to the frameworks and mechanisms of supporting economic development in each of the devolved territories of the UK. What is less clear is whether devolution has enhanced or hindered the capacity of the new institutions to deliver their economic strategies. The latter question is largely absent from the *Western Mail* piece above, which is preoccupied with structures and staffing. We seek to answer this question through empirical material and policy commentary collected between the years 1999 and 2006 – a seven-year window on economic governance in the immediate aftermath of devolution. We argue that this institution-building phase of devolution is the most interesting time period to study and present to a wider audience. The book is about the scale and nature of state intervention, which is non-trivial in a global world now in the midst of economic and state restructuring (see Callinicos, 2010). This chapter first provides a background to economic governance and devolution. It goes on to outline the Devolution and Constitutional Change Research Programme of the Economic and Social Research Council (ESRC), within which our research was situated, and then mentions our research methodology. The chapter concludes by providing an overview of the arguments and chapters to follow.

Economic governance and devolution/devolution and economic governance

The book is situated at the heart of debates about public policy: the specific concern is with *economic governance*: that body of literature associated with tracking the nature and practice of economic management, economic regulation and economic development. Notions of economic governance are found across academia and appear in such varied academic contexts as: heterodox, institutional and post-autistic economics (Lawson, 2003); policy studies in social and political science (Kooiman, 2003; Rhodes, 1997; Storper and Salais, 1997); conventions theory approaches to economic life (Storper and Salais, 1997); coordination approaches in economic sociology (Thompson et al., 1991); advances to the regulation approach (Goodwin and Painter, 1996; Goodwin et al., 2005; Jessop, 2002, 2008); associative institutionalist perspectives within geography (Amin and Thrift, 1994; Raco, 2003) and elsewhere (Keating, 1998; Keating et al., 2003); and a growing field of spatial planning (Allmendinger and Haughton, 2010; Healey, 1997; Tewdwr-Jones and Allmendinger, 2006). We present a deliberately broad reading of economic governance in this book that captures the ongoing interactions between markets, policies, institutions and networks, with our empirical attention focused on frameworks and mechanisms of economic development. The question of economic governance, then, refers to the mobilisation of available institutional and productive resources to develop a coherent sense of economic identity. Economic governance, moreover, is a distinctly geographical project: it is constituted in space and remakes the spaces of such constitutions in the process of performing economic development.

Academic writings in recent years have drawn our attention to different 'varieties' of economic governance, such as neocorporatist, neostatist, neo-Schumpeterian, and neoliberal approaches (Jessop, 2002, 2008; see also Coates, 2000; Hall and Soskice, 2001; Hollingsworth and Boyer, 1997). In the last case, the optimal mechanism for practising economic governance is to engage with open, competitive and unregulated markets, which have been liberated from most forms of state interference (Brenner and Theodore, 2002; Harvey, 2010). Of course, over the past century there have been no states in the West that have fully aimed at allowing free rein to markets: they have always, and in a variety of ways, aimed at organising them. On the other hand, there have been, and there can be, no markets that do not rely on some rules they cannot themselves set. The key point is rather that there are always both a plurality of modes of economic governance and a variety of forms of state. Despite this caveat, it is clear that neoliberal modes of economic governance have been in the ascendancy in recent years, spreading across the world as part of what Ridderstråle and Nordström (2003) call 'karaoke capitalism' or what Storper (1997) and Thrift (2005) might prefer to call 'reflexive capitalism'. Of course, although the general principles of neoliberalism are now widely established, there are variations in how these are implemented, as the Institute of Welsh Affairs' analysis of smart and successful regional economic development across the globe brilliantly highlighted a decade ago (see IWA, 2001). Late twentieth-century UK was characterised by neoliberal economic governance and its ongoing weaknesses played a large part in the Conservative Party's fall from power. The ascendancy of, and fall of, the Labour Party was based around a 'third way' alternative (Giddens, 1998): with faith being placed in the spatial and territorial reorganisation of the national state apparatus to deliver public policy and revive the state, the economy and civil society (Giddens, 2002).

Devolution – the relative transfer of power and responsibility from the nation state downwards to other units of government and governance – follows on from this philosophy. It was viewed, in large meaure, as a way of finding a third way to deal with some of the worst crises associated with neoliberalism. And of critical importance to this book, better economic governance *is* frequently cited as a justification of devolution. Decentralised approaches tailored to sub-national, regional and local circumstances are considered better able to address the continuing problems caused by entrenched territorial inequalities in growth, income and employment. Additionally, decentralised structures are expected to deliver an enhanced, democratised, political settlement that renders economic development institutions more open and accountable to local, regional, and sub-national territorial circumstances. These processes, however, do not operate in a spatial vacuum: territories are never empty but are filled with pre-existing policies and their legacies. The key point to make is that devolution has profound implications for the nature and practice of economic governance: it provides political space for adjusting and altering existing trajectories of economic governance. In turn, the 'success' of economic governance has consequences for further rounds of devolution, set within the limits of constitutional change. In short, devolution and economic governance are opposite sides of the same (capitalist state) coin. They could almost be considered recursive and are certainly dialectically intertwined. These points are, furthermore, generic to the advanced capitalist state and travel *beyond* the UK.

ESRC Devolution and Constitutional Change Research Programme

Since 1997, there have been several attempts both to fund and coordinate research on devolution and constitutional change. The two major research programmes have been the Leverhulme Trust Nations and Regions Research Programme (see Hazell, 2000) and the Devolution and Constitutional Change Research Programme (see Jeffery, 2007). The latter, directed by the political scientist Professor Charlie Jeffery, was a major investment in social science research, initially commissioned by the ESRC in 2000 and lasting until 2006, to explore the series of devolution reforms that have established new political institutions in Scotland, Wales, Northern Ireland, London and the other English regions since 1997. Our research was funded and supported by this ESRC research programme, hence the importance of detailing the aims and objectives of this initiative. As we suggested above, the establishment of the new devolved institutions has had far-reaching implications for society, for the political system and for the management of the economy in the UK. We were concerned mainly with the latter in our project, although as we have hinted, the success or failure of economic governance has held implications for the devolution project as a whole. The UK devolution reforms opened up a dynamic process, with radical institutional change interacting with the complex identity structures of a multinational state to open up new forms of governance and new ways of delivering public policy, such as economic development initiatives (Jeffery, 2002: 3). Devolution significantly altered the terrain on which economic development strategies were formulated and implemented. As a result, the UK had and, indeed, still has, five distinct and largely separate institutional structures for the promotion of economic development in Scotland, Wales, Northern Ireland, the English regions and London. Although the extent of institutional change brought about by devolution is clear (Cooke and Clifton, 2005; Goodwin et al., 2005), it is less certain whether devolution led to the emergence of better structures and mechanisms for economic governance (McGregor and Swales, 2005; Rodríguez-Pose and Gill, 2005). These contingent circumstances warranted detailed empirical investigations and the remainder of this book seeks to explore the findings of the research project that we conducted on such themes.

Views on the likely outcomes of devolution are only likely to be comprehensively known when historians look back at this era, and for now devolution has a considerable amount of 'unfinished business' as Jeffery (2007) put it. The much-cited definition of Ron Davies (1999), 'devolution – a process not an event', is certainly true here. Critics and sceptics, seeking to make early interventions and predictions, have seen the devolution dynamic as unstable, likely to produce conflict between different parts of the UK and end in the disintegration of the UK union (compare Marr, 2000; Nairn, 2000, 2002). Walker captures some of the tensions when he suggests that 'the market is a dream mechanism for proponents of diversity. Left to its own devices, it spreads income and wealth differentially. Advocates of the new localism should beware of becoming a fifth column for economic [neo]liberalism' (Walker, 2002: 6). With the freedom of capital movement and the institutionally charged capabilities of devolved territories to attract inward investment, the 'wimbledonisation' effect in economic development could be set to continue (Caple et al., 2003: 19). This is when firms within economic governance regimes only stay for a limited time-period, eat their strawberries, play their tennis matches, and then return home.

By contrast, policy advocates and optimists see the new territorial politics of devolution as revitalising and strengthening economy and democracy, in a union whose structures were outdated and moribund (Blair, 2000). The government's job is to set macroeconomic stability and devolution provides the right climate for tackling the five pillars of productivity – skills, investment, innovation, enterprise and competition – through institution-driven microeconomic reforms, which are open and accountable to the electorate (HM Treasury, DTI and ODPM, 2003: 3). The political foreword to this 'modern regional policy' in Labour's second term made this clear:

> Five years ago, the Government set out its central economic objectives of achieving high and stable growth and employment. Regional policy is at the heart of our efforts to reach this goal – ensuring that economic prosperity reaches every part of the country and that everyone, no matter where they live,

has the chance to make the most of their potential. For too long, too many nations and regions of the United Kingdom have been allowed to fall behind; for too long there have been huge differences in prosperity within regions; and for too long many people have been left out, their talents wasted. So we rejected the failed policies of the past and in their place developed a new framework for regional development for all nations and regions ... through devolution, we have ensured that ... decisions, which affect the lives of local people, are taken by their own directly elected and accountable representatives ... Modern regional policy must be locally led, which means substantially devolved. The Government's new framework, which espouses this principle, is already delivering results. (HM Treasury, DTI and ODPM 2003: iii)

The Devolution and Constitutional Change Research Programme was designed to build a critical mass of research capacity capable of assessing claims such as these in a rigorous and balanced manner. Projects were chosen to meet two specific challenges (Jeffery, 2002: 3–4). The first was to mobilise and develop insights from across the social science disciplines – political science, economics, geography, business studies, social policy, sociology and social anthropology, but also history and law – to get a fuller understanding of the devolution dynamic and its implications for the UK. The second challenge was to feed research into policy debates. Devolution has opened up uncharted territory for policy-makers around the UK to think reflexively and negotiate to either produce policy differentiation or policy convergence (Elliott et al., 2005; Keating, 2005), with the outcome being largely dependent on the strategies and tactics of economic governance actors and the environments within which they operate. The goal for academic research would be to provide some necessary 'route maps', identify potential pitfalls and problem areas, set out alternative options and create opportunities for policy learning through comparison with experience elsewhere (Jeffery, 2002: 4). We return to this issue in Chapter 7 of this book.

A note on method

We hope that this book will stimulate, tantalise and provoke readers to consider how processes of economic development are themselves embedded in transforming and transformative systems of governance. Our approach draws attention to more than just state regulation: it encourages us to think about the historically contingent and context-specific processes and practices of economic governance. In this context, we provide a window into the *dynamics* of economic governance: devolution offers a rare opportunity for understanding the state not as some lumbering bureaucratic monolith, but as a (political) process in motion, a point that we develop in Chapter 2.

This context-specificity has required a multi-method research design, deployed over a three-phase research project. Phase One involved the collection of data on the post-devolution institutions and policies of economic governance in order to produce a base line audit of existing practice in each UK territory. For each institution a documentary profile was constructed, containing information on, for example, personnel, terms of reference, organisational structures, consultation procedures, strategies produced, territory of operation and linkages with other agencies. In addition, the completion of Phase One involved an analysis of current economic development strategies, and the provision for each of a listing, and relative weighting, of its key themes and issues. Phase Two, which took nine months to complete, examined experiences of post-devolution governance in the four territories, through a series of contemporary case studies. Each case study was designed to explore how effectively the institutions of economic governance were able to meet the challenges of economic governance within their respective territories, by looking at the nature of intergovernmental relationships; the level of institutional cooperation and collaboration; and the realignment of policy responsibilities and working practices. In England we looked at the evolution of economic governance at a regional level in the East Midlands. In making this choice we were not claiming that the East Midlands were in any way representative of state restructuring – indeed one reason why we selected this area was precisely because it had been relatively lacking in territorial and institutional coherence at a regional scale, and the process of building new regional institutions allowed us to literally examine the 'peopling' of the state as this process unfolded over the first five years of the devolution settlement. In the other three devolved territories we also selected case studies that would allow us to analyse the unfolding process of devolution. In Wales we examined the introduction of Education and Learning Wales (ELWa); in Northern Ireland we looked at the formation of Invest Northern Ireland; and in Scotland we analysed the coordination of economic governance in the context of the development of ministerial task forces, joint performance teams and Local Economic Forums (LEFs).

Taken together, these case studies were designed to examine the capacity to act of the new structures of economic governance centred around the three dimensions of intergovernmental relations; scale and territory; and personnel. Each case study was undertaken using a combination of documentary analysis and semi-structured interviews. The interviews were undertaken with a wide variety of people working in, and connected to, the field of economic governance, ranging from ministerial, Chief Executive and Permanent Secretary level to those engaged in policy formulation and delivery 'on the ground'. For reasons of confidentiality we have chosen not to name the individuals we interviewed, but we were fortunate in that almost everyone we approached agreed to take part in the research, and we were able to speak with local and national politicians, board members and civil servants, as well as economic development practitioners. Each interview was taped and fully transcribed, before being transferred to qualitative software for sorting, storing and analysing, using over 250 separate codes to identify and retrieve different textual topics. Over Phases One and Two we conducted interviews with ninety-nine key actors involved in policy formulation and implementation. These interviews were supported by the analysis of policy documents, including institutional minutes, policy briefings and strategy papers. Phase Three was devoted to completing analysis, reviewing the implications of the findings for policy and academic audiences and writing the final report for the ESRC. In all we were able to use the empirical material collected and analysed in these three phases to produce twenty-four internal project reports, which were then drawn on to provide the empirical material in this book. Our research project funding ended in July 2003 and we continued the research analysis for a further year, publishing from this along the way (Goodwin et al., 2002; Goodwin et al., 2005; Jones et al., 2004, 2005; Goodwin et al., 2006a, 2006b; R. Jones, 2007; Jones 2008).

Outline of this book

Our aim in this book is to examine the key themes that helped to structure our research project on devolution and economic governance. Chapter 2 provides an assessment of a range of theoretical developments in the field of state restructuring, concentrating particularly on those which have been used to understand economic governance. Although there is a lack of a coherent body of theoretical work on UK devolution, we do have considerable conceptual insights into both economic governance and state restructuring at a more general level. The chapter examines key literatures on new regionalism, on multilevel governance, on the political economies of scale and on strategic-relational state theory. It sets out a modified strategic-relational approach (SRA) as the most appropriate conceptual framework for understanding current state restructuring in the UK, because of its emphasis on state strategy, on state personnel and on the link between state form and state strategy. The chapter draws out some key themes running through the rest of the book, namely: the formation of new institutions and strategies as an emergent state form; the changing territories and scales of governance; the importance of state personnel; and the ever-present tensions between cooperation and collaboration among different state institutions.

Chapter 3 examines the formation of new institutional structures following devolution in each of the devolved territories. It sets the scene by describing the pre-devolution institutional structure era. The chapter also examines the economic development strategies of these institutions and assesses whether there are major differences between the territories. Alongside this analysis of institutional and strategic development, the chapter explores the political pressures felt in each territory that led the newly devolved administrations to place their own stamp on policy development in the economic development field. This in turn has resulted in completely new configurations of economic governance; at both a political and administrative level within the new Parliament and Assemblies, and at an implementation level 'on the ground'. In sum, the chapter seeks to describe and account for the emergence of these new configurations.

Chapter 4 takes things forward by focusing on the ways in which these new institutions also represent a rescaling, as well as a restructuring, of the state. It discusses how we have witnessed a complex rescaling of economic governance, both vertically between scales, and horizontally between institutions operating over the same territory. However, the UK's asymmetrical devolution settlement, i.e. one whereby different powers and responsibilities have been settled (see Jeffery, 2007), has meant that these new spatial divisions are uneven across the four devolved territories. The chapter analyses this and the political and economic pressures resulting from such rescaling.

One of the claims made in Chapter 2 regarding the strength of the strategic relational approach, relates to its focus on state personnel as agents of continuity and change. Put simply, in a changing political and institutional landscape, it is those who work for the state who have had to literally 'make sense' of devolution. They have had to adapt to new roles within new organisations, relate to new territories of governance and understand new responsibilities, loyalties and working practices. Furthermore, it is these selfsame individuals who have also been the agents of change, helping to create new institutions and new strategies. The tensions here are clearly apparent in the *Western Mail* article that commenced this introductory chapter. Chapter 5 uses empirical and theoretical material to explore the ways in which devolution has created new scenarios for the unfolding of this dynamic and the dialectical relationships between state structures and state personnel.

Devolution has brought into play twenty-plus different structures of economic governance at the regional scale in the UK. One of the key questions for the UK polity and economy is the extent to which these different institutions compete or collaborate with each other. Using empirical examples drawn from the case study research, Chapter 6 explores the tensions that exist around this important question of collaboration and competition through a sustained discussion of the geographies of economic governance in Northern Ireland. In doing so, we we will seek to examine the way in which each of the empirical themes discussed in Chapters 3, 4 and 5 – organisations, territories/scales and state personnel – interact with each other to create a range of possibilities and challenges for economic governance under devolution.

Chapter 7, our conclusion, has two aims. First, it seeks to bring up to date the empirical discussion that appeared in Chapters 3–6. Second, it discusses the broader conceptual implications of our sustained empirical engagement with the SRA. In discussing these issues, we also seek to examine the implications of devolution for the notion of UK plc. Proponents of devolution, noted above, emphasise how the process has weakened political demands for separation, and thus strengthened the notion of the UK as a single entity. Our argument is that differentiated institutional capacities, which have resulted from devolution, have increased the already uneven patterns of economic success and failure within the component parts of the UK. The changing patterns of economic governance within the UK post-devolution, then, possess implications for political matters far wider than economic development. The conclusion critically asks whether the ability of the new economic development institutions to tackle the emerging economic tensions between different parts of the UK may, in fact, help to determine the very future of the UK as a political and economic union.

2
The theoretical challenge of devolution and constitutional change

Introduction

This chapter is concerned with developing conceptual frameworks to inform our understandings of the role of devolution in the contemporary reorganisation of the UK state by addressing the ways in which we can theorise the changes that have taken place within the devolved territories; all with respect to economic governance and economic development. This is because we feel that there has been little effort to locate an analysis of UK devolution into any *longue durée* of political economic transformation. A while ago, Nash (2002: 30) had a concern with the 'lamentable lack of theoretical and conceptual grounding' within research on constitutional change and territorial economic governance. Given that this disparaging comment was voiced only two years into the devolution research programme, perhaps it was a rather unforgiving assessment. Some ten years later though, having surveyed the published material from funded research programmes and other scholarly endeavours, we feel that its sentiment remains pertinent. Cooke and Clifton (2005: 440), writing on devolution and economic governance across the UK, for instance, note that there has been a 'copious literature on devolution but much of it proceeds only as far as textured case analysis, the elaboration of concepts, and in a few cases, conceptual frameworks'. Bradbury (2006: 563) shares this opinion, when he argues that 'there is reluctance among any scholars to theorise the subject at all' due mainly to an 'inclination of many political scientists to focus on limited empirical studies, thus failing to consider the big picture, a macro theory of political development'. In political science, there have been innovations for sure. Jeffery's excellent overview of devolution and its 'unfinished business', for instance, raises seven open questions, but makes little reference to the broader claims that can be made from the UK's devolution reforms. The claim that 'empirical genius without theoretical direction may produce an overall outcome that lacks structure and coherence' (Jeffery, 2007: 94) has a wider significance than its initially intended policy and political audience. As we argued back in 2005, devolution remains somewhat of a 'lost opportunity' (Goodwin et al., 2005: 423). We would argue that devolution increasingly presents an ideal circumstance in which to develop geographically informed theoretical debates on contemporary state restructuring. This chapter addresses this challenge.

A number of popular approaches to understanding the institutions of economic development are discussed in the chapter but are considered to be inadequate for explaining the variable geopolitical situations that have emerged within the UK. The chapter takes forward academic debate by extending Jessop's strategic-relational approach to the state, which has been very popular to position states, neoliberalism and globalisation. Jessop (1990, 1993, 1994, 2008, 2012) has famously suggested that the national state is being 'hollowed out'. We argue that it is no longer enough to simply refer to a multivariate 'hollowing out' of the nation state in an era of economic and political restructuring. Instead, devolution presents a unique opportunity to theorise the state as an institutional-materialist spatial matrix, which is currently being 'filled in' unevenly across the four territories, thus leading to an increasingly complex spatial division of the state (see Goodwin et al., 2005; Jones et al., 2005; cf. Shaw and MacKinnon, 2010). But before we commence this argument, it is important to first outline our understanding of the state, which should not be taken for granted.

Tracing the state

The most basic but least-asked question by all scholars, not just those interested in devolution, in thinking about the state, is how to define the 'properties' of the state. The most general feature of the state (premodern as well as modern and precapitalist as well as capitalist) is that it comprises a set of institutions concerned with the territorialisation of political power. This involves the intersection of politically organised, coercive and symbolic power, a clearly demarcated core territory, and a fixable population on which political decisions may be made collectively binding (such as the exercise of law and order and the collection of taxation and other sources of revenue) (see Mann, 1984, 1986). Thus, the key feature of the state is the historically variable ensemble of technologies and practices that produce, naturalise, and manage territorial space as a relatively bounded container within which political power is exercised to achieve various, more or less well integrated, and changing policy objectives. A system of formally sovereign, mutually recognising, mutually legitimating national states exercising sovereign control over large and exclusive territorial areas – the contemporary scenario – is only a relatively recent institutional expression of state power. Other modes of territorialising political power have existed, some still coexist with the so-called Westphalian system (initially established by the Treaties of Westphalia in 1648 but realised only stepwise, at times chaotically, and often subject to reversals, during the nineteenth and twentieth centuries), new expressions are emerging and yet others can be imagined.

The state, then, is distinct and different from, say, a multinational corporation, by virtue of its territorial integrity and its political legitimacy. The state is also different in the various roles that it can play. To know the state we need to also know the history and geography of capitalism. States can respond to the contradictions, dilemmas and problems of capitalism by creating the general conditions for the production and social reproduction of the capital relation, that is the environment for economic growth and development. The state does this in part by seeking to regulate uneven development and/or by responding to the effects of this, that is, uneven growth, change and restructuring. The state, though, is omnipresent. Due to its development and penetration into most spheres of life, it is everywhere and nowhere. This presents researchers with challenges of analysis and interpretation. Adopting these general parameters enables us to note that political power is not always exercised in and through territory and to explore the different modalities of territorialisation, deterritorialisation and reterritorialisation. For territory is not a given but something that gets constructed and institutionalised in different ways in different times and places. Recognising this from a geographical standpoint should exclude criticisms of 'spatial fetishism', that is, the belief that space as such had a linear causal efficacy in relation to the state. 'State/space' (Brenner et al., 2003) is a lot more contingent, as the terrain of the state is forged through the ongoing engagements between agents, institutions and concrete political and policy circumstances. The engagements change across time and space, which makes things even more interesting. Devolution and constitutional change provides us with a basis for taking this further, which is only one instance of state spatial restructuring (Shaw and MacKinnon, 2010).

Theorising the political geographies of state restructuring

In undertaking the project for this book, we were faced with how to theorise devolution and constitutional change from a state-centred perspective on economic development and economic governance. We took one particular entry point into this new theoretical venture, namely previous debates on the political geographies of state restructuring in the after-Fordist era. For although we might lack theoretical work on UK devolution, we do have considerable conceptual insights into state restructuring at a more general level. Indeed, in recent years there has been a growing concern in the social and political sciences to theorise the many ways in which economic and political geographies are being actively remade in the context of globalisation and the erosion of the Fordist–Keynesian national welfarist state settlement. Researchers have been contributing much to a number of 'new regionalist' literatures that are specifically concerned with mapping the emergence of new sub-national territories, scales and places of regulation and governance (see *Cambridge Journal of Regions, Economy and Society*, 2009; *Environment and Planning A*, 2001; Keating, 1998; *Regional and Federal Studies*, 2010). In contrast to 'boosterist' accounts of globalisation, which emphasise the death of the nation state and the end of geography, human geographers have emphasised the need to explore the complex connections between the institutionalisation of political activity, the changing role of the capitalist state, and the importance of territorially embedding continued capital accumulation within the context of economic competitiveness and social cohesion (see Brenner, 2004; Dicken, 2010; Jones and Jones, 2004). Such analysis suggests the need to consider the ways in which social, economic and cultural processes are institutionally mediated and actively produced through struggles occurring within and between different spatial scales. Some of these concerns are being shared by political scientists, whose work on multilevel governance seeks to capture the complex dynamics taking place with respect to territorial restructuring and political change in Western Europe (compare John, 2000; Marks, 1996; Pierre and Stoker, 2000; Scharpf, 1999). Multilevel governance (MLG) theorists, for instance, see state power and authority as 'dispersed' rather than 'concentrated' and political action occurs 'at and between various levels of governance' (Jones and Clark, 2001: 206).

We would suggest that key literatures on the new regionalism, on MLG and on the political economies of scale hold some useful pointers for those concerned with the contemporary economic and political geography of the UK, but we would also claim that these bodies of thought are incapable of fully understanding the processes of state restructuring that underpins much of these new geographies. This work has been well summarised, and extensively critiqued, elsewhere (see the accounts offered by Brenner, 2004; Jessop, 2002, 2008; M. Jones, 2001; Lovering, 1999; MacLeod, 2001a, 2001b; MacLeod and Goodwin, 1999a, 1999b) so we will restrict ourselves to drawing out some of the concerns which arise when these frameworks are applied to issues of devolution and state rescaling.

First, whilst the literature on the 'new regionalism' emphasises the central roles played by institutions, networks, trust and social capital in the maintenance of successful economies, it is less strong on analysing the continued role of the national state in nurturing and sustaining these institutional norms and networks. This may not be surprising given the heavy emphasis within this research on supply-side innovation and the replacement of formalised government with less formal networks of partnership and governance, but we still need to understand how the state helps to produce, reproduce and articulate these new sites and scales of economic governance. Second, MLG is stronger on the politics of the new sub-national institutions but overplays the vertical nesting of discrete policy competencies, at the expense of analysing the dense network of 'tangled hierarchies' (Jessop, 2001b) which mesh together to produce and implement policy horizontally across any one scale. MLG also tends to reify the different scales within these hierarchies, when in practice scales of governance are relative and are actively produced (not least by the national state). Third, the emerging literature within geography on the political economies of scale does stress the active constitution of spatial scale, but in seeing scale as the product of relational processes there is the danger of not appreciating how territorial fixity is created partly through processes of government and governance. Thus in many ways the process-based strength of this approach can become a weakness. This is a point that is confirmed by devolution research, which highlights how the production, or fixing, of scale is occurring through a number of context-specific institutions which are themselves bound up with the reconfiguration of national state competencies (Jones and Jones, 2004). Collectively, then, we would argue that these debates on the importance of sub-national institutions of economic governance need to heed Swyngedouw's (still valid) argument that 'although the thesis of state re-scaling has been advanced by a number of authors ... the *actual mechanisms* through which processes take place remain vague and under theorised' (Swyngedouw, 1996: 1500, emphasis added). We would suggest that a focus on such mechanisms – of seeing the state as a 'political process in motion' (Peck, 2001: 449) – leads us to pay more attention than hitherto to the continuing role played by political strategy in the production of new sites and scales of state governance (see Brenner, 2009a). This is clearly the case in a post-devolution UK, where the central state, together with each devolved administration, clearly has a key influence in structuring the scales and actions of a range of emergent new sub-national institutions.

The strategic-relational state approach

One theoretical approach which does stress state strategy is the strategic-relational approach (SRA) to state theory (especially Jessop, 1985, 1990, 1995, 1997, 1999, 2001a, 2002, 2008, 2012). This approach draws on Marxist accounts of capital being a social relation and applies this to the state as social relation so that the state is seen as neither a neutral instrument (equally accessible to all forces and useful for any purpose) nor a rational calculating subject (with a pre-given unity and clear purposes). State power is strategically and spatially selective and results from a continuing interaction between structures, strategies and balance of forces operating within and beyond the state. The state needs to be thus thought of as a 'medium and outcome' of processes that constitute its many interventions. The state is both a social relation and a producer of strategy and, as such, it does not have any power of its own, other than the forces acting in and through its apparatus. We develop this point further below, where we argue that the *political institutional geography of the capitalist state* is missing in devolution research. Our aim in this book is explore this missing link in conceptual and empirical detail.

Jessop has taken this basic SRA framework and developed it as a means of analysing the shifting contours of economic and political restructuring in Western Europe over the past twenty years (see especially Jessop, 2002, 2008). The SRA is, therefore, particularly useful for beginning to conceptually position the current round of variable state restructuring in the UK. It suggests that the nation state's dominance is being undermined by the three inter-related processes of 'de-statisation', the 'internationalisation of policy regimes', and 'denationalisation' in its long-run evolution from a Keynesian Welfare National State (KWNS) towards a Schumpeterian Workfare Post-National Regime (SWPR). In Jessop's account, the *de-statisation* of the political system is most clearly reflected in a functional shift from government to governance. This change is associated with a relative decline of the central state's direct management and sponsorship of economic and social projects, and an analogous engagement of quasi-state and non-state actors in public–private partnerships. *Internationalisation* refers not only to the more significant role of international policy communities and networks, but also to the heightened strategic significance of the international and global contexts within which state actors now operate and to the processes of international policy transfer as in, for example, the UK's adoption of 'workfare' from the USA. The *denationalisation* of statehood is reflected in a structural 'hollowing out' of the national state apparatus (cf. Holliday, 2000; Rhodes, 1994). As the nation state's capacity to promote economic development is being weakened through the processes of globalisation, international trade, financial deregulation, and space-shrinking technologies, so old and new state capacities are being reconfigured territorially and functionally along a series of spatial levels: subnational, national, supranational and trans-local.

Geographers have tended to focus on *denationalisation* at the expense of the other two inter-related processes, attracted perhaps by the spatial metaphor of 'hollowing out'. A trawl through the main human geography journals over the past ten to fifteen years is illustrative of this point. However, Jessop is very careful not to imply the inevitable decline of the nation state. In a deliberate echo of Ohmae's notion of the 'hollow corporation', Jessop points to its continuing importance:

> [T]he 'hollow state' metaphor indicates two trends: first, that the national state retains its 'headquarters' (or crucial political) functions – including the trappings of central executive authority and national sovereignty as well as the discourses that sustain them and overall responsibility for maintaining social cohesion; and, second, that its capacities to translate this authority and sovereignty into effective control are becoming limited by a complex displacement of powers upwards, downwards, and outwards. This does not mean that the national state loses all importance: far from it. Indeed, it remains a crucial site and discursive framework for political struggles; and it even keeps much of its sovereignty. (Jessop, 2002: 212)

Significantly, Jessop developed this thesis on state reorganisation through empirical work on economic governance during the 1990s, drawing the conclusion that these transformations have resulted in various sets of 'tangled hierarchies' (Jessop, 1998). The processes of constitutional change in the UK have altered this picture in two key ways. First, the 'tangled hierarchies' of governance, operating at various interlinked spatial scales, have, if anything, been made more complex. We can witness this growing level of complexity with regard to economic governance through the various chapters of the book. Even *before* devolution, a number of reports pointed out that the multiplicity of agencies involved in economic development, and their often overlapping responsibilities, proved to be a constant source of inefficiency and confusion (see Audit Commission,

1989; Environment, Transport and Regional Affairs Committee, 1997). Devolution has further complicated this picture. As we noted in the previous chapter, the UK now has five distinct institutional structures for the promotion of economic development, which hold important implications for the processes of de-statisation and internationalisation. Second, as we empirically chart throughout the remainder of the book, devolution *has* begun a critical process of formally building new architectures of governance *within* the 'hollowed out' structure of the UK state. Jessop hinted at this conceptually, when he wrote that the 'hollowed out' nation state

> *has a continuing role in managing the political linkages across different territorial scales*, and its legitimacy depends precisely on doing so in the perceived interests of the social base ... Moreover, just as multinational firms' command, control, communication and intelligence functions are continually transformed by the development of new information and communication technologies and new forms of networking, bargaining and negotiation, so, too, as *new possibilities emerge*, are there changes in how 'hollowed out' states exercise and project their power. (Jessop 2002: 212, emphases added)

Devolution, of course, has at once altered how the state manages its 'political linkages across different scales' and opened up 'new possibilities' in the exercise and projection of power. However, 'hollowing out' is perhaps not the most appropriate metaphor to explore the shifting political geographies of the British state. For as particular elements of the UK state (at the national scale) are 'hollowed out', the process of devolution has meant that at other (sub-national) scales they are being 'filled in'.

New state, new theories: from hollowing out to 'filling in'

We feel that the 'hollowing out' metaphor is *not* an appropriate one for two reasons. First, 'hollowing out' is often advanced as the explanation, i.e. we have witnessed devolution because the state is being 'hollowed out', when in fact it is precisely the 'hollowing out' which needs explaining. Second, 'hollowing out' is not uni-dimensional: as one element of the state is being hollowed out, others are indeed being 'filled in'. Under devolution we would suggest that 'hollowing out' and 'filling in' are twin aspects of the same process: you can't have one (and understand the state's shifting spatial architecture) without the other. Yet the very popularity of the 'hollowing out' concept leads to an analytical focus that directs attention away from this dual aspect. Using existing SRA accounts, we therefore have a somewhat one-sided treatment of a dialectical process, which is resulting in simultaneous de-statisation *and* re-statisation. All that is solid, including the state apparatus and its political institutions, does not melt into air because the state is 'incompressible': it can re-emerge at a different scale and with a different territorial form at different points in time (Poulantzas, 1978).

We feel that to develop strategic-relational accounts on the state, then, it is important to think spatially. We are not alone here. Shaw and MacKinnon (2010) also critique the use of 'hollowing out' and offer a modified version of our (Goodwin et al., 2005) notion of 'filling in'. In both our readings, 'hollowing out' has become a popular metaphor because it is deployed (usually implicitly) at a national scale, but as we discuss in subsequent chapters, the situation within the UK's devolved territories is far more complex and illustrative of asymmetrical 'filling in'. So there is an interesting paradox within the SRA. Although 'hollowing out' is a spatial metaphor, it is not sufficiently spatially sensitive, at least not in the way it has hitherto been deployed in Jessop's original thinking. This argument is acknowledged in Jessop's more recent work, which stresses the role of space in the reproduction of state power (see Brenner et al., 2003; Jessop, 2002, 2008). Jessop highlights 'counter trends' taking place within the de-nationalisation of the state, and the need to move beyond 'single causal mechanisms'. Later work suggests that 'hollowing out' brings with it 'increased scope for states in interscalar articulation' projects (Jessop, 2008: 210). This statement is not taken to a theoretical level *per se*, although Jessop would perhaps position his notion of 'metagovernance' (the coordination of coordination) as explanation. This link is not explicitly made, which still leaves a gap in the analysis and explanation of state spatial restructuring. 'Hollowing out' thus still remains central to Jessop's ongoing analysis and tends to be seen as a top-down – rather than a dialectical, iterative and negotiated – process. But as we discuss below, devolution and constitutional change is a multifaceted, multiscalar and multispatial process of state restructuring and remaking involving 'complex changes in the relations between different levels/scales and branches/departments of the state' (Peck, 2001: 447). Hence, as Peck adds, in an echo of Poulantzas's argument on incompressibility, we 'need to see "hollowing out" as a qualitative process of state restructuring, not a quantitative process of state erosion or diminution'. Thus with the advent of devolution and constitutional change, it is no longer enough to simply refer to the 'hollowing out' of the state. Future research also needs to concentrate on assessing the processes, practices and resulting geographies of 'filling in'. Some researchers are already addressing this challenge (see Shaw and MacKinnon, 2010).

This still leaves us with the problem of deploying (or reworking) adequate conceptual frameworks to grasp these complex qualitative processes of state spatial restructuring. It might be argued that the concept of 'hollowing out' implies 'filling in' and that the latter term is therefore unnecessary. After all, 'hollowing out' does refer to the ways in which state capacities are refigured functionally *and* territorially. But it is the implication that is the problem. 'Hollowing out' refers to a potential rescaling away from the national state, both upwards and downwards, at a series of levels from the local to the supra-national. In this sense it lacks specification. The use of 'filling in' as a concept draws attention to such specification, but focuses on the manner in which power is being transferred, and on the spaces it is being transferred to. In other words, the very process of 'filling in' is geographically constituted and spatially constructed, in contrast to 'hollowing out', which implies an abstract sense of restructuring at any number of potential scales. 'Filling in' also allows a specification of the relationship between different tiers of the state, and stresses the active and contested process of new state formation. Our theoretical priority should thus be concerned with the process through which particular spaces become (re)constituted, which necessitates a dialectical emphasis on 'filling in' as well as 'hollowing out'.

Modifying strategic-relational state theory to take account of scale

One of the great strengths of strategic-relational state theory is that it conveys an understanding of the state 'not as some lumbering bureaucratic monolith, but as a (political) process in motion' (Peck, 2001: 449). Moreover, in analysing this process, the SRA, as its name suggests, is at once strategic and relational. It stresses that state power, and indeed activity, can only be assessed relationally, as a set of social relations. In this vein, Jessop has famously argued that 'The state as such has no power – it is merely an institutional ensemble; it has only a set of institutional capacities and liabilities which mediate that power; the power of the state is the power of the forces acting in and through the state. These forces include state managers as well as class forces, gender groups as well as regional interests, and so forth' (Jessop, 1990: 269–70). Following this statement, it is possible to focus our analytical lens on the state as what we might term a 'peopled organisation', not a set of anonymous institutions referred to in some of the literatures identified above. We would maintain that there is more to this; this theoretical framework deployed also highlights the notion of strategy. The state is viewed as the site, generator and product of particular strategies. In other words, the state, and the policies and activities pursued through it, 'constitutes a terrain upon which different political forces attempt to impart a specific direction to the individual or collective activities of its different branches' (Jessop, 1990: 268). And in viewing the state as the site of strategy, it can be analysed as a territorially and functionally dispersed system, whose structural form and mode of operation are more permeable and suitable to some types of political agents than to others. For Offe, this often entails a tendency for the state to favour certain interests groups (usually capital); a process referred to as 'structural selectivity' (Offe, 1974). However, rather than being the result of some essentialist logic, whereby the state functions as if it were an 'instrument of the interest of capital' (Offe, 1984: 51), the structural selectivity of any state needs to be analysed as contingent upon the actions and strategic endeavours of a whole plethora of agents peculiar to specific places and times. The complex articulation of these processes of strategic selectivity means that:

> Particular forms of economic and political system privilege some strategies over others, access by some forces of others, some interests over others, some spatial scales of action over others, some time horizons over others, some coalition possibilities over others. Structural constraints always operate selectively: they are not absolute and unconditional but always temporally, spatially, agency, and strategy specific. This has implications both for general struggles over the economic and extra-economic regularization of capitalist economies and specific struggles involved in securing the hegemony of a specific accumulation strategy. (Jessop, 1997: 63)

This relational character of strategic selectivity also implies that the differential ability of social forces to pursue their interests through different strategies 'is not inscribed in the state system as such but in the relation between state structures and the strategies which different forces adopt' (Jessop, 1990: 260). This thinking can shed much light on the seemingly incessant rounds of post-devolution restructuring that we highlight through the remainder of the book, because this theoretical framework is inherently spatio-temporal. Considerations of space and time are etched into its formulation, although Jessop has perhaps been reluctant to pursue this in concrete research. We would suggest that this etching takes on three forms (cf. Jessop, 2001a, 2002, 2008; MacLeod and Goodwin, 1999b).

First, like all structures, and indeed institutions, states have a definite spatio-temporal extension: they emerge in specific places at specific times, they operate over particular scales and territories, and they have certain temporal horizons (see Jones and Jessop, 2010). States are in fact complex 'geographical accomplishments', which are forged through the interaction of economic and extra-economic systems and their social relations. Using a modified strategic-relational state theory can make us appreciate how devolution has served to make more complex the scalar and territorial geographies of the UK, leading to the creation of territorial mismatches and policy overlaps. Put simply, the modified SRA can help us focus on the spatial tensions inherent in devolution, most specifically in terms of collaboration and competition between the various new organisations of governance.

Second, some practices and strategies are privileged, and others made more difficult to realise, according to how they match the spatial and temporal patterns inscribed in the structures in question. Critically important here are the relationships between state structures and the strategies which given forces adopt. Once again, the modified SRA can enable us to tease out the relationships between new post-devolution strategies and particular territories and certain scales. It can also help us to highlight the efforts being made to dovetail strategies between territories and scales, but also the instances in which strategies – promoted within particular territories and at certain scales – compete, one with another.

Third, because of its peculiar territorial nature as an institution, the very forces that can legitimately gain access to particular parts and branches of the state are spatially bounded and to a certain extent scale-dependent. In this context, the modified SRA can draw our attention to the differential access of certain groups to the plural institutions of the state, post-devolution. Once again, access is territorial and scalar dependent.

The SRA, then, has the ability to reveal how the power of the social forces acting in and through the state, and their interplay with the state's institutional form, are dependent on sets of relations, which are geographically constituted and contested. And it is this brand of relational strategic and process-orientated analysis that social scientists can draw on in the immediate future as we seek to uncover the shifting sites and scales of state activity within an actively devolved system. Moreover, in addition to helping us to explore the newly devolved geographies of the UK state, we argue that the modified SRA is useful as a way of examining the political geographies of *all* states that contain regional and/or local tiers of government. Most especially, it can aid our understanding by encouraging us to focus on a number of important themes. First, whilst one might need to focus on institutions in order to conduct concrete research, there is a need to appreciate that one is not studying institutions *per se*, for their own sake, but rather one is studying them to uncover political, social and cultural dynamics they entail (and the way these are scaled). Second, there is a critical need to think about the processes that operate in between institutions, not just inside them. Institutions do not operate in a vacuum and, therefore, we must explore the dynamic relationships that exist between them. Third, there is a need to appreciate how scale is constructed horizontally (through territory and the connections between scales) as well as vertically through notions of multilevel governance. These horizontal relationships were especially apparent in the empirical material discussed earlier and should represent a key object of enquiry within geographical studies of the contemporary state. Finally, there is a need to develop an analysis which can fuse the spatial and the political, and a suitable modified strategic-relational state theory has the potential to help us do this. Devolution provides us with an ideal empirical opportunity for addressing these conceptual challenges. These conceptual challenges, in turn, have wider implications for state spatial restructuring in other eras.

Conclusions

This chapter has sought to provide a contribution to contemporary debates on state restructuring in the context of devolution and constitutional change in the United Kingdom. As noted in the previous chapter, at a basic level devolution has certainly been followed by a remaking, and indeed a rescaling, of the institutions responsible for formulating a variety of policies and strategies. These changes though have not just been the result of any simple transference of power and functions from the UK scale to each individual territory. What we are witnessing is a very complex rescaling of governance, both vertically between scales, and horizontally between institutions operating over the same territory, leading to what we might label an increased 'spatial division of the state'. We would contend that understanding this complexity requires an appreciation of 'filling in' as well as 'hollowing out'. This is partly because the asymmetrical devolution witnessed within the UK has meant that these new spatial divisions are themselves *uneven* across the four devolved territories. Attempts at rationalisation have occurred, both at a formal governmental level, and at a more local delivery level. But these have proceeded very differently in each territory. Whilst the concept of 'hollowing out' can be drawn on to situate the beginnings of these processes, notions of 'filling in' can provide an understanding of their differential and uneven outcomes. Moreover, the twin processes of 'hollowing out' and 'filling in' are recursive; each influences and is influenced by the other. Thus, the next round of 'hollowing out' from the central government is likely to be conditioned by the political, social, cultural and economic impacts of the current processes of 'filling in' within the locality.

Given that devolved organisations' structures, policies and strategies will have a direct impact on their ability to act and to achieve their stated goals, then a clear understanding of the conceptual and empirical character of the various processes of 'filling in' becomes imperative. We discuss this empirically in the chapters that follow. If this is the case, then the exact configurations of 'filling in' within the various UK territories post-devolution may well possess serious implications for the whole devolution project. We return to this important point in the conclusion to the book.

3
New politics/new institutions/new strategies

Introduction

The Labour Party returned to power in the UK in May 1997 after eighteen years of Conservative rule. But this was a different Labour Party to that defeated by Margaret Thatcher in 1979. As Tony Blair, the incoming Prime Minister famously remarked in a victory speech at London's Royal Festival Hall on election night, 'we were elected as New Labour and we shall govern as New Labour'. Among the policies which very clearly marked this government out as 'New' Labour, and as different to any of its predecessors, were those centred around constitutional reform. One strand of these focused on the operation of the UK Parliament itself, and especially on the reform of the UK's unelected second chamber, the House of Lords. A second strand tackled the constitution beyond Westminster, and became collectively labelled as the UK's 'devolution settlement'. Under this settlement, a Scottish Parliament was introduced, along with Assemblies in Northern Ireland and Wales. In England itself, various regional bodies were created, including a Greater London Assembly. By the summer of 1999, two years after they were elected, New Labour had devolved various elements of policy to these new institutions. The result was a number of far-reaching changes to the political, economic and cultural geographies of the UK state, together amounting to perhaps the biggest changes in state structure since the Act of Union in 1707. As we noted in Chapter 1, 'the carapace of Britain's ancient regime' (Gamble, 2002: 22) had been broken.

With this breakage came an unprecedented process of functional and territorial state restructuring. We saw in the previous chapter how a modified SRA can provide a suitable framework for analysing and interpreting changes in state activity. In particular we can draw on three interlinked aspects of the SRA to understand and account for the emergence of a plethora of new institutions and new policies across the

UK. Firstly, as we noted in Chapter 2, the SRA underpins a brand of relational, strategic and process-orientated analysis. The state is viewed very much as a political process in motion. Hence, the 'spaces of state power are not simply "filled", as if they were pre-given territorial containers. Instead state spatiality is actively produced and transformed' (Brenner, 2004: 76). And we would contend that devolution represents a perfect case of state spatiality being 'actively produced and transformed'. Secondly, such active production of state spatiality will inevitably be 'made at the point of interaction between the unfolding layer of regulatory processes/ apparatuses and the inherited institutional landscape' (Peck, 1998: 29). This draws our attention to the path-dependency involved in creating a new institutional structure and the manner in which past legacies influence future development. And thirdly, the SRA emphasises the interaction between state structures and political strategies in a complex dialectic between structures and social forces. As Jessop (1990: 260) notes, the differential ability of social forces to pursue their interests through the state 'is not inscribed in the state system as such, but in the relation between state structures and the strategies which different forces adopt'. Thus, the SRA will always view the state as a strategic terrain 'located within a complex dialectic of structures and strategies' (Jessop, 1990: 269).

This chapter looks at these twin aspects of structure and strategy. Initially, it sets the scene for this by charting the nature of the UK's devolution settlement, before looking at the new structures and institutions of economic development that have emerged across the UK since devolution. This section of the chapter builds on the concept of 'filling in' which we introduced in Chapter 2. There we set out the theoretical case for utilising the notion of filling in alongside that of hollowing out. In this chapter we will provide some empirical content for this theoretical framework and demonstrate our argument on filling in by interrogating the various ways in which the devolved bodies in the four territories of the UK – England, Scotland, Northern Ireland and Wales – have remade (or filled in) their institutional architectures of economic development. Finally, in line with a strategic-relational approach, we finish the chapter by looking at the different strategies which have been developed within and through these new state structures. This allows us to examine the interplay of structure and strategy in each of the UK's territories.

The UK devolution settlement

New Labour came to power in 1997 accompanied by manifesto commitments which promised devolution for Scotland and Wales and regional government for England. The programme of devolution, which gained legislative support over the next two years, has been labelled as 'one of the most significant features' of New Labour's first term in office (Driver and Martell, 2002: 54). Essentially, under the devolution programme (enshrined in separate Acts for Scotland, Wales and Northern Ireland), the government set down the powers which were 'reserved' for the Westminster Parliament to take decisions on, including matters of defence, international relations, fiscal and monetary policy, immigration and social security. Other matters were then devolved to a new Parliament in Scotland, and to Assemblies in Wales and Northern Ireland. Crucially for our research, economic development was one of the areas for which responsibility was devolved, along with matters such as health, housing, planning, transport, agriculture, sport and the arts (see Keating, 2002 for details).

The Labour Party had had a brush with devolution before, in the 1970s. After the second of two inconclusive elections in 1974, the party found itself with a tiny majority in Westminster and relied on support from Scottish and Welsh nationalist MPs to pass its legislative programme. In return for this support, devolution was placed on the political agenda but foundered after referendums were held in 1979. These required qualified majorities for devolution to go ahead and although in Scotland 52 per cent of voters voted 'yes' to devolution, a 64 per cent turnout meant this was less than the required 40 per cent of the electorate. In Wales, 80 per cent voted against devolution, stirred by a set of anti-devolution Welsh Labour MPs. New Labour learnt from what Driver and Martell (2002: 170) described as the 'experience of the devolution debacle'. The 1997 government also sought pre-legislative mandates for devolution through referendums but this time only a simple majority was required. The result was pro-devolution votes in Scotland, Wales, Northern Ireland and London. In Scotland, Northern Ireland and London, over 70 per cent of votes were cast in favour of devolution, while in Wales the result was much closer, with only a shade over 50 per cent voting in favour. Wales was also divided geographically. Eleven of its twenty-two unitary authorities voted in favour, while eleven (in the largely English-speaking areas of Wales) voted against. This split vote had repercussions for the way in which devolution was to proceed. As we shall see, Wales introduced a regional structure in many areas of its post-devolution governance, partly to ensure all parts of the country felt represented and were brought into the governing machinery.

Legislation followed each referendum to establish the new devolved governing arrangements. Crucially, these were different in each territory, and as a result the UK has established what has become known as 'asymmetrical' devolution. Thus although new state structures were introduced across the UK, they were given varying competencies and powers. The Scottish Parliament has primary legislative competence (i.e. law-making powers) over non-reserved matters, as does the Northern Ireland Assembly. However, Scotland has tax varying powers (by 3 pence in the pound up or down) while Northern Ireland does not, and in the latter there is a distinction between reserved matters which may be devolved at some point in the future and excepted matters which are kept permanently for Westminster (see Keating, 2002). Wales has an Assembly, but this has no primary legislative powers. Initially the Assembly concentrated on producing secondary legislation to provide further details to laws first passed at Westminster, but the Government of Wales Act 2006 granted the Assembly more powers to vary Westminster legislation. Legislative Competence Orders were introduced by the Act and are a type of secondary (or 'subordinate') legislation, which transfer powers from Parliament to the Assembly in defined policy areas, though still subject to the veto of the Secretary of State or the Westminster Parliament. To make matters more complex, the Northern Ireland Assembly was suspended between October 2002 and May 2007 when formal power was transferred back to the Northern Ireland Office at Westminster (although the Northern Ireland civil service remained a strong influence throughout this period). England saw two elements of devolution introduced by New Labour. The Greater London Authority – consisting of an elected Assembly and Mayor – was established in 2000, while eight regional development agencies (RDAs) were set up in 1999 and given power over economic development in their regions. Advocates of devolution hoped that these would be the forerunner of elected Regional Assemblies in England, but this idea has quietly faded away following the overwhelming defeat of the proposal to establish an elected North-East Assembly in the referendum of 2004.

As we noted in the previous chapter, these developments fit very well with what Jessop has described as the 'hollowing out' of the national state 'as its powers are delegated upwards to supra-regional or international bodies, downwards to regional or local states, or ... outwards to cross-national alliances' (Jessop, 2002: 235). Hence, hollowing out refers to the delegation of (non-reserved) powers away from the national level; in this case downwards to the four territories of the UK. This is where the concept of hollowing out stops. It makes no claims about the organisational or institutional forms, or strategies and policies, which may result as a consequence of such devolution. In this sense it refers to the beginning of a political process in motion. Further conceptual elaboration is required to understand how, and why, that process subsequently unfolds. This is why in Chapter 2 we developed the notion of filling in to help us account for the myriad ways in which the state becomes restructured and rescaled following the initial decision to devolve some powers to a new Parliament and Assemblies. It is to this restructuring that we now turn, using the example of economic governance to trace the post-devolution changes in the institutional architecture of the UK state.

Devolution, constitutional change and economic governance in the UK

This section provides an overview of the major changes which occurred to the institutions of economic governance across the UK following devolution. It should be read in conjunction with Figures 3.1 to 3.4, which provide institutional maps of the post-devolution structures of economic governance in each devolved territory. These provide snapshots of the major changes made to economic governance in the first five years of devolution. They are not definitive, but do clearly illustrate that different degrees of filling in occurred in different territories from 1999 when the devolved institutions first took power. As we hinted in the last section, however, the state is indeed a 'political process in motion', and as we shall see in the rest of the book, new structures of governance are 'emerging' all the time as a result of economic, political and cultural pressures. The snapshot presented here represents the situation at the end of 2005, and as we note in Chapter 7, there have been many changes to these institutional maps since then. However, they do serve to illustrate the way in which the state was restructured differently across different parts of the UK, and in the rest of the book we will explore the political forces and relations which lay behind such restructuring.

As we noted above, the UK's asymmetrical devolution settlement established new state structures in the form of a Scottish Parliament, and elected Assemblies for Wales, Northern Ireland and London. In some senses this process provided each territory with an outline of a new state form – or an architectural framework – whose precise shape and contents would be filled in in each devolved policy area by social and political forces acting within England, Northern Ireland, Scotland and Wales.

Significantly, Keating (2002: 5) claims that one effect of the devolution settlement is that 'over large areas of public policy there is now no "centre" at all'. Economic development – a matter devolved to each of the new territorial governments – is one such policy area and, in the absence of any 'centre', the new governments have been able to devise their own structures and strategies. They could, of course, have left the structures of economic governance untouched, and there was no necessary reason why state restructuring should have proceeded any further. The new Parliament in Edinburgh and Assemblies in Belfast and Cardiff could have simply taken charge of the existing structures. However, our empirical work revealed the considerable political pressures that emerged in each territory as the newly devolved administrations sought to place their own stamp on policy development – pressures which resulted in a completely new configuration of economic governance. But before discussing events after 1997, we briefly consider the pre-existing institutional and political scene in the four territories, as the processes and relations of devolution inevitably built on these legacies.

The structures of economic governance before 1997

England has been renowned as somewhat of an 'enigma' within the territorial politics of the UK, both before (Taylor, 1993) and after (Hazell, 2006) devolution. Nowhere is this more apparent than in the context of economic governance. At one level, the economic development of England has often been conflated with broader policies relevant to the whole of the UK. On the other hand, economic development has long been the responsibility of a plethora of local and regional institutions, ranging from local authorities, development agencies and development boards (Duncan and Goodwin, 1988) to regionally based selective assistance and grants (Townroe and Martin, 1992). As a result, many of the key institutions involved in economic development before 1997 in England were either based at a unitary UK scale or at a more local scale within England. The consequence of this is that there was little territorial integrity for economic development at the scale of England, and indeed no economic development strategy, or structure, existed for England as a single territorial entity. By 1997, employment training in England was delivered through a network of Training and Enterprise Councils (TECs), promoting a creed of entrepreneurship and suppy-side employability (Jones, 1999).

Scotland possesses a relatively long history in a UK context of economic development initiatives and institutional development, which can be partially related to its distinct institutional settlement and its diverse economic history. In the post-war period, the performance of the Scottish economy was below that of the UK mean and, therefore, a number of regional policy initiatives were instigated by central government as a means of redressing the problem. For instance, the Highlands and Islands Development Board (HIDB) was established in 1965 as a 'means of facilitating economic assistance in the Highlands and Islands of Scotland, an acknowledgement of the disadvantaged economic and social conditions in the locality requiring complementary regional planning initiatives to encourage indigenous economic activity and demographic stability' (Fairley and Lloyd, 1995: 43). In response to further economic decline and agitation from Scottish Nationalists, the government created the Scottish Development Agency (SDA) in 1975, once again as a means of enhancing economic development within Scotland. This was helped in its work by the transfer of responsibility for regional selective assistance in Scotland from the Department of Industry to the Scottish Office. However, to the Thatcherite UK governments of the 1980s these agencies were 'the embodiment of corporatist thinking that has typified Scottish policy for the last forty years' (Adam Smith Institute, 1983: 5) and, in a move to impose the new 'enterprise culture', the HIDB and the SDA were replaced in 1991 by Highlands and Islands Enterprise (HIE) and Scottish Enterprise (SE) respectively, both supported by a network of Local Enterprise Companies (LECs) (Industry Department for Scotland, 1988; MacLeod, 1996). The institutional autonomy of the Scottish Office allowed these companies to command powers over training, regeneration, innovation and land reclamation, as well as local economic development and enterprise. This was a much more coherent and 'joined-up' set of powers than anything held by single agencies in England, and led Scotland to develop policies centred around key sectors and economic clusters well before these issues appeared on an English agenda (Gillespie and Benneworth, 2002: 73). As we shall see, this relatively long institutional legacy in Scotland, facilitated through the gradual gaining of autonomy by the Scottish Office in this policy area, helped set the framework for the subsequent evolution of new institutions within the overall framework of devolution.

There has also been a long-standing recognition of Northern Ireland as a separate administrative entity within the UK state. A Parliament existed here between partition in 1921 and the installation, due to civic unrest, of 'direct rule' in 1972. At this point, the Office of the Secretary of State (NIO) was formed with overall responsibility for the government of the territory. The NIO dealt with a broad range of responsibilities from this period onwards, including: economic and social policy; constitutional and security issues, including law and order; political affairs; and policing and criminal justice. Thus, issues of path dependency come to the fore once again, since the Northern Ireland Assembly (NIA) has been given a considerably wider scope for action, including primary legislative powers, than the similarly titled National Assembly for Wales (NAfW). In terms of economic development, this meant that the NIO had a history of preparing and delivering its own policy agenda, tailored to the unique political situation of the province, and the Northern Ireland Economic Council was established in 1977 to provide advice to the Secretary of State on economic issues. By 1997 the Northern Ireland Civil Service had developed a comprehensive administrative structure within the Department of Economic Development, consisting of the Local Enterprise Development Unit (LEDU), set up in 1971 to support small and medium enterprises; the Industrial Development Board (IDB), established in 1982 to focus on larger enterprises; the Industrial Research and Technology Unit (IRTU), founded in 1992 to enhance the contribution of science, technology and engineering to economic competitiveness; and the Training and Employment Agency (T&EA), established in 1990 to promote training, skill development and lifelong learning.

Wales has a relatively short history of administrative devolution when compared to Scotland and Northern Ireland, if not England (Osmond, 1977). The Welsh Office (WO), the specific government office concerned with the territory of Wales, was formed in 1965. As in Scotland, a Development Agency (the WDA) was created during the 1970s to appease nationalist tensions. Set up in 1976, the WDA lacked the broad range of tools available to Scottish Enterprise and the NIO, but sought to turn this into a virtue by concentrating heavily on an aggressive marketing and inward investment policy. The WDA also capitalised on its position as the pre-eminent economic development institution by forging what Gillespie and Benneworth (2002: 73) call a 'privileged ... and close working relationship with the Welsh Office'. Alongside the WDA, the Development Board for Rural Wales (DBRW) was responsible for promoting economic development in rural mid-Wales, while the Land Authority for Wales (LAW) concentrated on land acquisition, assembly and site infrastructure. The other main strand of economic policy was centred on the role of the four Training and Enterprise Councils (TECs) and their role in promoting vocational training and human resource development within the business community (on these points see Morgan and Mungham, 2000). Here we see the close institutional ties pre-devolution between England and Wales. Despite the election of an overwhelming majority of Labour MPs throughout the 1980s, the Welsh Office was forced to implement Conservative training policies designed in Westminster. This of course, along with many of the structures described above, was to change with the implementation of New Labour's devolution programme.

Filling in: the reorganisation of post-devolution economic governance

As might be expected of new institutions seeking to make a political mark, significant changes were made to the institutional architecture of economic governance across the UK. Here we begin to witness the results of a range of new social and political forces operating in and through the state at new territorial scales. These results were felt at two main levels. Changes were made to the administrative and political structures within the new governments themselves, at a strategic and policy making level. These strategic political changes at assembly and parliamentary levels have been accompanied by varying degrees of state restructuring on the ground, at an implementation level. We will look at both of these aspects of restructuring, taking each of the devolved territories in turn to chart how their structures of economic development have been filled in following the transfer of powers under devolution.

The governance of economic development in post-devolution Northern Ireland

The performance of the economy was a critical feature of the devolved politics of Northern Ireland from the very outset of power sharing, for the task of creating a strong economy has taken on a particular inflection, over and above a concern with economic prosperity for its own sake. Here it is argued that one key way of promoting lasting peace and stability is through the development of a growing and successful economy, where access to its rewards is not dependent on sectarian identity. For instance the Northern Ireland Executive argued in its second Programme for Government that

> we are also acutely conscious of the religious, political and racial divisions within our community and also the impact of poverty on individuals and communities ... We are therefore committed to a society where communities pull together and inter-communal division is removed; in which people feel valued and respected and can share in growing prosperity; and in which there is equality of opportunity and justice for all. (Northern Ireland Executive, 2002: 5)

To reinforce the importance of economic development, two of the five

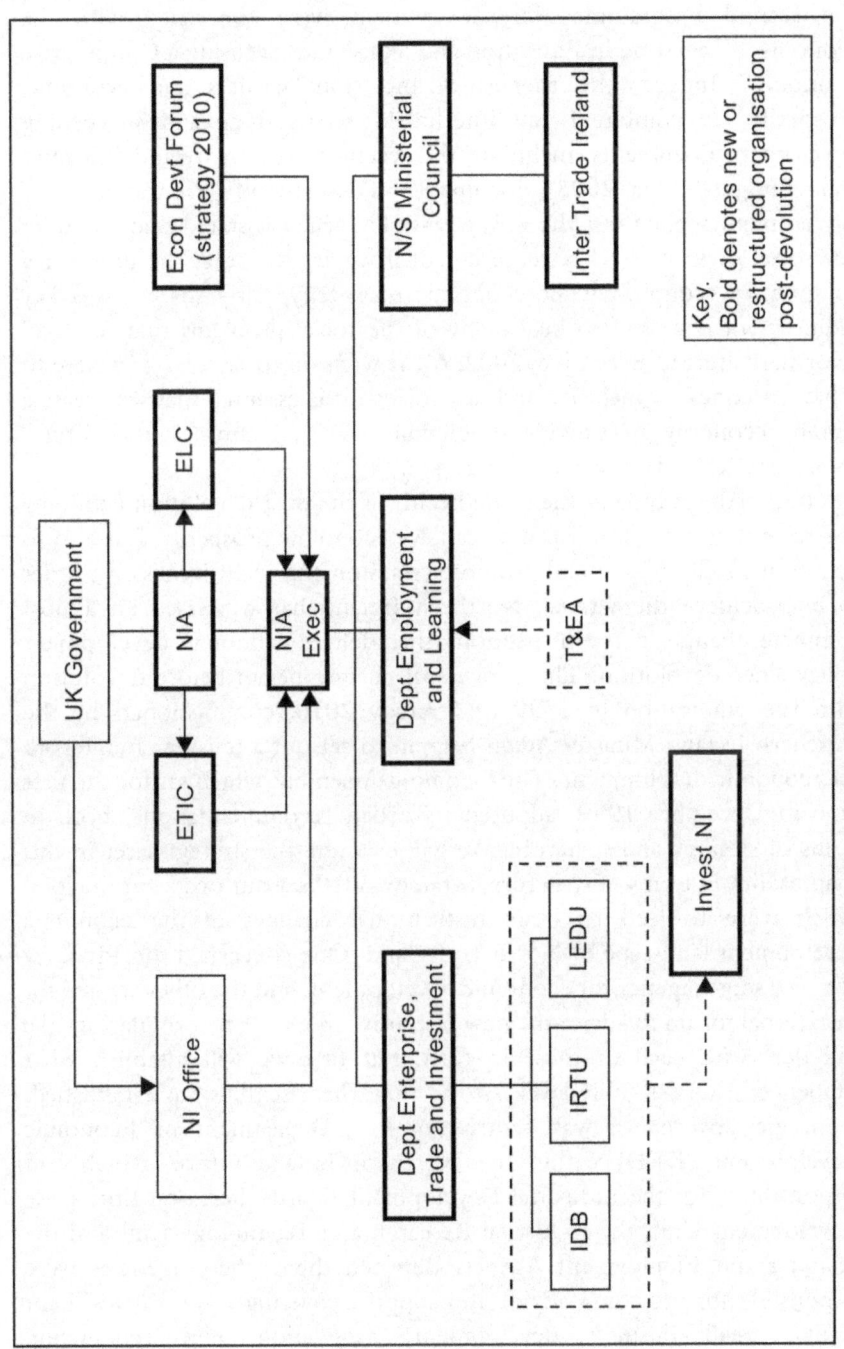

Figure 3.1 Structures of economic governance in Northern Ireland in 2005

priorities set out for government action by the Executive in both its first and second Programmes for Government were concerned with the economy – 'Investing in Education and Skills' and 'Securing a Competitive Economy'. Indeed, the themes of inclusion, fairness and economic prosperity are combined and interlinked across these and succeeding government documents, including the recent Northern Ireland Priorities and Budget 2005–2008 document. The second Programme for Government spelled out the linkages starkly, when it stated that 'tackling our social division is a key requirement if we are to create the basis for a competitive economy, while economic prosperity, fairly shared, is a key requirement if we are to heal many of the social problems that we face' (Northern Ireland Executive, 2002: 6). It went on to say that 'if we are to achieve a cohesive, inclusive and just society, it is essential that we create a vibrant economy to provide employment and wealth for the future' (Northern Ireland Executive, 2002: 43).

In Northern Ireland then, the health of the post-devolution economy was set out as critical, not just to achieve economic prosperity, but also to help heal social division and promote cohesion and inclusiveness. In order to help achieve these tasks, Northern Ireland has witnessed an almost complete change in the institutions that deliver economic development policy since devolution. This process of change began before devolution with the publication in 1999 of Strategy 2010, commissioned by the Northern Ireland Minister Adam Ingram to set out a ten-year framework for economic development. The incoming Assembly, which sat for the first time in December 1999, adopted its broad recommendations, both in terms of strategy and structure. We will examine the strategy later in this chapter, but in terms of structure, Strategy 2010 set out two key principles which were to lead to huge institutional changes in the economic development landscape of Northern Ireland. One concerned the advocacy of a new single agency for economic development, and the other argued for an external forum to advise the new Executive in its policy formulation. We will deal with each of these in turn, but first we will establish what happened at an assembly level. At the time the assembly was established, economic governance was centred on the Department of Economic Development (DED) within the Northern Ireland Office, which had responsibility for the Industrial Development Board, the Local Enterprise Development Unit, the Industrial Research and Technology Unit and the Training and Employment Agency. Between them, these agencies were responsible for providing advice and support covering inward investment grants, small business development, innovation, entrepreneurship, technological development, and training and employment services.

Under the inter-party agreement reached in December 1998 by applying the d'Hondt power-sharing principles of proportionality, the size of the new Executive was agreed at ten ministers, plus a First Minister and Deputy First Minister. Partly in order to increase the number of government departments to ten, the responsibilities of the old DED were split between two new departments – those for Employment and Learning (DEL), and Enterprise, Trade and Investment (DETINI). The former took the vocational training and employment services aspects of DED's work, and the latter had responsibility for inward investment, small businesses, innovation and technology transfer. Hence one of the major initial decisions on the structure of economic governance was partly determined by wider political issues concerning the Good Friday Agreement and power sharing.

Although comprehensive in nature, the structure of DED's responsibilities before devolution was somewhat unwieldy and Strategy 2010 argued for the establishment of a single lead economic development agency, which

> would sharpen the direction and delivery of overall economic development policy, presenting a clearer structure to users and removing the potential for confusion in the market place. It would simplify companies' dealings with the department [DED], and help to ensure that a clear and coherent policy message is presented to potential investors in Northern Ireland, whether indigenous or external. In addition, the integration of administrative services should yield worthwhile savings. (NIDED, 1999: 206)

Devolution presented the opportunity to implement this 'clearer structure'. As a senior civil servant commented about this reorganisation,

> We've reorganised the department [DETINI] ... this is about responding to the demands of today ... Why has the department reorganised? Answer, because the whole paradigm of having your resources dealt with, your policy dealt with in a devolved environment is different ... this is a devolved environment, local minister, locally accountable, he is going to be interested in knowing how policy is delivered.

As a result of the desire for a clearer and simpler structure, Invest Northern Ireland (INI) was established in April 2002 to operate as a Non-Departmental Public Body sponsored by DETINI. It took on the functions of the Local Enterprise Development Unit, the Industrial Development Board, and the Industrial Research and Technology Unit (see INI, 2001). In addition, this new 'sole' agency incorporated the role of the Company Development Programme (formerly with the Training and Employment Agency) and the business development functions of the Northern Ireland Tourist Board.

The other key recommendation of Strategy 2010, concerning the establishment of an advisory body, was also acted upon quickly. Indeed, by the time powers were transferred to the Assembly in December 1999, the new Northern Ireland Economic Development Forum (EDF) had already been set up to give advice and make recommendations on issues relating to the 'development and future competitiveness of the Northern Ireland economy'. The purpose of the forum has been to ensure that the 'social partners' (trade unions, employers, community and voluntary sector, further and higher education, local government and the agricultural sector) have an effective and meaningful role in influencing the formulation and implementation of economic development policy. In setting up the EDF, Adam Ingram had put forward the following economic argument:

> There is a recognition that shared knowledge and information is becoming more significant in the competitive strategy of companies. Knowledge-based competitiveness involves not only networks forged between businesses, but between businesses, education and research institutes. These links help ensure a flow of innovative ideas and highly skilled labour. (www.strategy2010.com/pages/ecodevforum.html, accessed 28 March 2007)

However, our interviews uncovered a significant role for the Forum in non-economic terms. It was viewed as important in securing 'buy-in' from non-governmental agencies; as one interviewee explained 'it was a case of getting lots of different views that have been accommodated within a common forum, towards a common purpose, and again that's where EDF sits, if you like, as drawing in partners'. But equally the Forum was also seen as something which could offer a broad oversight across different government departments. As one source put it, commenting on the establishment of the Forum, 'it was [a process] that actually engaged and helped gain the buy-in of all the social partners and members and also reflects the engagement and support of all government departments. So it really is a quite unique achievement, setting a picture, setting a scene, setting a framework for action by a lot of key players.'

This ability to join and link the work of different government departments became imperative after devolution, when the task of economic development was split between two new government departments, with their respective ministers and committees. As we noted above, DETINI took over most of the roles of the former Department of Economic Development, and the new 'lead institution', INI, is an agency of this department (see Figure 3.1). But alongside this, the new DEL has responsibility for higher and further education, vocational training, employment services, labour relations and training grants. Crucially, the Training and Employment Agency (T&EA), formerly a 'next steps' agency operating outside government under the remit of DED, was immediately absorbed back into the new DEL.

The rationale for this shift was also complex. The following quotes from three of those involved in the reorganisation illustrate administrative, technical and political reasons for the move.

> The T&EA was a next steps agency, and it was an executive agency before. When devolution came along we moved from the Department of Economic Development and became part of Higher and Further Education, Training and Employment, and they shortened the name to DEL. When the department was formed, the T&EA merged with higher and further education, the post-16 stuff. So it was a fusion of higher and further education and training and employment ... It was decided by the new ministers to bring all these things together, rather than have a small department with a big T&EA, and that's what happened, the agency was subsumed into DEL ... There's been no change in the status of people, but what has happened as a result is better cohesion in terms of policy-making, because you've got this post-16 remit together ...
>
> ... you could say that if Sean Farren hadn't brought T&EA in he wouldn't really have had a department at all ... a lot of the delivery mechanisms for education and training and learning are out there ...
>
> T&EA was the first next steps agency set up in Northern Ireland ... we wound it up because numerically it is 90 per cent of the staff of this department. The theory of next steps agencies is that they operate at arm's length from the minister on the basis of the framework document, which set up targets, reporting back to the minister quarterly and at the end of the year. But when you have a new minister who is full time, in a new devolved administration, anxious to get his hands on the levers of power and make a difference, unlike before it makes no sense to have those levers at arm's length. And so the agency didn't make any sense in political terms, and in terms of creating a new dynamic cohesive department, it made no sense in terms of that either. So we reviewed the situation and we moved from next steps status ...

What comes across strongly here is that whatever rationale is given – administrative, technical or political – the importance of devolution is clear in setting out a structure whereby local politicians and civil servants are indeed able to 'get [their] hands on the levers of power and make a difference, unlike before'. But what is also evident is the scope left to them to shape and develop such structures; to fill in the architectures of the state at the devolved level. As we have seen, in Northern Ireland this scope was used to completely restructure the institutions of economic development.

The governance of economic development in post-devolution Wales

Post-devolution Wales also accorded economic development a high political significance. Indeed, Rhodri Morgan, the First Minister for Wales, has argued that 'the most important task for any government is to create the conditions in which the economy can prosper' (*Western Mail*, 13 December 2001). In order to help provide these conditions, the National Assembly for Wales also established new departments and committees to oversee economic governance (see Figure 3.2). As in Northern Ireland there was a political desire by those who now had access to the levers of power, that these should be used to facilitate a coordinated strategy which would suit the new territorial scale of governance. Thus instead of being seen as 'effectively the regional office of Whitehall, [where] policy-making was essentially driven from London and we would just tweak it', a senior civil servant told us that devolution offered the opportunity of 'bringing political scrutiny and public direction' to the institutions of economic development. Hence there was a deliberate move to focus the activities of economic governance 'on the key goals of the National Assembly's strategic plan for Wales' (WDA, 2001: 1). Accordingly, the Assembly set up a new Ministry and Committee for Economic Development, covering national economic matters, including indigenous and inward investment, European economic policy (including structural funds), industrial policy and business support, tourism, and urban development and regeneration. For much of the life of the first Assembly (1997–2001), the First Minister also held the Economic Development portfolio, illustrating its political importance. The Assembly also established a new Ministry and Committee of Education and Lifelong Learning. The portfolio for this ministry involves the delivery of all publicly funded post-16 education, vocational training, and skills development policy.

As with Strategy 2010 in Northern Ireland, the Education and Lifelong Learning Department was also faced with implementing a pre-devolution action plan. In the case of Wales, the Education and Training Action Group (ETAG) had been set up after the General Election of 1997 amidst concerns over the quality of post-16 education and training following the collapse of traditional industries throughout the 1980s (Morgan and Rees, 2001; Rees, 2002). The Group produced an Action Plan (ETAP), prepared by the Welsh Office prior to the formal transfer of devolved powers in July 1999, which then went to the new National Assembly for final consideration. This gave an opportunity for the proposed reorganisation of training to be scrutinised by a new set of political and social forces. As Rees (2002: 108) puts it 'it is clear that the new [policy-making] mechanisms provided a vehicle through which these social groupings ... were able to exert important influences over the policy-making process in ways which had not been possible' before devolution. As a result, the role of business interests in the new arrangements was constrained, while local authorities and other public

NEW POLITICS/NEW INSTITUTIONS/NEW STRATEGIES

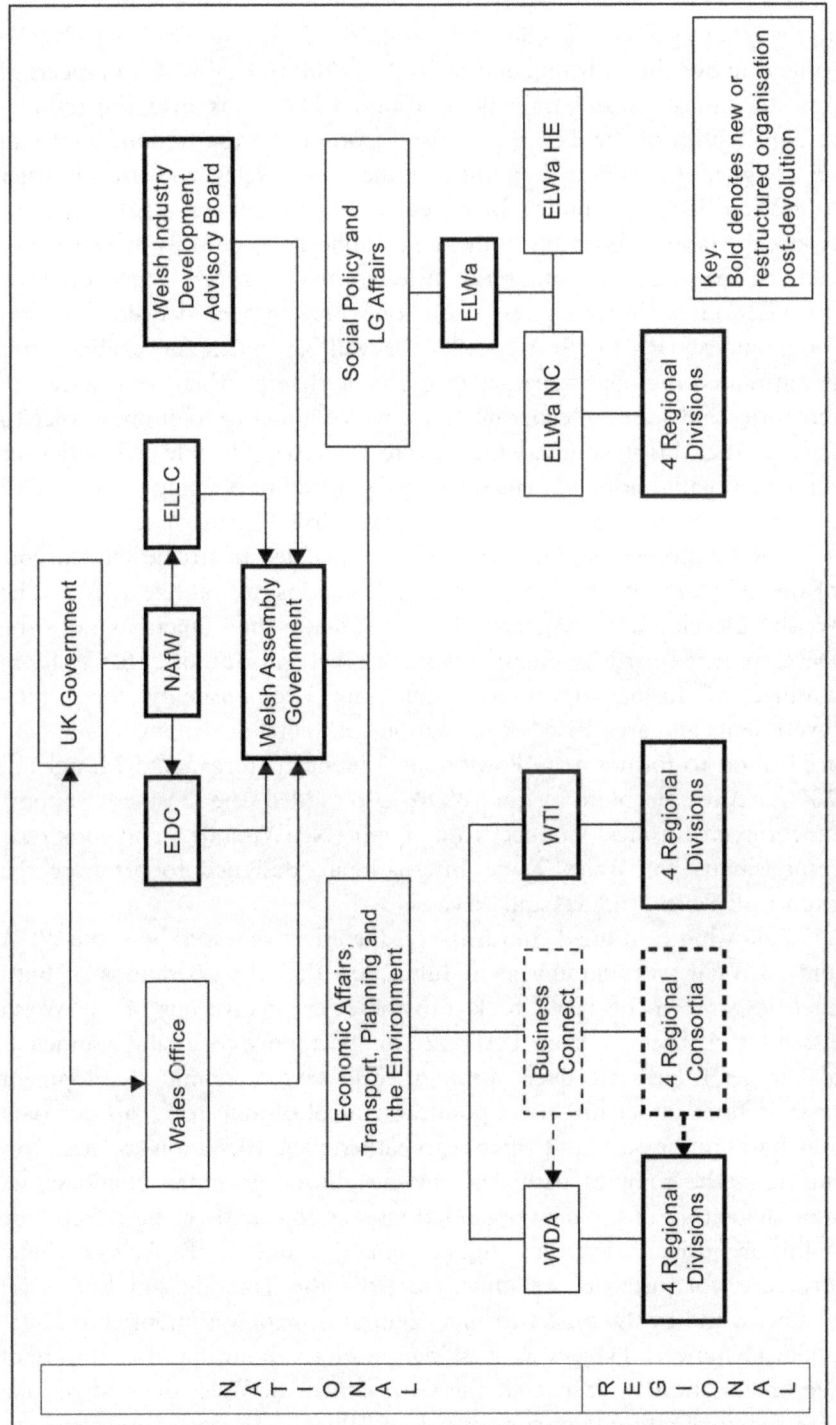

Figure 3.2 Structures of economic governance in Wales in 2005

sector groups gained influence. Education and Learning Wales (ELWa) was formed under the Learning and Skills Act 2000 to deal with all aspects of post-16 education and training in Wales. ELWa took over the training responsibilities of the TECs, and also incorporated the responsibilities of the Higher Education Funding Council for Wales and the Further Education Funding Council for Wales within its remit (see ELWa, 2001a). It was the largest Assembly Sponsored Public Body (ASPB) in Wales, but had no national headquarters, instead operating 'as a decentralised organisation with strong emphasis on the regional delivery of [its] programmes' (ELWa, 2001b: 42). We will say much more about this decentralised regional structure in the next chapter when we discuss the territories and scales of economic governance under devolution. Suffice to say here that this structure, which was to cause considerable difficulties for the new organisation, was largely a legacy of the re-opening of the ETAP discussions within the new political space afforded by the Assembly.

The Economic Development Ministry decided to strengthen the role of the WDA rather than invent a brand new institution like ELWa. The Welsh Development Agency had assumed the functions of the Development Board for Rural Wales and the Land Authority for Wales in advance of formal devolution, combining responsibility for capital investments and area-based regeneration with rural development and land acquisition to form a new 'Powerhouse' agency (Morgan and Mungham, 2000). After devolution, the WDA also added the business support functions of Business Connect to its remit (NAfW, 2001), and took over responsibility for Wales Trade International, designed to promote the export of Welsh products and services.

Following continued concerns over the effectiveness of both the WDA and ELWa it was announced in July 2004 that the operations of both agencies were to be taken back into the relevant divisions of the Welsh Assembly civil service from 1 April 2006. This move (officially branded as a 'merger') has effectively brought the key economic development organisations under the direct political control of ministers – an outcome which was unforeseen only three years earlier when ELWa was created. This illustrates the complex nature of post-devolution governance, and shows how the nature of the new organisations was constantly being affected by politically driven decisions right from the outset. ELWa's regional structure, for instance, was inherited from the Training and Enterprise Councils, and by the time a stronger central control was imposed in 2003, politically powerful voices were asking questions about the whole future of the organisation. A year later, the Government of Wales decided to take direct control rather than run the risk of failure in an arm's-length agency.

Somewhat ironically, one of our interviewees told us that ELWa always felt the Welsh Assembly was too prescriptive in the way it set objectives for the organisation:

> We're trying to get the Assembly to give us a little bit more freedom in that area actually. We would like to say to them, 'You agreed the corporate strategy and the operational plan with us, but don't manage us against the micro-indicators on that basis.' As I say, one of the things that we're looking at in the planning framework is that remit letter, which sets out the main aspects of strategy determined by the Assembly. As time goes on, hopefully they'll begin to trust us more and give us that little bit more freedom.

In practice, the reverse turned out to be the case, in what commentators have described as 'the biggest Welsh Government shake-up since the creation of the National Assembly in 1999' (Osmond, 2004: 2). Rhodri Morgan, the First Minister for Wales, justified the move in the following terms: 'The shape of the Assembly Government will become more governmental ... it will give us far more firepower ... and less of a distinction between making policy and implementing it' (cited in Osmond, 2004: 2). The Economic Development Minister was perhaps more forthright in hinting that disagreements over the strategic direction of the economic development organisations lay behind the move (Osmond, 2004: 3). A paper presented to the Welsh Cabinet in March 2004 by the Finance Minister Sue Essex stated that 'we need to consider how we can improve and strengthen the process of giving strategic direction to Assembly Sponsored Public Bodies (ASPBs)' (Osmond, 2004: 3). In the end, the outcome of such consideration was to take the ASPBs back under direct political control, in what has been labelled as the 'bonfire of the quangos' (*Western Mail*, 2004). From 1 April 2006, ELWa, the WDA and the Wales Tourist Board (WTB) were all 'merged' with the Welsh Assembly Government, creating two new departments to oversee economic development – the Department for Enterprise, Innovation and Networks (incorporating the WDA and the WTB) and the Department of Education, Lifelong Learning and Skills (incorporating ELWa).

In interpreting this process we can go back to the ideas of Jessop, and the strategic-relational approach to state theory, which we discussed in Chapter 2. We noted there how the relational character of strategic selectivity implies that the differential ability of social forces to pursue their interests through different strategies is dependent upon the relation between state structures and the strategies which different forces adopt. In this case, the Welsh Government decided that the only way they could guarantee to implement their chosen strategies was to take these agencies back under public control – as arm's-length sponsored public bodies ELWa and the WDA could not be relied on to carry out Assembly policies. The result is a greatly enhanced politicisation of both economy and civil society in Wales. As Kevin Morgan (2004: 15) puts it, such politicisation means 'that all roads will lead to and from the Assembly, rendering Wales a less pluralistic and more state-centric society than ever before'. Thus, what we witnessed in Wales was what might be termed a 're-statisation' of economic governance, rather than the de-statisation that commentators usually associate with devolution, again confirming the complex and contingent nature of these political processes of 'filling in'.

The governance of economic development in post-devolution Scotland

The Scottish Executive also provides an instance of how the political impetus provided by devolution can stimulate institutional organisational change. One interviewee characterised the pre-devolution situation as one of 'benign neglect', where the institutions of economic governance received written guidance from a minister in the Scottish Office operating as part of a UK Government, but were then left to 'get on with it'. He went on to add that '[devolution] is a positive development because ... one of the weaknesses of the Enterprise Networks was because ministers didn't really intereact with them ... they were developing their own strategies ... and felt almost isolated'. In contrast to this, devolution afforded the political space for ministers to have 'close involvement' with the work of the Enterprise Networks, and give them 'a clear direction'. To put in place this involvement and direction, the incoming Scottish Executive established a single department to oversee all aspects of economic governance (see Figure 3.3 and also Lynch, 2001; Parry and Jones, 2000). The Enterprise and Lifelong Learning Department (ELLD) was set up, along with an Enterprise and Lifelong Learning Committee (ELLC), which acted in a scrutiny capacity within the new Parliament. This took over most of the responsibilities of the business and industry policy functions of the former Scottish Office, together with responsibilities for Lifelong Learning and Further and Higher Education policy. Thus, post-devolution decisions in Scotland offered a contrast with those in Wales and Northern Ireland, where two departments and ministries were set up to govern economic development. Other key developments within the Scottish Executive include the formation of Ministerial Taskforces, including one launched to give greater ministerial oversight at a national level of the operation of Local Economic Forums and the creation of the Joint Performance Teams (JPTs) to set 'stretching' targets for the delivery agencies of Highlands and Islands Enterprise and Scottish Enterprise.

NEW POLITICS/NEW INSTITUTIONS/NEW STRATEGIES

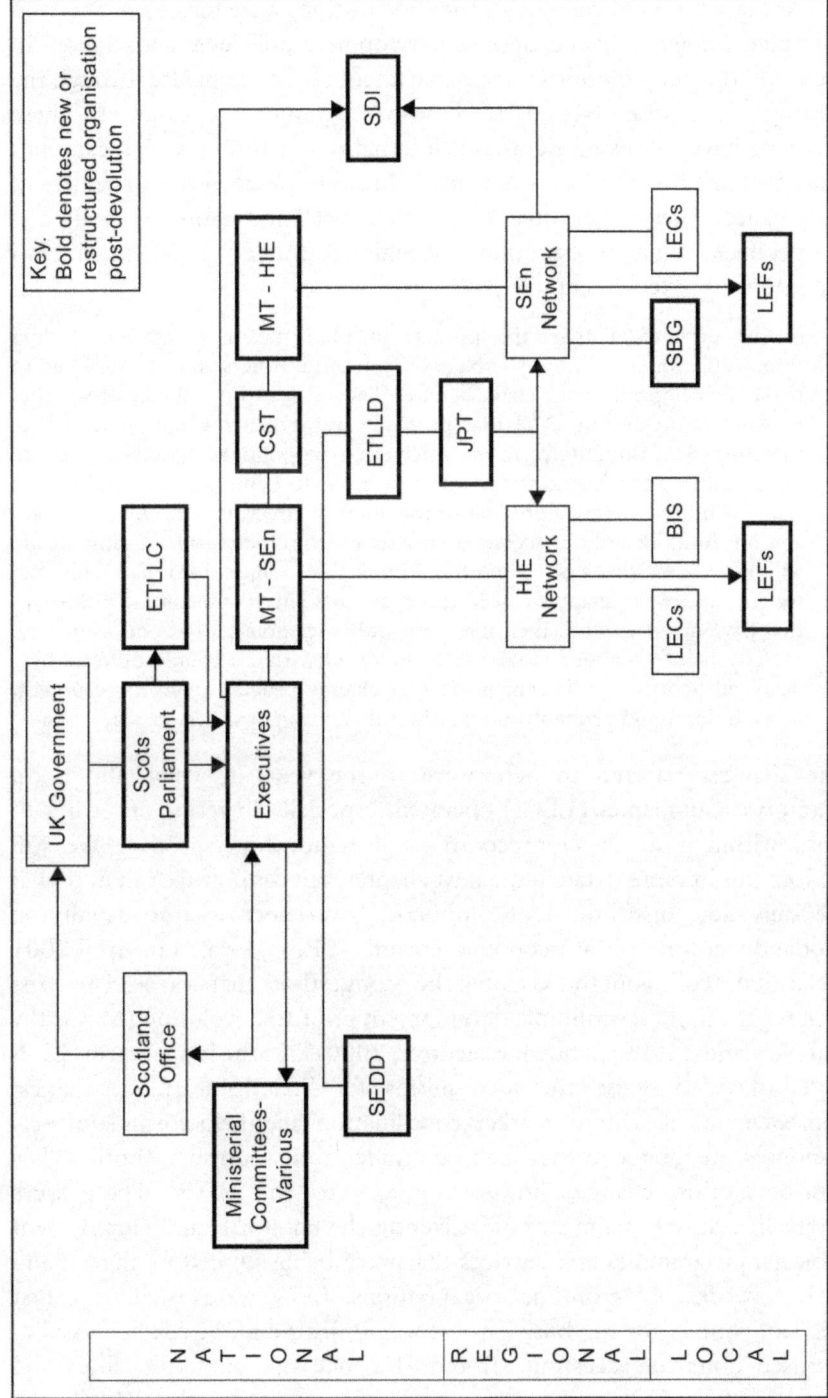

Figure 3.3 Structures of economic governance in Scotland in 2005

As Figure 3.3 indicates, fewer new institutions were formed in Scotland to implement and deliver economic development policies at a local level. In the main, the new committee and department chose to operate through the existing Enterprise Networks. However, despite appearances, these networks have witnessed significant internal restructuring, which can once more be linked to the forces operating through the devolved structures of governance. They were required to be 'less local' and 'more regional', and to operate within a more pronounced regional strategy. As one member of the Enterprise Networks put it,

> in the process of that, the process of them taking ownership, feeling responsible for [the Enterprise Network], feeling ownership of it, they had to make their imprint, make changes on it. They also had the choice of whether to wind it up or not. And that probably was a genuine option they had, therefore Scottish Enterprise in anticipation of political changes started to make some of the changes themselves in order to demonstrate: 'We live in a real world here, we are a product of the political environment. Our legitimacy and our funding and our accountability stems from there, so let's show we are willing to make changes' – almost as a survival technique. If SE had said: 'No, we are exactly the shape we need to be, and it's you, the incoming politicians that have got it wrong', then there was only ever going to be one winner ... the advent of a Labour Government followed within a couple of years by a devolved Scottish Parliament made that change process much more urgent, much quicker and probably more radical than it might otherwise be.

The changes referred to here were to the ways in which the Local Enterprise Companies (LECs) operated, especially in terms of having to work within a much more coordinated regional perspective. We will explore this in more detail in the next chapter, but for now we can note that the only new institutions of economic governance in post-devolution Scotland were the Local Economic Forums (LEFs), formed in April 2001 to facilitate cohesion and counter the 'congestion' that was said to exist with regard to local economic development prior to devolution (McCarthy and Newlands, 1999; Scottish Executive, 2000a). In the longer term, LEFs were asked to revise the mechanisms for lifelong learning, suggest improvements to labour market coordination and help formulate local responses in policy areas such as trade and tourism. Another key post-devolution change, however, relates to the LECs. These were originally created as a means of delivering the enterprise and employment projects, programmes and services that were being funded by the SE and HIE networks. As 'frontline' organisations, LECs were usually the first point of contact for the business sector and firms and, in effect, served as localised units for accessing SE and HIE network services (Fairley and Lloyd, 1995). Following recommendations made by the ELLC, the

Executive changed the constitution of LECs from private sector companies limited by guarantee, to being public bodies (Scottish Executive, 2000a, 2000b, 2001). LECs were reformed into subsidiaries of SE and HIE, and as such their staff are employees of these core organisations. In a move similar to the 're-statisation' of ELWa and the WDA in Wales, the aim of carrying out this organizational change was to make the LECs more accountable to the new devolved governance by bringing them within the legislative framework of the new Parliament. However, as we shall see in the conclusion, by 2009, both LECs and LEFs had been abolished, yet another example of the tendential nature of governance institutions. One other major post-devolution change took place in 2001 when the institutions concerned with Scotland's international trade and development roles were merged. Locate in Scotland, the institution concerned with attracting foreign investment into Scotland (see MacLeod, 1996), and Scottish Trade International, concerned with encouraging the trade of Scottish goods abroad, were merged into one institution, Scottish Development International. This single institution has taken on the functions of both its predecessors and demonstrates a more holistic attitude to Scotland's overseas linkages, post-devolution.

The governance of economic development in post-devolution England

England was always an 'enigma' within the territorial politics of a devolved UK. Despite devolution, there were no economic governance structures that operated at the scale of England. As we noted earlier, the post-devolution organisation of economic development in England was sandwiched between the government's various UK-wide policies and the activities of regional scale institutions such as the Government Offices and the Regional Development Agencies. As a result England was not subject to the same kinds of territorial political pressures felt within Northern Ireland, Scotland and Wales to reform its institutions of economic governance. Instead, the impetus for reorganisation originated elsewhere. Ongoing pressures from civil society at the regional level, particularly in the north-east, helped to provide the political momentum for the creation of nine Regional Development Agencies (see Mawson, 1998; Robson et al., 2000; Tomaney, 2002). This momentum had been building since the establishment of the Welsh and Scottish Development Agencies in the 1970s (Caborn, 1996) but it now coincided with the acceptance of a powerful academic and policy discourse which argued that in an increasingly globalised world the 'region' was the best scale at which to pursue economic competitiveness (Cooke and Morgan, 1998; Storper,

1997; for a critique see Lovering, 1999). The incoming Labour Government wasted little time in putting this discourse into practice, and established the Regional Development Agencies, to provide 'new opportunities in the English regions to enable them to punch their weight in the global market place' (DETR, 1997: 1). Given the subject-matter of this book, it is doubly significant that the functions of the RDAs were restricted to economic development. First, it shows the importance of scale in building institutions of economic governance, and we will explore this further in the next chapter. Second, it indicates that for England, or at least for those regions beyond London, devolution was a fairly restricted activity, being administrative rather than electoral and limited to this one policy area. Indeed, as one of the Prime Minister's early biographers put it, 'in England, [Blair] does not expect devolution to go beyond regional development agencies' (Rentoul, 1996: 467; see also Harrison, 2006), and this indeed proved to be the case.

The statutory powers and functions of the RDAs – to further economic competitiveness, efficiency, investment, employment and skills within a framework of sustainable development – were set out in the Regional Development Agencies Act of 1998, and those in the English regions became fully operational in April 1999, followed by the London Development Agency in July 2000. The 1998 Act also allowed for the creation of voluntary non-statutory forums called Regional Chambers (quickly renamed Regional Assemblies (RAs) in most cases), which were to scrutinise and monitor the work of the RDAs, although in London this monitoring role is performed by the elected Greater London Assembly. In addition to establishing RDAs and Regional Assemblies, New Labour increased the power of the Government Offices for the Regions (GOs). These had been set up in 1994 by John Major's Conservative Government, and were designed to coordinate the work of Whitehall departments in each region. Originally the GOs brought together the work of the Departments of Environment, Transport, Trade and Industry and Employment, but on taking office New Labour expanded their remit and by 2004 the GOs were bringing together the activities of nine central departments.

This regional triad of RDAs, GOs and RAs formed the key institutions of New Labour's devolution programme in England. Proposals for economic development (and other policy areas) to be controlled by elected Regional Assemblies were comprehensively defeated in a referendum held in the north-east in November 2004. Almost 80 per cent of voters rejected the proposal that the region should have an elected Regional Assembly, ending the chance of elected devolution in England for the foreseeable future. Interestingly for us, opinion polls revealed that one reason why the opposition was so strong was an adherence to the county scale of local government, which would have been abolished had the proposal for a Regional Assembly gone ahead – an example of the social relations operating in and through existing scales and territories of governance preventing new scales and territories from being realised. Reorganisation of economic governance in England has also taken place through the restructuring of a number of Whitehall ministries; some in the aftermath of New Labour's second election victory in 2001, and some as the result of Westminster scandals and resignations in 2002. First, the Department for Education and Employment (DfEE) was restructured and its functions transferred to a Department for Education and Skills (DfES) and the Department for Work and Pensions (DWP) (previously the Department of Social Security). Second, the Department of Transport, Local Government and the Regions (DTLR) was also restructured. A separate Department of Transport (DoT) was (re)created, and responsibility for local government and the regions was given to the newly formed Office of the Deputy Prime Minister (ODPM), although the Department of Trade and Industry (DTI) took over from the DTLR as the sponsoring department for the RDAs. The ODPM did gain responsibility for urban and regeneration policy, the Single Regeneration Budget programmes and European Regional Development Funds from DTLR. Thus, in the second Blair administration, three Whitehall departments had significant responsibility for regional economic development policy within England; the DfES, DTI and ODPM (see Figure 3.4). None were to last. By 2006 the ODPM had been replaced by the Department of Communities and Local Government (DCLG), and a year later, when Gordon Brown assumed the Premiership in June 2007, the DTI was replaced by the Department for Enterprise and Regulatory Reform and the Department for Innovation, Universities and Skills (DIUS). The latter department also took over some of the powers of the DfES, with the rest going to the Department for Children, Schools and Families (DCSF).

We have already noted how the DTI and the ODPM shared the responsibility for delivering England's post-devolution regional economic development agenda. The other major development took place with respect to Learning and Skills Councils (LSCs). Within the DfES, LSCs were established in April 2001 but were planned before devolution, following New Labour's review of the TECs. They were responsible for the planning, funding, and management of post-16 education and training outside of the higher education sector (DfEE, 1999). Significantly, below a national-level LSC, a network of 47 local LSCs was established at a

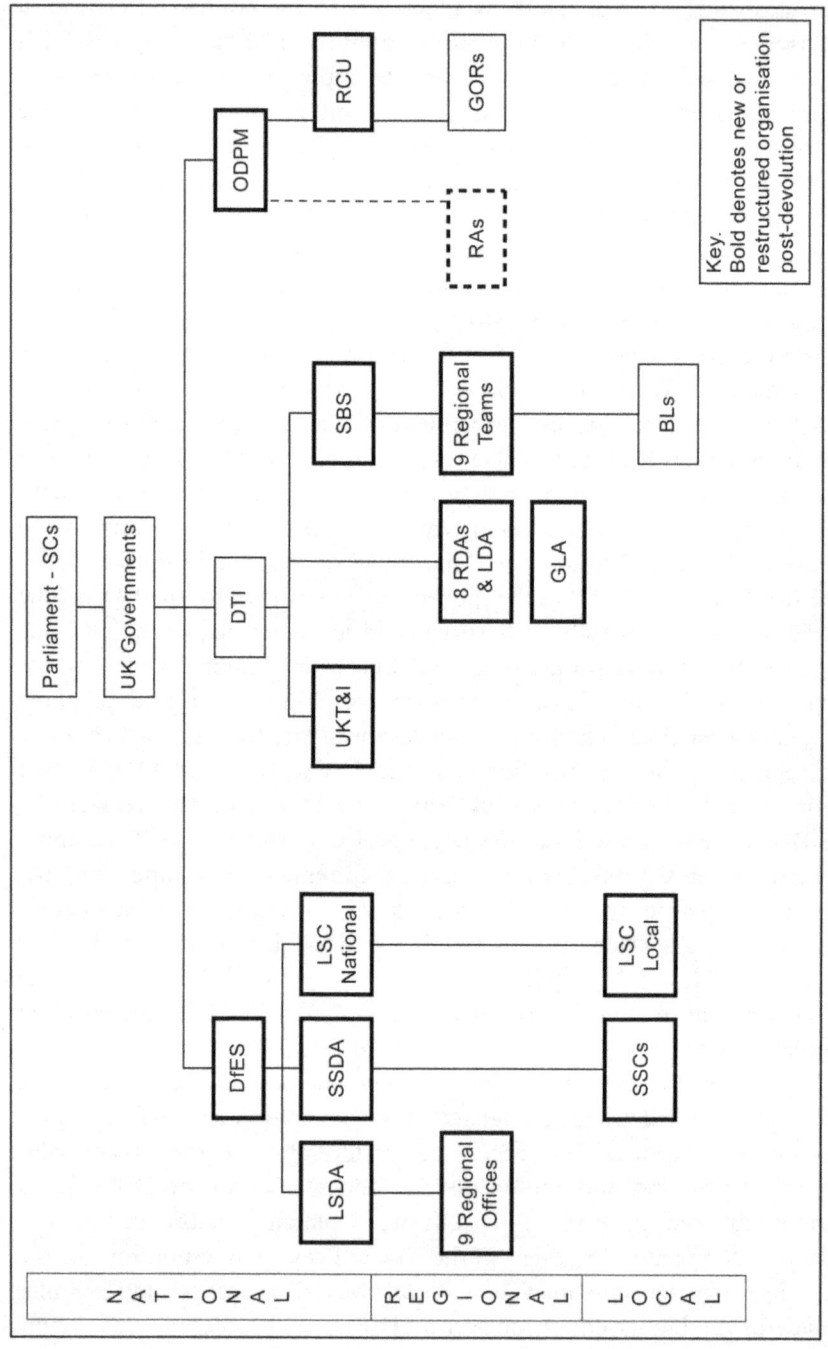

Figure 3.4 Structures of economic governance in England in 2005

sub-regional scale. LSCs took over the function of the Further Education Funding Council for England (FEFC), responsible for funding colleges and other institutions in the FE sector; the work-based training tasks of the Training and Enterprise Councils; the funding of school sixth forms; and the responsibility for adult and community learning – previously based with the Local Education Authorities. In tandem with the RDAs, the LSCs were at the front of the government's drive to secure effective economic development in England by harnessing the benefits of a 'knowledge-driven economy'. By 2008, however, their closure had also been announced, to be replaced in 2010 by a Young People's Learning Agency and a Skills Funding Agency. And in the biggest change of all, the abolition of the RDAs themselves was announced by the incoming Coalition Government in May 2010. We return to this theme in the conclusion.

The sum total of this change resulted in a complex series of differently scaled economic governance institutions operating on the ground in England. The spatial tensions inherent in devolution came to the surface when we examined the issues of collaboration and competition between them (see also Jones et al., 2004). As one prominent regional politician said to us with respect to setting up sub-regional partnerships in the East Midlands region:

> I think that East Midlands Development Agency and Government Office East Midlands didn't actually assert the fact that they needed two principles ... proper coverage of the region and no overlap. If you create partnerships, you don't want gaps or overlap, do you? The current structure has got gaps and overlap ... all I'm saying is there is gap here, gap here, overlap here, not a good framework for delivering.

He went on to illustrate the difficulties of joining up all these different scales of governance in terms of policy implementation:

> So anyway, there are some pluses and minuses. On the plus side you would suggest that if they get the regional framework right, and work properly with pre-existing sub-regional partnerships to help deliver, then you could get a win-win situation. You get your vertical integration, you get action on the ground, and regions are a bit remote to deliver. So let's get that delivery bit closer to where it can actually impact. But you could actually end up with the worst of both worlds, if you neutralise the effectiveness of those regional partnerships and you don't retain adequate capacity to drive a regional strategy and a proper regional perspective, and I'm a bit fearful that we are on the edge of that worst of both worlds scenario at the moment.

As we noted above, the other territories have witnessed more significant post-devolution changes at an implementation level, but somewhat ironically these have been driven by a desire to impart the kind of territorial coordination that seems a problem in England. We will return to these issues in the next chapter. For now we can sum up this section by emphasising the huge diversity of post-devolution structures of economic governance in the UK. England, Scotland, Wales and Northern Ireland have put in place significantly different institutional architectures. However, as we saw in the introduction to this chapter, it is important to emphasise the complex interplay between institutional structures and the strategies they adopt. It is to the latter that we now turn.

Post-devolution strategies of economic development

In contrast to the diversity of institutional structures, there was a remarkable degree of unanimity in the strategies of economic development adopted by each devolved territory. All stressed the improvement of productivity and enhanced competitiveness as their goals. All highlighted an increase in entrepreneurship, an improvement in skills and learning, and the development of ICT and digital connectivity as the key means of reaching these goals. But perhaps this is not so surprising. As one of our respondents said,

> We scoured the world looking for something a bit different. One of the team, who'd been on holiday to Hawaii, above and beyond the duty, called in at Hawaii Economic Development Department and brought back a brochure that talked about 'We must focus on innovation, we've got some natural in-built abilities here, oceanography and a range of other things, we could have spin-outs from that. University of Hawaii is a blah blah blah, but we do actually have problems with low-skilled people, tourism industry's taken a bit of a hit, we do need to strengthen this, what about the movie business, couldn't this be a great place for locations'. And I thought, 'Change the name, and change some of the sectors and clusters, and you've basically got it.' Go over to Atlanta, New South Wales, you go to Queensland ... there are no new solutions.

However, while there are 'no new solutions', and economic development departments globally seem to be adopting the same policies and plans, the political space created by devolution has been used to provide different inflections within the same broad approach. These have stemmed from the distinct political, social and economic circumstances faced by each territory, as well as from the different strategies that were inherited by the new governments upon devolution. We can also witness shifting strategies within each territory, as their economic development institutions have been re-appraised and their initial plans renewed within a post-devolution polity.

In Northern Ireland, for instance, Strategy 2010 was published early in

1999 to set out a ten-year framework for economic development, and the incoming Assembly – established later in 1999 – adopted its broad recommendations. Many of those involved in economic development in Northern Ireland recognised the particular problems faced by the province. Commenting upon the position of the Northern Ireland economy, the following source drew attention to its bias towards low-value activities. He argued that 'the key problem has persisted for a long time. [It is] well documented and it is the problem of low productivity, relatively low incomes. Problems less so than in the past are unemployment and particularly long-term unemployment. [There is] still an over-dependence on traditional low-value-added sectors like textiles and clothing, and food sector where growth is relatively slow.' Other respondents pointed to the economy's over-reliance on the public sector. One stated that 'you can argue that our business base is too small, our economy's lopsided in terms of the public sector, and the GDP associated with that sector, compared to some more successful economies. That's not because the public sector is too big, the private sector is just too small', while another reinforced this point when he argued that

> Northern Ireland has got a very high percentage of people in public sector employment. That's probably not sustainable in the long term, and that's dangerous for any economy. So while we've been glad to have it, it doesn't do a lot for the GDP target and it doesn't do a lot for competitiveness and it doesn't do a lot for innovation and it certainly doesn't do a lot for making a region like Northern Ireland a world-class region.

Our interviewees also pointed to the specific nature of the 'dependency culture' which had been fostered by Northern Ireland's particular circumstances, and to the ways in which this had hampered economic performance:

> There has been this reliance on government assistance throughout the 'troubles'. People get used to that so-called 'grant culture' ... People now realise, I think generally, that there's a need for change and unless we do change, we're going to lose jobs. You think about jobs that we're losing from our traditional industries, we've got to replace them. However, everyone says, 'Yeah, absolutely, develop entrepreneurship, develop the enterprise culture, that's what we need', but this isn't what you might call an enterprising economy, people don't start small businesses ... When push comes to shove, there's still a lack of will there, but gradually, we're getting to believe in people and I think we can do that through this movement away from capacity building to capability building, and the movement away from grant-dominated assistance to repayable forms of assistance.

Devolution offered the opportunity to reassess the levers of economic support in order to tackle the 'problems' of a low-value, public sector-orientated economy, and Strategy 2010 argued that a more dynamic and prosperous Northern Ireland economy could be encouraged through emphasising and developing enterprise, self-reliance and a heightened international perspective via a focus on knowledge, innovation and skills. The document also emphasised the fair distribution of the benefits of future economic development across the community, and argued for an increase in the resources available for skill development and other 'soft' infrastructure rather than providing grants and physical infrastructure such as premises. In all these respects the document was a significant forerunner of the themes that were to appear consistently in government documents after devolution. However, although its five core 'principles' were expressed succintly – in that the strategy should promote equality and social cohesion, create a knowledge-based economy, foster enterprise, be outward-looking and emphasise self-help – the document specified sixty-two separate recommendations for action. Practitioners found this somewhat unwieldy and one respondent told us that

> One of the biggest difficulties that the present DETINI had with 2010 was to try and make sense of the list. There's sixty-odd things to do, you can't possibly be doing that, it's much too complicated. So what they've tried to do is they've tried to sort out headings, sub points and to prioritise the list essentially, perfectly sensible ... You see the basic ideas, what people will publicly agree are the most important features of all of this, are known. Grants culture, and this and that. That's all generally agreed. It's just doing something about it.

In order to 'do something about it', the agencies of economic development further refined their structures, strategies and working practices following the suspension of the Assembly. Strategy 2010 was replaced as the key strategic document by the Economic Vision for Northern Ireland, published by DETINI in 2005. Although the essential 'vision' was the same – 'improving our global competitiveness through increased value-added leading to increased market share in products and services' (DETINI, 2005: 8) – this was a much slimmer and focused document, which set out four key drivers as a means of closing the productivity gap between Northern Ireland and the rest of the UK and other European competitors. These drivers were: increasing investment in research and development and promoting innovation and creativity; promoting and encouraging enterprise; ensuring people have the right skills for future employment opportunities; and ensuring modern infrastructure to support business and consumers. A set of key priorities was attached to each driver.

In addition, at a policy level DETINI also published a Regional Innovation Strategy to think/create/innovate, and together with DEL produced an Enterprising Education Action Plan. At a more operational level, INI developed annual Corporate Plans, as had InterTradeIreland (set up to develop North/South trade and business links), and it also produced an Accelerating Entrepreneurship Strategy. Structurally, INI had five 'local' offices, and worked through these to collaborate with groupings of local authorities to produce Regional Action Plans, and it also worked in partnership with local enterprise agencies at the local level. Gradually the development and implementation of these strategies helped to put the flesh on the economic governance framework created by devolution.

Wales too has seen the gradual evolution of its economic development strategies, and it has also attempted to tailor its policies to the particular circumstances of the territory. These were well set out by one of our respondents in the following terms:

> Basically, we've got two big problems, with a little third one added on top. One, we haven't got enough people in work, and two, those we have got in work tend to be in the wrong industries. Those, although not by UK standards, low productivity, we tend to have actually a large share of people in relatively low [value] activities and occupations. So what we've got to do is get about 100,000 people into the workforce, and the million people we've actually got already in the workforce, we need over a period of time to move them into higher added value businesses ... The one added on top of that, is that everyone else is doing the same thing. So what we've got to have is a unique selling point, and it's harder for Wales to have a unique selling point arguably than some other parts of the UK or Europe because our profile in the world is relatively low, certainly by comparison for the right reasons in Scotland and the wrong reasons in Northern Ireland. We don't hit the headlines for the right or wrong reasons and therefore if you want to become more global, more competitive and do the sorts of things we're talking about, then that requires us to do something about profile as well.

This type of diagnosis led to a post-devolution strategy with a twin emphasis on economic growth and training. The former was set out in the National Economic Development Strategy *A Winning Wales*, whilst the latter was expressed through the Skills and Employment Action Plan. The latter took its cue very much from the former, but as one respondent put it, these documents were seen as 'twins':

> There was pressure to produce an action plan for employment for Wales ... We basically said that employment is both demand and supply and really you need to mesh them both together. There's no point in just having an action plan for employment, because if there's no demand you've got a problem. So the economic development strategy was being developed at the time, so what we basically said was we need to embed the skills agenda and training agenda into that ... so we were working very closely with them ... The monitoring of both of those strategies has been done [together] ... so there's a great sort of

working togetherness between the economic side and the training side on developing that agenda. Also, the Economic Development Committee would have a presentation on the Skills and Employment Action Plan, and be able to input into it. So there's that cross-working, cross-fertilisation of stuff going on.

As in Northern Ireland, devolution offered an opportunity to rethink the strategies of economic development. One of our interviewees explained that post-devolution, economic development had 'become softer in a way. Before devolution, I would have said that the economic agenda was inward investment, and getting ministers on as many trips as possible, to fly the flag, you know, and fly them round all over the globe ... But [it used to occur] without much real understanding of the softer side of economic development ... skills soft infrastructure, make people employable.' As a result of this 'softer' agenda, training – or rather learning – has come to the fore. Another respondent also linked this shift to the establishment of a devolved government in Cardiff Bay:

> I think that what's happening now is that the lead by the National Assembly has led to a re-visiting of strategy. Most people accepted that the right strategy through the 70s and 80s was essentially one based on low factor cost. So I think there has been a change of emphasis ... in terms of looking forward to recognising the global economy and European enlargement, Wales has to compete essentially on the basis of innovation-led strategy which features the skilling of the workforce, including management. [ELWa is] centre stage now. Since 1997, investment in learning, and I prefer to use the word 'learning' rather than education and skills, has moved from the Cinderella of the economic development, to being seen as one of the ... key components of economic development.

A Winning Wales was published in January 2002 and contained ten priorities on which efforts would be focused. These were: supporting businesses; encouraging innovation; encouraging entrepreneurship; setting a fresh direction towards a greener economy; establishing Wales in the world; making Wales a learning country; creating strong communities; improving transport; supporting rural Wales; and promoting information and communication technologies. As a backdrop to these priorities, the document stressed the importance of spatial planning as a context for economic development. Thus, these priorities, 'relate both to the creation of increased prosperity and to its wider distribution across Wales' (WAG, 2002: 9). As we shall see in the next chapter the issue of a regional approach to economic development was to loom large in Wales. Indeed, several of these priorities drew on an expanded notion of the economy to recognise that economic development must also entail social and cultural development. Thus the explicit intention to create strong communities, improve transport, support rural Wales and set a fresh direction took us beyond a narrow firm-based focus. Interestingly, each of the targets set out at the end of the document was linked to one of the economically focused priorities, rather than to any of the more generic ones.

These targets were set out for 2010, and were to increase Welsh GDP per person to 90 per cent of the UK average; increase employment by 135,000; increase financial and business services employment by 20,000; increase business R&D expenditure to more than 1 per cent of Welsh GDP; raise the stock of Welsh businesses to the UK average per 10,000 people; reduce the proportion of adults without qualifications to one in ten and increase the proportion with a Level 4 qualification to over three in ten; match UK export growth; increase tourism expenditure by at least 6 per cent per year; increase the proportion of Welsh businesses using e-commerce to the UK average; and increase household disposable income to 95 per cent of the UK average. To take account of this timescale spanning the rest of the decade, Rhodri Morgan, the First Minister, declared in the preface that *A Winning Wales* was 'a 10-year strategy'.

Despite this, the document was 'revisited' in November 2005 with the publication of *Wales: A Vibrant Economy* (W:AVE), a new Strategic Framework for Economic Development. The new framework had just two priorities in place of the previous ten. These were to increase employment still further, so that over time the Welsh employment rate matched the UK average, even as the UK employment rate itself rose; and raise the quality of jobs so that average earnings increased and closed the gap with the UK average. These were overwhelmingly endorsed in a three-month public consultation stretching into February 2006, and W:AVE provided 'the broad economic development agenda for the Assembly Government as reshaped by the mergers, including the direction of future support to business' (WAG, 2005: 1). Although the next step was to develop an implementation agenda with 'clear action plans, timetables and revenue streams' (Department for Enterprise, Innovation and Networks, 2006: 57), the connection between structure and strategy is again clear, with the reformed institutional structure that saw ELWa and the WDA moved into the Welsh Assembly accompanied by a revised economic development strategy. But unlike Northern Ireland, where Strategy 2010 outlined and foreshadowed a new economic development structure, in Wales the revised strategy was prompted by the new structure. As the Minister for Economic Development and Transport puts it in the Foreword to W:AVE, 'the forthcoming mergers of the Welsh Development Agency, Wales Tourist Board and ELWa with the Welsh Assembly Government, provides the right setting for revisiting our economic development strategy to ensure that it remains fit for purpose for the next phase' (WAG, 2005: 1).

Although Scotland has seen fewer changes in its institutions of economic development than the other devolved territories, the new Parliament wasted little time in formulating its own strategies. By June 2000 it had published *The Way Forward: Framework for Economic Development in Scotland* (FEDS) which 'was designed to provide an integrated and coherent framework within which the promotion of Scottish economic development may be taken forward' (Scottish Executive, 2000c: x). As such FEDS was a broad strategic document, setting out a structure within which operational policy statements can be placed (such as *A Smart, Successful Scotland* for the Enterprise Networks or *Skills for Scotland* containing the Skills Action Plan). Like its Welsh and Northern Irish counterparts, it stressed that policies must be tailored to the particular concerns of the Scottish economy, and noted that an essential element of a successful economy would be the ability to 'shape solutions in ways which are most relevant to Scottish circumstances' (Scottish Executive, 2000c: 10). In this case, tackling low productivity was identified in the document as of particular importance, and this was confirmed by our respondents. One said that 'productivity no doubt is a massive challenge' and another said the 'big agenda in Scotland ... firstly ... is productivity ... you know we are well behind, even our best companies are fairly substantially behind the world's best practice in productivity levels, and it's that core productivity agenda'. Other specific weaknesses identified in FEDS included low levels of innovation, R&D and business start-ups, poor levels of training, infrastructural deficiencies and population out-migration.

The priorities put forward to tackle these were concentrated on the supply side of the economy, as might be expected. Indeed, FEDS was explicit that such policies maximised the input that the Scottish Executive could have on economic development. Hence it gave priority to strengthening the basic education system; improving transportation and electronic infrastructures; supporting enterprise; ensuring regional development; and reducing social deprivation and improving health. It also pointed out (17) that the main macroeconomic policy levers which affected the demand side of the economy, such as monetary, fiscal and exchange rate policy, were all reserved powers, and thus were not within the control of the Executive. As well as carefully demarcating the boundaries between devolved and reserved powers, FEDS was also keen to outline the respective roles of the private and public sectors. Indeed, it is unusual for a document of this nature in that it clearly established that the public sector should intervene in order to 'promote economic equity or economic efficiency where the normal operation of the market fails to do so effectively' (28), and it went on to point out that the public sector also had a role in establishing and maintaining 'the institutional structures that allow markets to operate' (28) and in 'facilitating the development of institutional networks – both formal and informal – that are not always self-generated within the private sector' (29). The document also explicitly stated that it was designed as an evolving strategy, to be 'refreshed' on a two- to three-year cycle. In practice, the electoral cycle ensured we had to wait four years before the next version was published in 2004.

Although the new Framework acknowledged that the fundamental strategic direction remained unchanged, there was an increased emphasis in the refreshed document on managing public finances, raising environmental sustainability, demographic change and utilising the planning system (Scottish Executive, 2004: 8). Of the five previous priorities, only two remained unchanged – 'basic education and skills', and 'electronic and physical infrastructure'. The former priority of enterprise support was strengthened to include 'entrepreneurial dynamism' and 'research & development and innovation', whilst the final new priority was simply expressed as 'managing public sector resources more effectively' (Scottish Executive, 2004: 8). The issues of regional prosperity, social deprivation and health were removed from the list of priorities. This represented a more focused and sharper vision, but the inclusion of public sector finance, sustainability and planning as key issues also tied the strategy more closely to the wider activities of the Scottish Executive itself. Following the publication of the new Framework, *A Smart, Successful Scotland* was also 'refreshed'. Its three essential themes remained the same – 'growing businesses', 'learning and skills' and 'global connections' – but the new document emphasised and clarified its relationship to FEDS. This is important, as we found several practitioners who were unsure of the relative roles of the two original strategies. As one of them put it,

> FEDS, that again is something that's influential ... then coming down the other way [is] *Smart, Successful Scotland* ... So *Smart, Successful Scotland* will be an umbrella [strategy] along with FEDS and there will be a number of things flowing beneath that, business birth rate, the global connections strategy that you've got, approaches in the whole learning and skills agenda, approaches in commercialisation, a whole range of things. One of the issues is how are these things put together?

At first, there seemed some confusion about just how they were 'put together'. One respondent viewed FEDS, and not *A Smart, Successful Scotland* as relevant to the work of local authorities, while another felt the opposite, claiming that 'SSS gets more mentions in local authority circles than FEDS does'. Others thought that FEDS had been superceded by

Smart, Successful Scotland. The 2004 version of *A Smart, Successful Scotland* clarified the relationship. It stated in the Ministerial Foreword that

> A *Smart, Successful Scotland* concentrates on the promotion of enterprise: on business growth and on the skills of individuals underpinning that. But we are making clearer that SSS is informed by, and dependent on, FEDS. FEDS, updated recently from its first publication in 2000, provides our overarching economic development strategy. SSS takes forward several of the key priority areas in FEDS to provide our enterprise strategy.

Here we have another example of the dialectic between structures and strategies, an emphasis that is opened up through a strategic relational approach. In this case, the opportunity presented by a new strategy was used to clarify to the institutional structures the roles of both itself and other strategies; to make it clearer to all just how 'these things are put together'.

The UK's asymmetrical devolution settlement means that Scotland, Wales and Northern Ireland each enjoy different powers and responsibilities. As a consequence, the operations of the Whitehall departments are also uneven. Some ministries, like Defence and the Foreign Office retain UK-wide responsibilities, while others like the Home Office cover some of the UK, but not all of it. A third batch of ministries, such as Health have effectively become English-only departments. Those responsible for post-devolution economic development – the DTI, the ODPM and DfES – fall into this latter category. Despite this, however, England remains the one territory of the UK not to have its own economic development strategy, as the responsibility for this was devolved to the RDAs. In essence, England had nine separate economic development strategies.

The 1998 Regional Development Agencies Act charged RDAs with providing a strategic focus to economic development in their region by producing Regional Economic Strategies (RESs). They did not, however, have a free hand in this and had to work within guidelines laid down by central government, which provided advice to RDAs on the development, content and implementation of their strategies. The guidance stressed that each RES should focus on areas where there was a need for specifically 'regional level' action. According to the guidance, each RES should provide

- a regional framework for economic development, skills and regeneration which will ensure better strategic focus for and co-ordination of activity in the region whether by the agency or by other regional, sub-regional or local organisations;

- a framework for the delivery of national and European programmes which may also influence the development of Government policy; and
- the basis for detailed action plans for the agency's own work, setting the wider aims and objectives for its annual corporate plan.

In terms of the more detailed content of each RES, the guidance stated that the strategies should:

- provide an analysis of the regional economy;
- identify priorities for action and identify which organisations should be responsible for delivery;
- set a 5–10 year plan outlining the RDA's aims, objectives and policies, with a particular reference to improving business competitiveness and productivity, marketing the region as a location for FDI [Foreign Direct Investment] projects, regeneration (especially in coalfield areas) and skills;
- identify areas suffering from social deprivation and exclusion and set out the reasons for this;
- outline the contribution the strategy will make to sustainable development;
- identify clusters of business that are, or have the potential to be, of regional significance;
- set out plans for developing strategic sites in the region;
- take account of rural issues.

Given these broad guidelines it is not surprising that the initial round of strategies, produced between April and September 1999, were fairly similar across the English regions (see Robson et al., 2000, for details). As in the devolved territories, they concentrated on promoting supply-side measures. Each of the nine strategies contained a commitment to develop existing industrial clusters, and each also vowed to increase the supply of start-up and venture capital. The majority of the strategies sought to provide incubators for business start-ups, encourage spin-out companies from higher education, develop new industrial clusters, secure sites for new investment, build networks linking higher education and business, encourage the growth of the social economy, establish innovation centres and develop ICT skills. Nevertheless, part of the government's rationale for establishing the RDAs was a recognition that there was no single economic development solution that could be applied across England, and underlying the Guidance outlined above was a sense that the RESs needed to reflect the individual circumstances of each region. Thus, the remoteness and rural character of some of the East of England was reflected in the stress its strategy placed on internet and broadband access, while in London the creative industries were emphasised as a means of opening access to global markets.

Our research in England concentrated on the East Midlands, and its

RES, published in 1999 as *Prosperity through People*, set out the following vision for the region (EMDA, 1999). It maintained that 'by 2010, the East Midlands will be one of Europe's top 20 regions. It will be a place where people want to live, work and invest because of our vibrant economy, our healthy, safe, diverse and inclusive communities [and] our quality environment.' The introduction stated that the RES was a 'key component of an emerging *Integrated Regional Strategy* (IRS) for the East Midlands'. Uniquely amongst English regions, the East Midlands RES was placed from the outset within a wider strategic regional framework. As a result, the strategy recognised that economic priorities could only be achieved through integration with other regional social, environmental and spatial strategies and policies. The East Midlands RES (EMDA, 1999: 14) focuses on five strategic objectives:

- *Excellence in Learning and Skills*: creating a learning region which results in a workforce that is among the most adaptable, motivated and highly skilled in Europe.
- *Enterprise and Innovation*: developing a strong culture of enterprise and innovation putting the East Midlands at the leading edge in Europe and creating a climate in which businesses can prosper.
- *Information Communication Technology Revolution*: creating an ICT capability for everyone in the region to ensure information and knowledge is used to maximum benefit.
- *Climate for Investment*: providing the right conditions in the East Midlands for a modern industrial structure based on a combination of indigenous growth and inward investment.
- *Sustainable Communities*: empowered to create solutions geared to their own needs, thereby supporting a socially inclusive region.

The East Midlands RES was also distinctive in that it set out a fairly detailed timetable for delivering the strategy. The timetable was divided into three parts. In the first 100 days the strategy aimed to meet twenty-six of its 'commitments' or priorities for action, with EMDA acting as the lead partner in delivery on most of these commitments. The strategy also set out a short- and medium-term timetable covering two-year and five-year time horizons. These were less detailed 'aspirations'; for instance, 'meet training targets agreed between the East Midlands Lifelong Learning Partnerships and Government' (a two-year aspiration) and a 'marked improvement in levels of basic, ICT and transferable skills' (a five-year aspiration). Interestingly, the strategy also stated that the RDA would adopt a 'sub-regional approach' as a central component of its delivery strategy. Existing sub-regional partnerships would be 'encouraged to revisit current economic development strategies for their areas' and develop 'cross-fertilisation and cross-boundary working among partnerships and with partnerships from neighbouring regions' (EMDA, 1999: 29). The RES suggests that key components of the strategy could be delivered through sub-regional partnerships, although only after partnerships had gone through a process of 'accreditation'. We will examine this further in the next chapter when we look in detail at the spatial aspects of economic development.

In line with a commitment given in the original strategies, each RDA had to revise and update the documents at least every three years. In the East Midlands we were told that the RDA concluded that the initial document did not require a 'fundamental change' but, instead, 'changes of emphasis [were needed] for the new strategy'. The revised RES, published in 2003 as *Destination 2010*, again stressed that it was 'a high level strategic framework' which was 'intended to be the blueprint for economic development over the next seven years' (EMDA, 2003: 7). However, the key objectives and priorities had subtly changed. In the original RES, EMDA had set out two overarching 'outcome priorities': economic success and sustainable communities. In the revised version these were labelled (p. 20) as 'aspirations', and the outcome of 'economic success' had been replaced by the aspiration of delivering 'a competitive region'. This change is perhaps understandable, given the difficulties of delineating economic success. Below the two outcome priorities, the original RES set out the four 'key drivers' of economic success encompassing four of the five strategic themes listed above. These were learning and skills, enterprise and innovation, ICT revolution, and a climate for investment. In Destination 2010, the ICT revolution had lost its position as a key driver, and was repositioned as a cross-cutting 'connecting theme' (21). Enterprise and innovation and a climate for investment retained their position as key drivers, but learning and skills was changed into employment, learning and skills. This suggests a greater emphasis on employment issues, and indeed in the revised document specific targets were set to address unemployment. Overall, the notion of the East Midlands as a learning region had been replaced with a greater prominence on developing workforce skills. The other key change was to replace the 100-day commitments and two- and five-year targets with a range of more specific targets and priorities in order to reflect the three tiers of government targets. Tier 1 contained national objectives that provided an overall context for activities undertaken by all nine RDAs, Tier 2 had high-level regional outcome targets that added measurability to the national objectives and Tier 3 milestones were detailed output targets negotiated separately with each RDA. Our interviewees felt that these strategic developments had matched a shift in the organisation.

As one of them put it

> We've [EMDA] actually gone a long way to rebalance our priorities from where we started from. We did start from huge spend on re-generation and huge spend on land and property. We've moved a long way to the softer-end stuff – the enterprise and innovation, the learning and skills side of the agenda that we started back in 1999. There is a much stronger sense of strategy and stronger sense of direction, stronger unity of purpose. And a much stronger sense of where we are actually trying to get to, which didn't exist before.

This takes us back to Jessop's notion that state projects are needed to give elements of the state some measure of internal unity and guide its actions (Jessop, 1990: 315). Here we see the clear manner in which an evolving strategy provided a stronger sense of unity and purpose to an institution that did not exist three years previously.

Conclusions

This chapter has examined the structures and the strategies of economic development that have been put in place across the UK since devolution. As we have seen, devolution provided the impetus, and the political space, for both elements to be almost completely refashioned. We witnessed new institutional frameworks emerge across the UK, both at a policy-making and an implementation level. As a result, the structures of post-devolution economic development varied widely from territory to territory. But these new institutions also felt a political imperative to rewrite their economic development strategies. Interestingly, despite the institutional differences, these each covered very similar ground, emphasising the 'softer' elements of learning, skills development and employability, alongside a focus on industrial clusters, digital connectivity and entrepreneurship.

So we are faced with a situation of similar strategies being implemented through a diversity of institutional and political structures. As we pointed out at the beginning of the chapter, state spaces are actively transformed by the continual operation of this dialectic between state structure and state strategy. The rest of the book is concerned with how this dialectic has unfolded across the UK since devolution. We begin in the next chapter by looking at the crucial role played in such unfolding by the twin elements of territory and scale.

4
Territories and scales of economic governance

Introduction

We saw in the previous chapter how devolution in the UK ushered in a host of new strategies and institutions concerned with economic development. In this chapter we want to explore how these new institutions represent a rescaling, as well as a restructuring, of the state or, perhaps more accurately, we want to explore how state rescaling is part of the very fabric of state restructuring, and how it is difficult to achieve the latter without the former. This is because the scalar organisation of the state not only provides a site for the playing out of political strategies, but also provides a crucial mechanism though which such strategies may be enacted (see Brenner, 2009a, 2009b; Jessop, 1990; MacLeod and Goodwin, 1999b; Pemberton and Goodwin, 2010). By its very nature, devolution is a geographical process and by definition it refers to the rescaling of state activity. As Blacksell (2000: 171) puts it, devolution is 'the process of devolving power from central to more local levels of government'. However, this is not just a simple transfer of power from one level of the state to another, from the UK Parliament in Westminster to Assemblies and Parliaments in Cardiff, Belfast and Edinburgh. As we shall see, it also involves a rescaling of institutions within each of the UK's four devolved territories. The result is a complex reconstitution and rearticulation of various scales and forms of state activity.

We should not, of course, be surprised at this. Brenner (2004: 76) has drawn our attention to the ways in which 'historically specific configurations of state space are produced and incessantly reworked'. In other words, new geographies of the state, or 'new state spaces' (Brenner, 2004) are constantly being produced as part and parcel of the shifting nature of state institutions and political strategies. But Brenner (2004: 76) warns us that the 'spaces of state power are not simply "filled", as if they were pre-given territorial containers'. Instead new state spaces are actively produced through 'sociopolitical struggles articulated in diverse institutional sites and at a range of geographical scales' (Brenner, 2004: 76). Our research sheds some empirical light on these propositions. It enables us to see how the processes of devolution are part of this 'incessant reworking' of state space, but also how they are a key moment within it. We can also see how the territorial reconfiguration of the state is open to political contestation, and how new state space is indeed 'actively produced' at a variety of geographical scales through a set of diverse struggles within multiple institutional sites. Moreover, the SRA we traced in Chapter 2 enables us to think beyond a relatively straightforward shift from one scale to another, and instead focuses us on multidimensional relations between scales and across territories (see also Mansfield, 2005). It is these complex relations that we seek to draw out as we once more work through some examples of state rescaling and restructuring in each territory of the UK.

But before we do, we need to spend a short time clarifying our concepts of territory and scale, and exploring the relationship between them. Jessop et al. (2008: 392) refer to territory and scale as two of the most salient 'spatial dimensions' to consider when exploring the social relations of contemporary political–economic restructuring but they also call for 'conceptual clarification' that 'can be used to generate more precise, substantial, and substantive analyses' (Jessop et al., 2008: 397; see also Jones and Jessop, 2010). The principle of territoriality 'entails the enclosure, bordering, and parcelization of social relations' while that of scaling 'entails the vertical differentiation of social relations' (Brenner, 2009a: 31). Both elements are critical when analysing the UK's devolution settlement, but we have to avoid viewing either in isolation from the other. The notion of territory 'denotes segments of terrestrial space that have been demarcated and organized in terms of political power' (Jessop, 2009: 95), and is obviously foundational for any analysis of the state. In Western Europe, from the Peace of Westphalia in 1648, states were 'understood to occupy mutually exclusive, non-overlapping, contiguous, and sovereign territorial spaces' (Brenner, 2009a: 37). For our purposes, of more importance than this 'inside'/'outside' separation of national sovereign states is the internal division of the state into territorially demarcated sub-national jurisdictional areas. In the UK these internal political divisions have a long history and the current round of devolution is the latest phase in the uneven development of the state itself (Duncan and Goodwin, 1988). Through devolution Northern Ireland, Scotland and Wales gained jurisdictional authority over particular policy arenas within their own territories, including economic development and, as we shall see, this set in motion a complex series of events which reshaped the territorialities of governance in the UK.

In addition to altering the territorial geography of the UK state, devolution has also resulted in a fundamental rescaling of state activity – both within and between the four territories which make up the UK. If territory refers to the areal or horizontal 'reach' of the state, the notion of scale refers to the vertical differentiation of the state into a hierarchy of different scales that stretch from the global to the local. A rich array of empirical and theoretical work (Brenner, 2004; Jessop, 2002; Jones and MacLeod, 2004; Kiel and Mahan, 2009; Mansfield, 2005; Swyngedouw, 2000; Uitermark, 2002; While et al., 2004) has shown how the recent reconstitution of the state under contemporary capitalism has increasingly involved a reworking of the state's 'scalar architectures'. In Brenner's terms (2009b: 126), 'no longer, then, are the scales of statehood conceived as stable platforms of institutional organisation' but, instead, 'state scalar structures are now understood to be historically malleable: they may be ruptured and rewoven through the very political strategies they enable'. A fundamental task of this chapter is to trace how the political strategies entailed within devolution have 'ruptured' and 'rewoven' the scalar structures of the UK state, putting in place new vertical linkages and hierarchies between different elements of the state. In doing so we can add specification to how the twin processes of rescaling and reterritorialisation have been implicated in, and contributed to, the more general reshaping of the UK state. We can also link back to Chapters 2 and 3, and anticipate the material in Chapter 5, by exploring how the emergence of new territories and scales of economic governance provide opportunities for the emergence of new political forces and new state strategies. As Jessop (2009: 93) puts it 'approached from a strategic-relational perspective, actually existing spatial configurations offer a whole series of different strategically selective possibilities to stretch, compress, and otherwise develop social relations over time as well as space' (see also Pemberton and Goodwin, 2010). We will now explore how these 'different strategically selective possibilities' were realised around the issue of economic governance.

The devolution settlement and new territories and scales of governance

In the previous chapter we considered the new institutions of economic governance brought about through devolution and we touched on some issues of territoriality then. In this chapter we want to bring these territorial issues centre stage and consider how they combine with new scalar relations in the making of new state spaces. As we saw in Chapter 3, the devolution settlement consisted of a dual movement. New institutions were established following successful referendums and government legislation – a Parliament in Scotland, Assemblies in Wales, Northern Ireland and London, and Regional Development Agencies and Chambers in England – and powers over certain matters were then devolved to them. The result inevitably altered the territorialities of governance in the UK. Responsibility for policy areas such as agriculture, economic development, education, environment, health, planning and transport was transferred from the UK Parliament to the devolved institutions in each territory. Devolution, however, was asymmetrical – not all powers were transferred to each territory, and the nature of the institutions was also different (see Keating, 2002 for details). Powers for police and justice, for instance, have been transferred to Scotland and Northern Ireland but not Wales, and Social Security has been transferred to Northern Ireland but not Scotland or Wales. One of the reasons we chose economic development as the policy area to study was because it was transferred to each territory, including to the devolved institutions in England. This enables us to compare the outcome across the entire UK, something we could not do for other policy areas.

However, territorial reconfiguration did not stop at the territorial and scalar level of England, Wales, Scotland and Northern Ireland. Indeed, one key feature of the state restructuring that was witnessed during this intense period of change was a further round of territorialisation within each of these four nations. As we shall see in the sections below, this produced nine economic regions in England, four in Wales and two in Scotland, alongside sub-regional and local partnerships in each territory. The result was not four territories of economic governance across the UK, but many many more as the four nations began the task of setting up their own local and regional institutions. As to be expected given this level of territorial recomposition, the scaling of economic governance also underwent considerable change. Vertical relations were now stretched through local, sub-regional, regional, national and international networks, and rearticulated between different institutions operating at different levels. Crucially, such territorial and scalar recomposition was the outcome of political manoeuvres and contestation within each of the four UK territories. It is to this link between state strategy, scale and territory that we now turn as we seek to uncover the unfolding process of post-devolution economic governance in the UK. Given that we are devoting a later chapter to Northern Ireland, we will use examples here from England, Scotland and Wales to illustrate this link, beginning with the latter.

Territorial and scalar restructuring in Wales – the case of ELWa

We noted in Chapter 3 that one of the distinct features of economic governance in Wales after devolution was the formation of ELWa. This was a new institution set up by the Learning and Skills Act in 2000 to take responsibility for all post-16 education and training in Wales. This insitution was unique in the UK, as in all the other territories vocational training was provided separately from post-16 school education, further education and higher education. In Wales all were combined in the new institution. Given this wide-ranging remit, and the fact ELWa was the largest ASPB in Wales, the institution had a high profile and political visibility. However, the Welsh Assembly Government decided to set up ELWa with no national headquarters, instead emphasising the regional delivery of its programmes. Initially ELWa had two wings, one dealing with higher education, and one dealing with further education and training. We will concentrate on the latter, known as ELWa-National Council, as it was by far the largest element of the new organisation. Its emergence can be traced to a recognition of the importance of supply-side, skills-driven policies within Wales's post-devolution economic development strategies. This was in contrast to much of the previous two decades, where economic development had focused heavily on attracting inward investment and the provision of industrial and business premises. The shift found formal recognition in the production of the National Economic Development Strategy (NEDS) (NAfW, 2002) – the first economic development strategy of the new National Assembly Government. One person involved in the production of the strategy commented:

> One of the things we argued very strongly with the National Assembly last year when we saw the original NEDS draft, and the subsequent drafts ... was that we felt we needed to avoid making the mistakes of the past, which tended to be initiative-based. Big projects to develop business parks, which are needed, and transport infrastructure, communications, it's not that they're not needed, but what we said was if we're really going to make a lasting change in Wales, we've really got to look at the population of Wales as a whole.

Importantly, ELWa was fully aware of its position as the new cornerstone of economic development strategies in Wales. One of its employees told us that

> It's critical ... that [ELWa]'s been the major piece of institutional reform from the Assembly. There is a recognition in the Assembly that investment in

learning is part, a central part, of the economic agenda and so ... we've generally seen a shift in the mind set of politicians, whereas if you go back five years, economic development was largely seen as inward investment and some business support ... Since 1997, investment in learning, and I prefer to use the word 'learning' rather than education and skills, has moved from the Cinderella of the economic development, to being seen as one of the three key components of economic development.

Here we see state strategy and institutional change coming together to provide the organisational structures felt to be necessary to deliver the strategy. However, this was far from straightforward, partly because ELWa-National Council, in contrast to its name, was anything but national. Arguably the most important scale for the organisation over the first few years of its existence was that of the region. The decision to establish ELWa on a regional scale can partly be explained by political sensitivities towards devolution in Wales, and a corresponding concern to avoid concentrating the headquarters of national organisations in Cardiff and the predominantly English-speaking south-east, at the expense of Welsh-speaking mid-Wales and north Wales. It also reflects the political structures and strategies which existed around this policy area in pre-devolution Wales. In this instance ELWa had taken over responsibility for skills and employment training from the four TECs, which were regional bodies. Prior to the formal transfer of devolved powers an Education and Training Action Plan had been produced in July 1999 by the Welsh Office. During its production, with devolution on the way, the TECs and local authorities were able to lobby effectively to preserve a regional dimension to the delivery of training. As one politician told us,

> the TECs put up a very strong resistance in lobbying very powerfully, very effectively. The Council of Welsh TECs certainly became effective as a lobbying body and the CBI were also backing them and saying 'The last thing we want now is a reorganisation, get on with your job without reorganising', was their attitude.

In short, the political forces acting in and through the old pre-devolution state were able to guide and influence the institutional and territorial form of the new post-devolution state. It is indicative that the 'reorganisation' that was resisted was a territorial and scalar one. The institutions themselves changed completely, but their territorial reach and scalar differentiation were preserved as the process of 'filling in' the structures of post-devolution Wales began in earnest.

The four formal ELWa regions which emerged from these political debates – North Wales, Mid-Wales, South-West Wales and South-East Wales – mirrored the new National Assembly's four regional committee areas, and were also coterminous with the regional structure of the Welsh Development Agency, which had responsibility for promoting indigenous economic growth and attracting inward investment. On the surface, it seemed as though a new institutionalised territorialisation of governance was emerging in Wales at this regional level. Both elected and unelected institutions were organising structures around these four 'regional' territories, which in scalar terms were placed between local authorities and the national all-Wales level. ELWa then initially established four regional offices rather than one national headquarters, each one attached to a regional advisory committee, whose chair was also a member of ELWa's National Council Executive. These regional committees were comprised of people with experience in learning, skills provision, business, local government, trade unions and the voluntary sector. Each was responsible for drawing up annual Regional Statements of Needs and Priorities and liaising with the various locally based Community Consortia for Education and Training which lay inside their boundaries. The regional scale appeared to offer a way, in the words of one ELWa official, of meeting 'the need to make decisions at a local level as much as possible'. Again we see political strategies being reflected in the territorial structure of the state. The regional committees in particular, according to one interviewee from mid-Wales, were seen as having an important function:

> the production of the Regional Statements of Needs. The document guides ... the [National] Council's investment programme in each region of Wales, the advisory committee's role in that is extremely important ... what we've tried to do is relate the main goals in ELWa, as the National Council has set within its corporate strategy and plan, and try to apply what we think are the priorities in Mid-Wales, to those goals. And there are certain sorts of specific aspects to each region, there are deficiencies which the members of the advisory committee recognise, and you know, bring to the table.

Regional committees, and indeed the whole regional structure of the National Council, thus played an important role in enabling the National Council to tailor its policies and strategies, within defined limits, to the more specific needs of the various regions of Wales. However there was a 'national framework' of organisational aims and objectives within which the regional structure operated. The challenge, as one ELWa employee explained to us, was 'to balance being within a national framework and having that sort of homogenous approach ... but at the same time being able to reflect things locally'. The need to ensure an appropriate level of national guidance was reflected in the decision to determine the use of regional office funding at a central level. As another respondent put it, 'there is a need to get a balance between the all-Wales bit and the regional bit. It would be wrong to carve up budgets regionally: "There's your money, do what you like with it", because that would entirely defeat the whole bloody purpose of trying to approach issues on an all-Wales basis, so getting the balance right is the key.' However, 'getting the balance right' proved difficult. Indeed the territorial and scalar structure of ELWa posed very real logistical difficulties in enacting its strategies, as the following individual made clear:

> We're distributed so within my directorate and within my teams I've people in all the different offices. Team Leaders in our offices, and that obviously means that on a practical level it's much much harder to operate in a very integrated way, because with people around you, you can talk immediately. So a great deal of effort and resources are used travelling around Wales. I think the implications of saying we're an all-Wales body with no headquarters makes communications more difficult.

Clearly, in this respect, the scalar and territorial dynamics of filling in economic governance in Wales have led to considerable transactional costs within the organisation. These are magnified when we consider that ELWa was not just dealing with internal tensions and communication difficulties, but rather was attempting to fit into an existing institutional landscape which was full of other organisations operating at different scales across different territories. The following interviewee pointed to the difficulties of inter-institutional working in just one small part of north-east Wales:

> We've got the National Strategy in the Assembly for economic development [NEDS], we have each of the local authorities with an economic development plan, we have the Objective One partnership in North Wales with its Objective One Plan, we have the Urban Two Plan in Wrexham as well, we have the annual plans of ELWa, North Wales Division and the WDA. Really it was a matter of saying 'Right, let us try to get all those together let us see where the gaps are, let us see where are the opportunities to work as North Wales.'

Other respondents told us about the difficulties ELWa found when working with the local Community Consortia for Education and Training (CCETs), charged with providing the regional offices with information on local education and training needs. As one National Council employee noted:

> CCETs, well it's a question isn't it? We need to decide what the CCETs are for, we need to decide what to do with them ... There have been tensions, well documented, with the CCETs ... we need to work out what role the regional committees and the CCETs can play in our new structure and, as I said, the interface is not perfect. We're designing some of the new policy areas in the face of these new structures.

Morgan and Rees (2001) have shown how the tensions between regional ELWa and local CCETs have partly arisen because of the conflict between a regionally based business interest and a locally based local authority interest, illustrating that different levels and territories of the state are more or less amenable to access by different types of social forces. This is something we will return to later in this chapter, but for now we can simply note the significant operational and political tensions that were revealed in the post-devolution structure of economic governance in Wales. Indeed, the creation of ELWa shows how the spatial and scalar materiality of an organisation possesses direct implications for the way it operates. In particular, the initial primacy of the regional structure adopted by ELWa led to what we might term regional 'rhythms' in the way it operated (Jessop, 2001a) – rhythms which seem to have been detrimental to its more national concerns. Partly as a reflection of this, ELWa's territorial and scalar structure was reorganised only a few years into devolution. In 2003 the significance of the regional scale was reduced and all corporate directors were based in the South-East Wales office, with the regional offices concentrating on delivering services to learners in the various regions. Significantly, part of the reasoning behind this change of emphasis was to 'enable faster decision-making' within the organisation (ELWa, 2003a), suggesting that the previous territorial structure was an inhibitor to this.

However, despite these internal changes, questions continued to be asked over the performance of ELWa, and in July 2004 it was announced that the operations of ELWa (and the Welsh Development Agency) were to be taken back into the relevant divisions of the Welsh Assembly civil service. As we noted in Chapter 3, this was carried out in 2006, effectively bringing the key organisations of economic development under the direct political control of ministers in the Welsh Assembly Government. This outcome could not have been foreseen only six years earlier when ELWa was created in a blaze of publicity to tackle the economic problems of Wales. It does, however, illustrate the complex nature of post-devolution governance, and demonstrate the constant interplay between political forces and strategies and the organisational structure of the state that they seek to control. Of key interest here is the articulation between territory and scale. What was important in the early uncertainties of ELWa's operation was not just the insertion of a new regional territorialisation of the state in post-devolution Wales, but the scalar relations between this regional level and the National Council on the one hand and the local CCETs on the other. As Jessop (2009: 103) has pointed out, 'the key issue for a research agenda ... is the manner and extent to which the multiplying levels, arenas, and regimes of politics, policy making, and policy implementation can be endowed with a certain apparatus and operational unity horizontally and vertically and how this governance problem affects the overall operation of politics and the legitimacy of the new political arrangements'. For horizontal and vertical unity, we can read the articulation between territory and scale. In the case of ELWa this operational unity could not be endowed – either horizontally across the regional offices, or vertically between the different scales of operation – and after a short time the entire organisation was brought back into the political control of the Welsh Assembly Government as part of its civil service. At this point a new state strategy was implemented which once again altered the territorial configuration of the state. This articulation between scale and territory will now be explored further as we look at the post-devolution processes of economic governance in England.

Regional economic governance in England: seeking appropriate scales and territories of operation?

We saw in the previous chapter how the devolution of economic governance in England was centred on the creation of the nine Regional Development Agencies in 1999 (see Map 4.1).

The regional scale of governance had become formalised earlier in that decade, when in 1994 the Conservative Government redrew the map of Standard Regions in England (Hogwood, 1996) to create regional territories for new Government Offices for the Regions (GOs). These were designed to coordinate the work of Whitehall departments in each region, originally bringing together the Departments of Environment, Transport, Trade and Industry and Employment. This in itself was an interesting reterritorialisation around the work of central government departments, and it paved the way for the formal institutionalisation of regional governance under New Labour, as the RDAs were literally mapped onto the GO territories (with the slight exception of the Merseyside GO which was incorporated into the North West RDA). This regional structure represented the territorialisation of New Labour's economic strategy, which had always made an explicit connection between regionalisation and economic performance. Originally set out in opposition by New Labour's Regional Policy Commission (1996), this was a strategy which emphasised indigenous supply-side growth mobilised via regional-level institutions. In this way, all regions would be candidates for economic growth, rather than just the lagging ones. As New Labour put it:

> We believe that in an increasingly inter-dependent world in which the UK economy faces more intense competition, the best way to meet the challenge to increase economic performance in all our regions is to empower them to harness their full economic potential. This is being achieved by devolving

TERRITORIES AND SCALES OF ECONOMIC GOVERNANCE

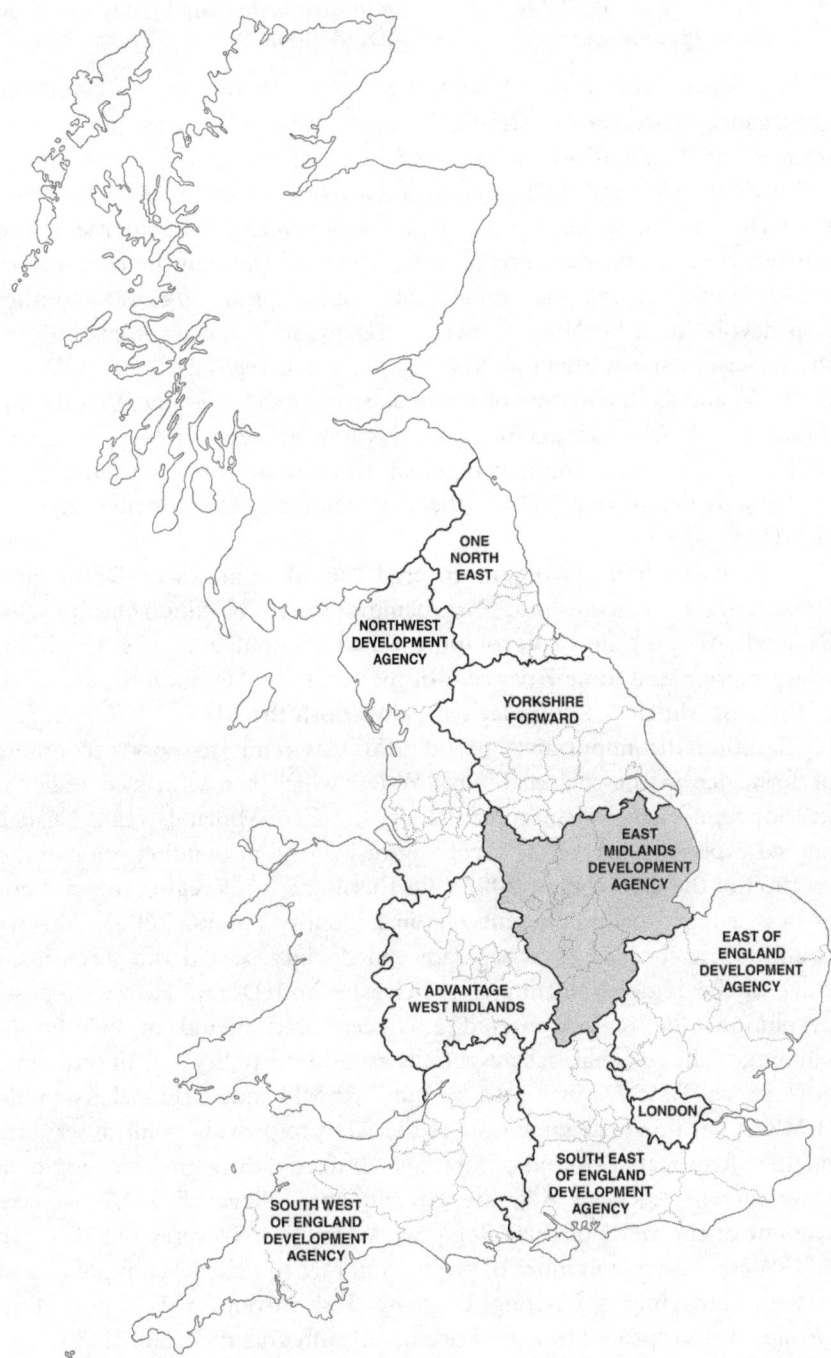

Map 4.1 Map of English RDAa

greater freedom, flexibility and funding to each region and locality to exploit their indigenous sources of growth. (ODPM, 2005: 9)

Unlike Wales, Northern Ireland and Scotland, there were no economic governance structures – or strategies – at the scale of England. Instead, the territory of 'England' was sandwiched between the government's various UK-wide policies, and the strategies and activities of the RDAs. This made the RDAs critical agencies in the delivery of economic development, and this territorialisation was enacted in policy terms through the compulsory delivery of Regional Economic Strategies, producing yet another post-devolution articulation between strategy, scale and territory. Indeed, the government saw them as 'the key players at regional level' (ODPM, 2005: 5) and as 'the drivers of regional economic development' (ODPM, 2005: 9). We will now explore how this link between strategy, scale and territory played out in this new regional structure by looking in more detail at the activities of one RDA – the East Midlands Development Agency (EMDA).

The East Midlands region covered the six counties of Derbyshire, Leicestershire, Lincolnshire, Northamptonshire, Nottinghamshire and Rutland. At the time of devolution it had a population of 4.2 million, which represented some 7 per cent of the UK total. Significantly, the GDP of the East Midlands region lagged below both the EU and UK averages, highlighting the importance of the EMDA's remit to boost economic performance in the region. Unlike Wales, which had witnessed regional development agencies since the 1970s, the East Midlands region had a limited experience of regional working or institution-building prior to the creation of the GOs (Foley, 2002). Furthermore, it is a region that did not possess a territorially coherent regional identity (Jones, 2003). The six counties saw themselves as separate and distinct, as did the three main cities in the region, Nottingham, Leicester and Derby. However, post-devolution, the region entered a concentrated period of institution-building at the regional scale, especially around the policy area of economic governance. EMDA was joined by the East Midlands Regional Assembly (EMRA), set up at the same time as the RDA to provide political scrutiny of the Regional Economic Strategy. Indeed, through the Regional Development Agencies Act, the government obliged all RDAs to take account of the views of their Regional Assemblies. To carry out this task EMRA established a number of groups and fora to help develop policy and strategy, including a Lifelong Learning Task Group, a Transport Task Group, a European Strategy Forum, an Integrated Regional Strategy Policy Forum, and a Regional Assembly Economic Review Group. New Labour expanded the remit of the Government Offices for the Regions after devolution, to bring together the regional activities of nine Whitehall departments, and the Government Office of the East Midlands (GOEM) completed the key trinity of regional economic governance institutions.

As in Wales, however, the region's territorial governance structures were not restricted to the regional scale. Indeed, a whole plethora of agencies and institutions were established at a more local scale to deliver and translate regional-level strategies. First, six Sub-regional Strategic Partnerships (SSPs) were set up by EMDA, based in Lincolnshire, Greater Nottingham, Northamptonshire, Leicestershire, North Derbyshire/North Nottinghamshire and Welland. These were created as a way of ensuring that EMDA's Regional Economic Strategy could be delivered in local communities at a sub-regional level. SSPs were responsible for drawing up local strategies and were seen as key partners in delivering many of the major outcome targets of the Regional Economic Strategy. EMDA Chairman, Derek Mapp (EMDA, 2002: no page), viewed SSPs as: 'key regional agents for economic development at the local level – they will support and shape the East Midlands strategy in future years and encourage partners to work for change on the ground. They hold the key to translating our Region's Economic Strategy into sub-regional action.' The connection between strategy, territory and scale is again highlighted. Local-level institutions, working over smaller territorial areas, were felt to be necessary to deliver and 'translate' the broad regional strategy into practice. Second, there were five Learning and Skills Councils (LSCs) in the East Midlands, covdering the counties of Derbyshire, Leicestershire, Lincolnshire and Rutland, Northamptonshire, and Nottinghamshire. LSCs were established in April 2001 to plan, fund and manage post-16 education and training outside higher education (see DfEE, 1999). Unlike Wales, where ELWa performed both tasks, in England, Higher Education was delivered separately from further education and vocational training. Third, Local Strategic Partnerships (LSPs) were supported by the GOEM and were charged with encouraging various actors – public sector agencies, local government, the voluntary and community sectors, businesses and local residents – to improve the social and economic viability of local communities. Finally, the various local authorities within the East Midlands area also took some responsibility for pursuing the economic development of the region. This responsibility was discharged mainly through the various social, environmental, and economic partnerships that the local authorities were members of. Significantly, the local authorities set up their own regional-level institution – The East Midlands Regional Local Government Association – to represent the interests of the region's local authorities and prepare Regional Planning Guidance and the Regional Transport Strategy.

In the East Midlands, then, the result of this whirl of institution-building in post-devolution England was a complex mix of organisations and agencies operating over different territories and at different scales, with the associated dangers of conflicting and overlapping territorial and policy responsibilities. In an effort to avoid these dangers, EMRA produced an Integrated Regional Strategy (IRS) in December 2000. As in the other eight English regions, the immediate context for the IRS was the production of a regional sustainable development strategy. As such, the Integrated Regional Strategy sought 'to apply the National Sustainable Development Strategy' to an East Midlands context (EMRA, 2000: 1; see also EMRA, 2005). However, EMRA also took the opportunity to use the IRS as an overarching regional strategic framework that could act to draw together other regional strategies, integrate regional policy-making, provide a framework for developing future regional policies and strategies, and outline how 'regional policy gaps' may be filled. The framework for the Integrated Regional Strategy is summarised in Figure 4.1.

Intriguingly, although not couched in this conceptual language, the diagram in the IRS (EMRA, 2000: 32) is a schematic representation of the horizontal and vertical unity, which Jessop (2009: 103) refers to and, as such, it explicitly recognises the need to draw together the territorial and scalar elements of economic governance. The framework shows an awareness of the importance of developing integrated policies in a multilevel policy-making and governmental environment. It stresses, for instance, the importance of vertical and horizontal policy coordination and relationships at all spatial levels between the European and the local. The adoption of such a framework reflected an enlightened approach towards the coordination of governance in the East Midlands, but as in Wales it proved harder to put into practice than describe diagrammatically. One problem, as in Wales, was the difficulty of unifying scales and territories through different institutions working to deliver the same overall strategy. The delineation of spheres of interest and policy responsibilities assumed a great significance in a region that very quickly became cluttered with organisations. A GOEM official described the following example to us: 'there are a couple of topics the RDA and Assembly work on and similar areas where we work on. So what or who has responsibility for what can be tricky. The more we worked on it, the more we decided it wasn't actually going to help anybody until everyone understood more about what was going on in the region.'

While this refers to the difficulty of territorial coordination, the issue of coordinating policy activities also arises in the context of the different vertical scales of economic governance. Indeed one EMRA official raised

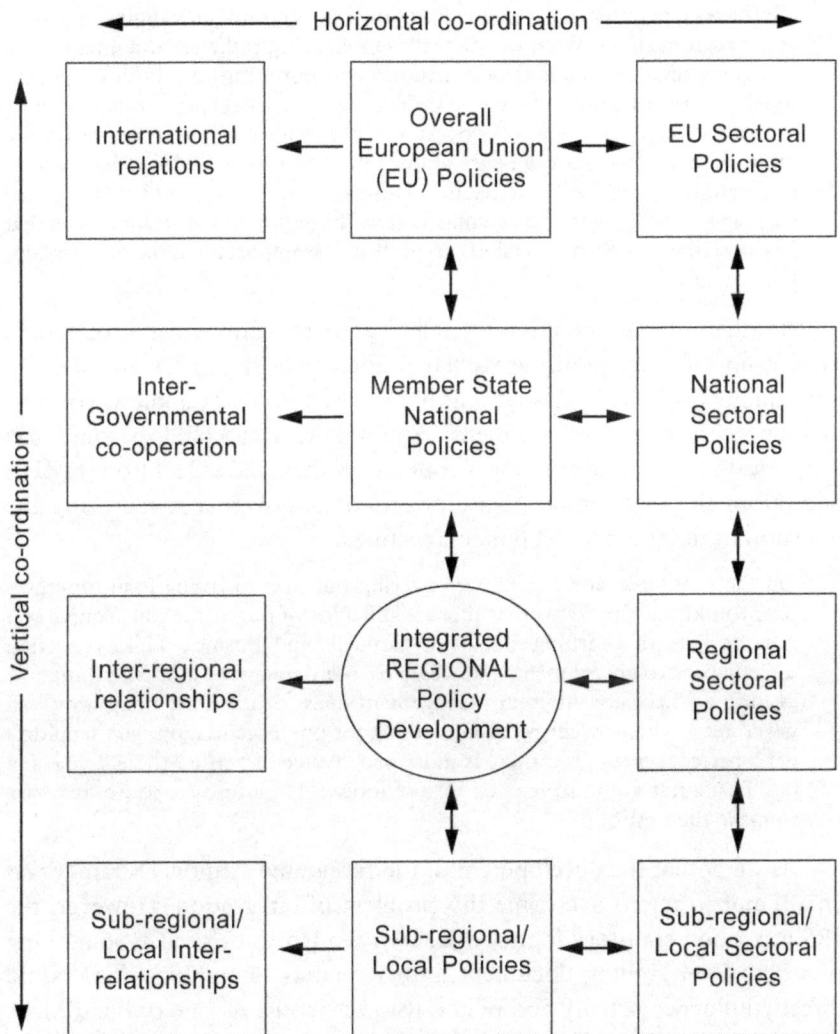

Figure 4.1 EMRA's Integrated Regional Strategy

concerns that the building of horizontal relationships was being done at the expense of vertical ones:

> We [have] been obsessed with the horizontal integration, how things fit across, at the regional level. What we are really emphasising is the vertical integration, you know the sub-regional, local, national and European, and I think a part of moving forward now is to say it isn't good enough to get a tidy and fully integrated regional framework, because if it doesn't connect to reality on the ground it's useless. So a big part of our integration now is about that vertical integration ... So building relationships with those local and sub-regional partnerships will always be as important as those horizontal relationships that I've described ... So partnerships vertically are as important as the partnerships horizontally.

Another of our interviewees referred to the difficulties involved in joining up different policy areas. He argued that 'if you try and join up everything, you never get anything bloody well done. You know, you just end up with a pile of spaghetti. You know, you could become too sophisticated ... and everything atrophies.' A third individual from EMDA pointed to the fragmented nature of economic governance following the insertion of new actors and policy structures:

> On the economic side I think we're trying our best to [bring it all together] but, you know, the fact is that there is still a lot of fragmentation. You've still got the likes of Learning and Skills Councils and Business Links reporting directly back to government, and we do try our damnest to influence things ... as long as there are different management lines for different things you will never get a perfect synergy. Even working for one organisation, you wouldn't get a perfect synergy but there is more of a chance of getting there if you join up. That's not going to happen for the foreseeable future ... so we just have to make the best of it.

As we noted, the development of the Integrated Regional Strategy was an attempt to try to overcome this problem of integration. However, the IRS was a non-statutory framework and it tended to be used as something of a high-level guiding document, rather than as something which could directly influence activity and policy at lower levels. As one of our EMRA interviewees put it, 'the Assembly could have driven an IRS concept till the cows come home, but unless you have the buy-in then they wouldn't have captured the EMDA resource into that approach'. This was confirmed by a respondent from the Government Office, who commented that 'I think that partnership development would have all happened without the IRS ... I think, you know, you would find plenty of people that would argue, you know, that it's all a bit too high level.' Here again we see the dilemma in seeking strategies that are able to operate meaningfully in drawing together territory and scale. It would seem that those which cover particular territories find it difficult to reach up and down a scalar hierarchy, whereas those which seek vertical scalar integration find it hard to provide purchase across a particular territory. Certainly we found that devolution in the East Midlands had produced a complex set of new institutions working at different scales and over different territories, and the search for a unifying strategy proved elusive. Work by Pike and Tomaney (2009: 24, 26) in the north-east of England has confirmed this view. They have maintained that 'by 2004, the emergent state spatiality of regionalization and regionalism had faltered leaving a pattern of territorial governance of bewildering complexity' and that 'projects of deliberately rescaling the state ... had fragmented into a much more messy morass of competing spatial imaginaries promoted by a web of institutions and individuals from within parts of government centrally, regionally and locally'. The problem in England was that the regional agencies inserted into the economic governance structure after devolution – the RDAs, Regional Assemblies and reformed Government Offices – found that they had to establish sub-regional structures to deliver their policies, but they lacked any means of providing integrated strategies to guide the work of these more local institutions. We will now turn to see whether Scotland was any more successful at joining up strategy, territory and scale.

Scales and territories of economic governance in post-devolution Scotland: the search for coherence

In a UK context, Scotland has had a relatively long history of economic development initiatives and governance institutions. As we noted in Chapter 3, the Highlands and Islands Development Board was established in 1965, followed by the Scottish Development Agency in 1975. Territorially, these twin agencies split Scotland diagonally in two, with the HIDB covering the sparsely populated north and west of the country and the SDA covering the eastern, central and southern part of Scotland from the Moray Firth to the English border. Each covered around 50 per cent of Scotland's landmass, but the HIDB accounted for less than 10 per cent of the population. This territorial division survived the major reorganisation of economic governance in 1991, when Highlands and Islands Enterprise and Scottish Enterprise were created, replacing the HIDB and SDA respectively. These twin agencies had responsibility for skills training, regeneration, innovation, land reclamation and local economic development and business assistance, presenting a much more territorially coherent structure than in the rest of the UK. Both Scottish Enterprise and Highlands and Islands Enterprise were 'legally required to decentralise much of their operations and budgets to local partnerships'

(Fairley and Lloyd, 1995: 62), which led to the formation of private companies known as Local Enterprise Companies (LECs). Prior to devolution then, the territorial and scalar organisation of economic governance in Scotland was relatively simple – with two key agencies covering the whole country territorially, occupying the centre of a vertical scalar system between the Scottish Office and the Local Enterprise Companies.

The process of devolution did not greatly disturb this picture. Highlands and Islands Enterprise and Scottish Enterprise remained in place, as did the Local Enterprise Companies. However, significant changes were made to the operation and organisation of this structure. As a senior LEC employee in the Scottish Enterprise area put it:

> Well, it's complex in the sense that you have, if you like, a disaggregated structure, you know, which combines the central body and the Scottish Executive based in Glasgow, but which operates through a network of LECs which are regional rather than national or thematic responsibilities. It's a product of the early 90s Conservative Government of that time. The rationale behind it ... was to bring more local flavour and accountability into the setting up of regional companies. And it was to bring more private sector participation and leadership in economic development. That's why the LECs were set up as sort of quasi-independent companies. That structure is changing quite dramatically and quite significantly ... On paper it still looks the same, there's a central body and 12 LECs which carry out about 80 per cent or so of operational activity. The method of operation is becoming more coherent or consistent. More aligned to national priorities than it ever was before ... Instead of each LEC developing its own suite of products we have a much smaller, more rational mix of products and services that we offer on a more national basis.

Under devolution then, the basic structure of economic governance remained the same but the operation changed. The same LEC employee went on to explain that

> What you had initially was a pretty loose network. Yes, there was a single organisation called Scottish Enterprise, and all the people working in it were employees of Scottish Enterprise, but the LECs ... were seen to be capable of operating quite independently, separately, devising their own strategies for their own area ... The degree of control from the centre was relatively loose and at arm's length ... The situation now is the national body, Scottish Enterprise, nationally exercises a much greater degree of control, as it were, on what can and can't be done by LECs, both in terms of corporate functions like HR and communications [and in] defining a much narrower range of products and services that we can offer, trying to establish a standard of service quality across the country ... So although on paper the structure looks the same, the method of operation both in terms of corporate services and delivery is very different to what it was.

Other interviewees confirmed the influence of the new political structures on Scottish Enterprise. Significantly, some of these individuals also drew attention to the significant contribution made by Scottish Enterprise's new leader in helping to push through a degree of centralisation within the organisation.

> The incoming Chief Executive ... very much accelerated that process because his arrival coincided with the political changes. So one of his key jobs initially, probably his key job initially was to get close to the new administration, the new Executive, understand what they wanted, what their expectations were and drive through changes that his predecessor was already making but maybe making in a bit of a political vacuum ... Robert, when he took over, because it coincided with political changes, was able to define and drive the change process much more vigorously and aggressively than was previously possible.

The same trend towards a centralisation of economic governance and a concomitant reduction in the latitude afforded to LECs was apparent in Highlands and Islands Enterprise. Significantly, the process of centralisation was felt more keenly in Highlands and Islands Enterprise in financial terms. One of our interviewees from a Highlands and Islands LEC told us that 'recently the LEC has been taken much more into the control of Highlands and Islands Enterpise itself and because that has happened the [LEC] board was saying "Well, what are we supposed to do, you're now even more in HIE's pocket than you were before ... HIE now own our cheque book", it's not the stuff to get excited about, but the board got really uptight about the fact that we no longer controlled the cheque book.'

Where did these centralising pressures come from and how were they made visible and executed? Many of our interviewees reported the direct political pressures felt after devolution. As one put it, pointing to how the time horizons of economic development were becoming more aligned to the time horizons of the electoral cycle, 'I think [devolution] has brought us closer to the immediate needs of customers and the immediate needs of Members of the Scottish Parliament ... I think it's probably brought us very much into horizons of a year or two, rather than the horizon of 5, 6, 10 years hence.'

Other interviewees pointed to the central role played by Scotland's new economic development strategy *A Smart, Successful Scotland*, published in 2001. As we saw in the previous chapter, this was the new government's operational policy for the two Enterprise Networks, and it broke new ground by setting out key performance indicators for both networks as a means of establishing a central direction for their activities. As an employee of Scottish Enterprise put it, 'the *Smart, Successful Scotland* document is actually the first time that the Scottish Government, the Executive or the Scottish Office has actually put a set of what you might call guidelines into the public domain about what should be happening in economic development'. The same individual, rather wistfully, stated that 'up until then it was truly arm's length, we [Scottish Enterprise] were able to do it ourselves'. Another senior figure in Scottish Enterprise pointed to the way in which *A Smart, Successful Scotland* extended the influence of the Scottish Executive. He stated that the document 'is a fairly clear statement of what we should be doing but it is also a clear statement from the Executive to the Enterprise Networks that this is what we want to do, as well. So, for example, our Chairman does repeatedly and frequently say "That's the game plan that we have been set by the Executive and it's our job to get on and try and deliver that".'

Scotland appeared to have been able to join up strategies, territories and scales in a much more successful manner than either England or Wales. This was not just about structures and organisations, but was also linked to the political culture that devolution fostered. The development of a 'Scottish' frame of reference and an economic governance landscape focused on the new Parliament were also influential. As one of our respondents put it:

> I think that devolution does give you a different audience; an audience in terms of decision-making that is a Scottish audience rather than a UK-wide audience. There's a much greater understanding of what's going on in the small-scale picture. They know what you are talking about. So I think devolution definitely has had an impact. You've also got, because of the constituency MSPs, you've got elected members coming from a much smaller area, much more aware of the specific issues within that and driving it through the parliamentary process.

Another explained how the devolved structure had led to a greater interest in, and transparency of, economic development issues:

> I think it has increased the transparency of what we [Scottish Enterprise] do. Let's just take an example in Westminster. Then, you might have a debate on the Scottish economy or the Scottish industry policy, I don't know, once a month. Now it's one every few days, the media are much more in your face on a lot of these things. So the whole environment I think, of economic development, has become one which is much more high profile … So the profile has been raised, expectations have been raised, both I think within MSPs and also within the wider public as well. As a result of that then we have seen a, I would say, a significantly greater level of interest and influence coming from the Scottish Executive … into economic development than we've probably seen before. We work much closer with them now than we've ever done before, and that's a good, positive thing. There's much more interest in setting up targets, in setting the direction for us, setting the vision for us and

largely we are now – we jointly decide upon the best way to go forward on things and then Scottish Enterprise kind of goes and implements.

Two further post-devolution changes helped to further this coherence, and cement the notion of doing things jointly. The first was the creation of a Joint Performance Team (JPT), established at the same time as the publication of *A Smart, Successful Scotland*, and designed to bring together staff from the Enterprise Networks and the Scottish Executive to articulate and measure overall progress towards the goals set out in *A Smart, Successful Scotland*. One of our interviewees explained its objectives by stating that 'I think the purpose of the JPT ... is to look, in the broader sense, at the outcome issues, at the output issues, and see whether ... those two together, suggest that economic interventions need to be re-directed because the existing interventions are not having the desired effect.' The shared membership of the JPT between Highlands and Islands Enterprise, Scottish Enterprise and the Scottish Executive meant that each organisation bought into and accepted the analyses and conclusions of the team, as the following quote makes clear:

> I guess just a feeling that there was work requiring to be done and we needed to get together a team of officials from our respective agencies who would actually roll their sleeves up and get on with that. So the lady from my team is the Chair of the Evaluation Group and she's responsible for taking that forward. Our opposite member from Scottish Enterprise chairs the Measurement Group and so on. So it's a question of just getting a small number of hardworking people together around the table and planning how we actually do the measurement.

The JPT framework provided a sophisticated performance measurement regime, and while other parts of the UK developed methods and systems for measuring and evaluating performance, the Scottish JPT model represented the most comprehensive and 'partnership'-based approach. Evaluation elsewhere was often viewed as top-down surveillance, and failure to meet targets in the RDAs in England resulted in grant penalties. In Scotland the evaluation focused on 'overall' outcomes agreed by the Enterprise Networks and a key role of the JPT was to disseminate best practice to key economic development actors across the country.

The second post-devolution innovation was the introduction of Local Economic Forums (LEFs), set up to identify and remove overlap and duplication of business support services within each LEC area. The creation of LEFs brought together for the first time a range of local economic development actors, and provided an important opportunity for the exchange of ideas and information. One of our interviewees commented that the role of LEFs was to 'get all these agencies under one roof, working and talking together, and trying to come, to the mutual benefit of everyone, trying to come to satisfactory conclusions for some of the problems we have', while another said the intention was to 'get them all together in a room, and the Scottish Executive seizes the initiative by laying down the remit [of LEFs]. The remit is "Get your heads together, get it sorted, sort out the confusion".'

LEFs were voluntary partnerships drawn from public sector agencies and local businesses, and in addition to streamlining business support they were charged with developing local economic development strategies consistent with *A Smart, Successful Scotland*. Two Ministerial Taskforces were established, one in the Scottish Enterprise area and one in the Highlands and Islands, to monitor progress and highlight areas of best practice, and a Central Support Team was set up to provide advice and information to the LEFs. There were debates as to whether LEFs added another element of complexity into the economic governance framework, especially as they had no dedicated budgets or administrative resources, instead relying on LECs to provide the necessary support. However an Audit Scotland report of 2004 found that LEFs had successfully delivered local actions and delivered most of the financial benefits expected of them, although there was a more mixed picture on effective communication and the elimination of overlap and duplication (Audit Scotland, 2004: 2).

Overall Scotland did succeed in setting up an economic governance structure which was aligned between strategies, territories and scales. The relatively long history of the Enterprise Networks meant that the pre-devolution framework was built upon rather than restructured. New dedicated processes – the Joint Performance Teams, the Ministerial Taskforces and the Central Support Team – were inserted to bind different elements together, and *A Smart, Successful Scotland* provided a good example of a strategy that was delivered and monitored through workable performance indicators. The coterminosity of LECs and LEFs produced a streamlined structure, and along with the well-established division of the Enterprise Networks resulted in a scalar structure that went from twenty-two LECs and LEFs to two Enterprise Networks to a single Executive Committee and minister. The move to a more corporate and 'nationalised' policy structure after devolution also helped to give the economic governance system more focus and coherence and the general consensus from our interviewees – whether located in the Executive, in the Enterprise Networks or in LECs/LEFs – was that such a system had succeeded in finding a balance between central strategy and direction, and local delivery and discretion.

Conclusions

This chapter has charted the multiple changes in the scales and territories of economic governance following devolution. What is immediately apparent is the way that these have taken completely different forms in the different parts of the UK. In this sense, the process of devolution, which ushered in a Scottish Parliament, Welsh and Northern Irish Assemblies and the English RDAs was only the precursor to a further set of complex changes which altered the shape and form of the state, both horizontally and vertically. Horizontally, new territories of regional operation were introduced in Wales and England, and each of these in turn then set up new territories of policy delivery at the sub-regional level. In contrast, Scotland did not alter its territorial organisation at all, keeping the pre-devolution shape of territorial governance at both regional and local levels. Highlands and Islands Enterprise, Scottish Enterprise and LECs all operated across the same territories pre- and post-devolution. Unsurprisingly, the insertion of these new territories of governance in Wales and England also transformed established formations of state scalar organisation, and both witnessed a far more messy and complex vertical hierarchy of state institutions. Local/sub-regional/regional and national-level organisations were asked to develop policy and operational unity, and the majority of key actors that we interviewed found this lacking in both respects. In contrast, most of those we spoke to in Scotland felt that the vertical and horizontal elements of the state had been successfully brought together. What we have witnessed empirically is a complex 'filling in' of the state, both vertically and horizontally within each devolved territory.

This took place differently in each case, and these differences were in turn driven by a set of political strategies that were developed by the devolved administrations in each country. In Scotland these paid careful attention to sets of performance indicators that were jointly developed at central and regional level. In this case the strategies did help to impose vertical and horizontal unity, but only because they focused on organisational as well as policy development. In England and Wales the strategies were less concerned with organisational unity, and as a consequence state personnel found them much harder to implement. As we have hinted throughout this chapter, it is state personnel, working over various territories and at particular scales, who are crucial in such implementation. Territories and scales of governance do nothing in and of themselves. It is state personnel, albeit working in particular territories and through relations at different scales, who attempt to put these strategies into practice. We will now turn to explore this in more detail in Chapter 5.

5
Peopling a devolved UK state

Introduction

The process of filling in that we have discussed in preceding chapters is one that has been taking place through the reconfiguration of organisations and territories and scales of economic governance. The period between 1999 and 2006, the main empirical focus of this book, witnessed the formation of new organisations of economic governance and the rationalisation or dissolution of others. As befitting a monograph written from a geographical perspective, we have also been at pains to illustrate how this process of organisational realignment possessed territorial and scalar ramifications. Post-devolution reorganisations of the UK state have led to the emergence of different territorial and scalar configurations of governmental power. The contemporary UK state, nonetheless, is more than merely an assemblage of inter-connecting organisations and bureaucracies possessing territorial remits and scalar associations. It is also, self-evidently, a peopled organisation. As well as being filled in in organisational and territorial contexts, it is clear that the UK state has also been filled in by its various state personnel. Our position on this issue is quite simple. State personnel of various kinds have had literally to make sense of the often large-scale organisational and territorial changes that have affected their working conditions over the past few years. At the same time, it is these state personnel that have been, in large part, the effective agents of change within these large-scale developments. As Heffernan (2005: 605) succinctly puts it, 'insitutions cannot be understood without exploring the actors who occupy them, while actors cannot be understood without examining the institutions they inhabit'. In this context, a consideration of the peopled aspects of the filling in process is imperative if we are fully to understand the unfolding dynamics of the devolution project within the UK.

The following section will outline briefly some of the academic work that has sought to consider the role played by people within the state apparatus. To date, work in this area has been relatively limited. Admittedly, some contributions from both Weberian and neo-Marxist positions have begun to allude to the significance of state personnel of all kinds for the reproduction of state forms. This new emphasis has been developed further in more anthropological work on the state, which has examined both the peopled character of state forms (e.g. Bratsis, 2006; R. Jones, 2007), the impact of the state on the everyday lives of citizens (e.g. Painter, 2006), as well as the interaction between the two (e.g. Corbridge et al., 2005). We maintain that recent work within a broadly neo-Marxist tradition offers valuable insights into the important recursive relationship between state personnel and state organisational and territorial forms. Furthermore, it is a body of work that complements and augments our view of contemporary devolution within the UK as a contingent process of filling in the state. Following this conceptual discussion, the chapter proceeds to examine the more empirical contexts within which these themes have been evident. First, we explore the role of state personnel in shaping some of the new organisations of economic governance that have been created in the UK in the period between 1999 and 2006. In this discussion, we seek to show how state personnel were actively involved in determining the organisational makeup, policies and strategies of new organisations of economic governance in the various devolved administrations. Second, we examine how state personnel were also instrumental in the reproduction of new scales and territories of economic governance in the UK. State personnel, through their actions, reaffirmed and problematised the emerging geographies of economic governance. Third, we discuss how state personnel embodied the connections being forged between different devolved state organisations. State personnel, in this way, were at the forefront of a key policy and academic goal of creating more 'joined-up' forms of governance within the UK as a whole and in each of the devolved territories (Ling, 2002). Significantly, state personnel also had to deal with the difficulties of developing these more coordinated forms of governance over recent years. Finally, we discuss how state personnel were associated with the territorial and national, if not always explicitly nationalist, contexts for the whole devolution process. The territorial identities of state personnel, we contend, could influence these individuals' attachment and commitment to the devolved organisation within which they worked as well as to the broader devolution project within their territory.

Thinking about a peopled state ...

Weberian state theory has traditionally advocated a relatively agency-centred approach to studying the state and has, therefore, tended to emphasise the importance of examining the role of state personnel in the reproduction of state forms. Max Weber, for instance, argued that a political organisation is considered a state 'in so far as its administrative staff successfully upholds a claim to the *monopoly* of the *legitimate* use of physical force in the enforcement of its order' (1947: 154, original emphases). Michael Mann (1984, 1986) has built on these ideas by arguing that any conception of states should incorporate a number of different elements, an important one being the existence of a set of institutions and their related personnel. This neo-Weberian perspective has been furthered by Giddens (1985: 8), who contends that states, as 'power systems', always embody 'relations of autonomy and dependence between actors or collectivities of actors'.

Max Weber, as well as noting the significance of state personnel for state organisations, also alluded to the qualities of different categories of state personnel. He argued that two kinds of official played an important role in the reproduction of the state. The state as a rational bureaucracy is peopled by a certain type of functionary, referred to as an 'administrative' or 'genuine' official. This individual is 'the narrowed professional, publicly certified and examined, and ready for tenure and career. His [*sic*] craving for security is balanced by his moderate ambitions and he is rewarded by the honor of official status' (Weber in Gerth and Mills, 1991: 50). For Weber, therefore, modern state functionaries demonstrate certain rational qualities. As well as being rational, these individuals are also educated and trained to a certain level in order to deal with the technical rules and norms that undergird the state bureaucracy (Weber, 1947: 331). The counterpoint to the faceless modern state bureaucrat lies in Weber's discussion of the notion of charismatic leaders. These individuals display extraordinary personal qualities, which are used to generate enthusiasm for particular state projects and strategies. Charisma, therefore, as a 'balancing conception to bureaucracy' (Weber in Gerth and Mills, 1991: 52), concerns the *personal* qualities of select leaders. It is something that is more an attribute of a second type of state functionary, namely that of the 'political' official (Weber in Gerth and Mills, 1991: 90–5).

While there is undoubted value in this Weberian conception of a peopled state, we contend that the manner in which people are incorporated into Weberian state theory leaves a little to be desired (see also R. Jones, 2007). The individuals that help to reproduce state forms and state territories must fit into one of either two different categories. They are either charismatic and visionary state leaders or faceless and depersonalised state bureaucrats. In addition, these individuals are deemed to be immune from any outside interests since it is this professionalism that enables various state actors to sustain the autonomy of the state (for alternative arguments, see Hobson, 1998). We would maintain that state actors have more socio-economic, political and cultural complexion than is allowed for within Weberian state theory. These socio-economic, political and cultural characteristics allude to a stronger connection between state personnel and the society that they govern. If this is the case, the role of state personnel in reproducing state forms must also be more variegated than what is suggested within Weberian state theory.

One body of work, which emphasises the embeddedness of the state within the broader society, is Marxist and neo-Marxist state theory. Despite this strength, it would seem that conventional Marxist state theory has demonstrated a somewhat contradictory attitude towards the role of people within the capitalist state. During the 1970s, much ink was spilled on deciphering the relative impact of individual agency and deeper socio-economic structures on the fabric of the state, particularly in the context of the so-called Miliband–Poulantzas debate (Hay, 2006). While Poulantzas, especially in his early writings, viewed the capitalist state as the product of the deeper socio-economic structures associated with the capitalist mode of production (Poulantzas, 1969), Miliband (1983) conceived of the state 'in terms of the inter-personal alliances, connections and networks of the state "elite"' (Hay, 2006: 71). At one structuralist extreme, therefore, it is the broad, relatively generic and definitely 'unpeopled' language of 'class', 'capital' and 'state' that has been used to examine the manifold connections between state and society (e.g. Offe, 1984). Converesely, instrumentalists such as Miliband (1969, 1983) have been keen to emphasise the existence of 'social connections between those holding positions of economic power and the state elite' (Hay, 2006: 61).

Following Hay's (2006) intervention, we maintain that there is considerable scope to move beyond the reductionism of both these structuralist and instrumentalist viewpoints. Structuralists do not take any heed of the significant input that can be made by state personnel to the reproduction of state forms, either through their role as reproducers of pre-existing state organisations or in terms of their possible contribution to the development of new state organisations, strategies and policies. At the same time, instrumentalists such as Miliband can be accused of underplaying the embeddedness of state actors within class categories, which are themselves the product of 'objective structural locations within the relations of production' (Hay, 2006: 71). The challenge must be, in this respect, to move beyond this dualism between structure and agency (Giddens, 1984) in order to examine the scope afforded to state personnel, within broader socio-economic structures, to influence the reproduction of state forms (see Block, 1987 for one option).

We believe that the SRA discussed in Chapter 2 offers the most theoretically rigorous way of emplacing state personnel within contemporary devolved state forms, as well as the broader socio-economic structures within which they reside. One of the great strengths of the SRA is that it conveys an understanding of the state 'not as some lumbering bureaucratic monolith, but as a (political) process in motion' (Peck, 2001: 449). Equally significantly – especially with regard to the concerns of this chapter – it demonstrates the fact that the state should be viewed as a 'peopled organisation', rather than something that is governed by an abstract institutional or structural logic. Moreover, the role of people – as 'state managers ... class forces, gender groups as well as regional interests, and so forth' (Jessop, 1990: 270) – is crucial to the unfolding of the state's strategic selectivity in particular places and at certain times. The SRA, therefore, acknowledges the roles played by 'state agents' and broader structural imperatives in configuring the state's institutions and strategies (cf. Bertramsen, 1991). State personnel, in this context, are *not* passive agents but can actively influence the organisational and strategic terrain of the state. At the same time, the opportunities afforded to these state personnel to affect such changes are circumscribed by the pre-existing state forms – both organisational and territorial – within which they find themselves.

A key conditioner of state agents' interactions within the state over recent years has been the process of hollowing out of the state (Jessop, 1990; see also Rhodes, 1997). State agents have sought to influence the specific trajectories taken by national states with regard to the de-statisation and denationalisation of state activities, along with the internationalisation of policy regimes. Within broad constraints, state personnel can decide which state functions are de-statised, which policy regimes are transferred from one state to another and which functions are transferred to transnational and subnational state organisations. At the same time, state personnel are heavily involved in regulating the different aspects of the territorial process of filling in that occurs within states. Within sub-national territories, state personnel, in their own contingent and specific ways, may influence: processes of further de-statisation or, alternatively, re-statisation; an alternative engagement with international or subnational policy regimes; further denationalisation (see Jones et al., 2005). The point that we would want to stress is that the exact configuration of de-statisation, internationalisation and denationalisation processes taking place within particular territories is dependent, first, on different state personnel working individually or in concert with one another and, second, on the pre-existing state forms that structure the actions of these individuals (Archer, 1995; Jessop, 2001a).

But in addition to its focus on the connections between state personnel and state organisations, the SRA can also been utilised to examine the territorial contexts of state power (see Brenner, 2004; Brenner et al., 2003; Elden, 2005; Jones, 1997; MacLeod and Goodwin, 1999a, 1999b; Peck and Jones, 1995). A temporally and spatially sensitive reading of the SRA provides an insight into the way in which the 'success' or 'failure' of the strategic endeavours of state personnel and other agents is, at least in part, dependent on their access to particular territories and scales of governance. But while a spatially sensitive version of the SRA can lead us so far, we also believe that its examination solely of the way in which state spaces condition the actions and strategies of various state actors underplays the potential for state actors – in various guises – to shape the spatial and territorial form taken by the state. As Lefebvre (1991: 1; see also Soja, 1989) has shown, state space is something that is produced through a combination of different processes that are combined together in a triple dialectic: *spatial practices*, which relate to the material form of social spatiality; *representations of space*, reflecting spaces of ideological power, utopias and visions; and, *spaces of representation*, concerning clandestine spaces of resistance or the space of inhabitants and users (Soja, 1996). Crucially, the whole emphasis placed by Lefebvre on the *production* of state space draws our attention to the role of people within the process. State territories do not just exist: they must be reproduced, transformed and contested through the actions and practices of people, either as individuals or in concert with other people. State space is the product of the actions of these state officials (*hommes de l'État*):

> The state and territory interact in such a way that they can be said to be mutually constitutive. This explains the deceptive activities and image of state officials (*hommes de l'État*). They seem to administer, to manage and to organize a natural space. In practice, however, they *substitute* another space for it, one that is first economic and social, and then political. They believe they are obeying something in their heads – a representation (of the country etc.). In fact, they are establishing an order – their own. (Lefebvre, 2003: 87, original emphases)

What this means, in effect, is that state territories are the product of the 'narrations' of state officials. The production of state territories, moreover, cannot be seen 'as external to practice' (Lefebvre, 2003: 87). The continual 'becoming' of territories comes about as a result of the practices and ideologies of a variety of state personnel operating at a variety of different scales.

Despite the obvious value of Lefebvre's contribution, it can also be criticised for the way in which it maintains that the state, through its officials and apparatus, tends to produce a homogeneous state space, one that is at odds with the 'chaotic features as the space generated by "private interests"' (Lefebvre, 2003: 86). State space, according to Lefebvre, is both homogeneous *and* broken but spaces of dystopia, difference and opportunity are said to emanate solely from outwith the state apparatus. The representation of (state) space that originates from within the state apparatus and its officials is one of blandness and uniformity. The problem with such a viewpoint is that it tends to reify the state apparatus, in terms of its organisational structure and its territorial reach. Yet if we think of the state as a peopled organisation, then it is likely that different branches of the state, and different state officials, will promote alternative and heterogeneous representations of (state) space (cf. Jessop, 2002). If state officials play an active role in reproducing state territoriality, then the resultant state spaces must be plural in character. Other advantages accrue from adopting this modified Lefebvrian approach. First, in emphasising a heterogeneous, contested and variegated understanding of state territoriality, it is possible to promote an alternative to the more static and pre-given conceptualisations of territoriality that appear in much of the contemporary geographical literature (e.g. Amin, 2004; Amin et al., 2003). Second, adopting such a viewpoint is useful as a way of avoiding what Agnew (1994) has referred to as a 'territorial trap', in which the territoriality of the modern state is viewed as an unproblematic, flat and isomorphous space (see also Delaney, 2005: 57–8).

State territories, therefore – as products of a variety of different interest groups, a variety of state officials and a variety of state organisations – are always multiple in character. Whilst states seek to promote an illusion of national territorial homogeneity – through the existence of nationally based organisations, or the promotion of national projects and strategies – they are fundamentally plural in nature. Nowhere is this multiple territoriality of the state more evident, we would maintain, than in the context of the convoluted political geographies of the devolved UK state. Importantly, it is state personnel who play a key role in producing this heterogeneous territoriality of the state.

As well as being sources of academic debate, discussions of the connections between state personnel of all kinds and emerging devolved organisations of governance have also been apparent in more popular and policy contexts. In the period discussed in this book, for instance, much was made of a so-called Blairite project, in which strong associations were drawn between the person and personality of the Prime Minister and the objectives and style of his Labour Government (see, for instance, Foley, 2004; Gray, 2004; Heffernan, 2005; Hennessy, 2000, 2005; Lee and Woodward, 2002; Needham, 2005). While comments such as 'personal temperament *and* ambition are central to the Blair style' of government (Hennessy, 2000: 387, original emphasis) allude to the largely intangible connections that were said to exist between the Prime Minister and the broader political characteristics of the party that he led, it is clear that the most significant connections between Blair as leader and the broader Labour Government emerged in the context of the perceived emasculation of Cabinet government and a alleged centralisation of governmental authority within the Cabinet Office itself and its related policy and communication units (see in particular Hennessy, 2005; Lee and Woodward, 2002). With the emergence of a so-called 'presidential' style of government (Foley, 2004; Heffernan, 2005), Tony Blair was said to have acted as both a driving force behind, and symbol of, the Labour Government's political priorities. In more mundane contexts, too, it has been argued that the changing working conditions of civil servants has impacted on the process and outcomes of government. Since the 1980s, the civil service in the UK has undergone a sustained period of reform, which has impacted in numerous ways on their working conditions. Most significant, in this respect, was the First Steps programme that was implemented during the late 1980s (Pyper, 1995: 72–8). The programme led to the creation of a number of quasi-private agencies, which took over service delivery and the implementation of policy from government ministries and departments. In broader terms, it also signalled the development of a more 'federal' or 'balkanised' civil serice 'containing a multiplicity of fairly discrete component parts, within which managers have significant freedom of manoeuvre' (Pyper, 1995: 77). While some commentators have argued that such changes have led to the creation of a civil service that is 'under stress' (Foster, 2001: 725), we would contend that it also illustrates a situation in which civil servants possess more licence to shape a differing implementation of policy in their respective departments and/or agencies. Furthermore, the process of devolution has served to heighten the stresses and opportunities that are available to civil servants with regard to their effect on the formation and implementation of strategies and policies (see Carmichael, 2001; Laffin and Thomas, 2001; Parry, 2001). The scope for state personnel to promote, alter or resist various state projects and strategies was thus, in all probability, enhanced under devolution.

Our research on the process of filling in that has occurred with regard to economic governance in the UK since devolution also illustrates the different connections between state personnel and new state organisations and territories. We begin by discussing how state personnel shaped, and were shaped by, the new organisations of economic governance in the devolved territories. Building on this, we then move on to discuss how state personnel were implicated in the reproduction of new and complex territories and scales of devolved governance, particularly in the context of ELWa. The following section focuses on another issue by examining how state personnel also attempted to act as 'bridging mechanisms' between different organisations of economic governance. The final section then deals with the connections between state personnel and the debates concerning territorial and national forms of identity that were, and continue to be, part and parcel of the process of devolution in the UK.

State personnel and the formation of new organisations of economic governance

The development of a sense of coherence within organisations of economic governance, as well as a strong and positive link between new organisations of economic governance and the people that staff them, was viewed as a key aim in a post-devolution UK. As we showed in Chapter 3, the process of devolution led to the proliferation of organisations of economic governance and all of these, to a greater or lesser extent, emphasised the need to develop a strong organisational culture that could provide a sense of purpose for the people working within them. At the same time, state personnel of all kinds within these organisations were viewed as key progenitors of this organisational mission. This interlinkage between state personnel and new state organisations arose in a number of different contexts.

In general terms, much was made of the role of the leaders of devolved bodies in affecting the trajectories of devolution within the different territories (in more conceptual contexts, see Evans, 2006). Debates concerning the link between elected leaders and the perceived success or failure of the devolution project were prominent in Scotland. Devolution in Scotland, although viewed initially as a trailblazer for the other devolved territories, was perceived by many as being something of a damp squib. Mitchell (2001: 45) for example, stated that the 'high hopes attendant on the creation of the Scottish Parliament have given way to a more realistic assessment of its potential'. An important element within the perceived lacklustre performance of the Parliament, it was argued, was the lack of leadership shown by the Scottish Executive. Donald Dewar, the first First Minister for Scoland, in particular, was derided for being an individual who did not possess the enthusiasm to ensure that the Scottish Parliament and the Scottish version of devolution was pushed to its limit (Mitchell, 2001: 49). His close connections with the Labour Party on a UK level, according to many critics, compromised his willingness to challenge it in any significant way. Following the death of Donald Dewar, Henry McLeish, the new First Minister for Scotland, sought to portray the new administration as one that could kick-start a Parliament that had been stalled in first gear. Under the banner of 'Team McLeish', he sought to promote a distinctly Scottish take on institutional arrangements, policy innovation and symbolic politics. His progress was hampered, nonetheless, due to an apparent lack of political foresight and a series of embarrassing political clashes with the Labour Party in London (Mitchell, 2001: 54). In Dewar's and McLeish's periods as First Minister, we witness the role of key state personnel in shaping the evolution and reproduction of state forms. Both engendered varying attitudes towards devolution in Scotland but their contributions to the development of the Scottish Executive were strangely similar. They were both unable to energise the Scottish Parliament into the progressive, distinctive and forward-looking organisation that the Scottish electorate had expected on the eve of devolution (Mitchell, 2001: 45). The election of a minority SNP Government in Scotland in 2007 – with its leader Alex Salmond currently First Minister of Scotland – may well have signalled the emergence of a new series of connections between the political leadership of the Scottish Parliament and the alleged vitality of the broader organisation.

Similar debates took place in Wales, most notably in the context of the public consternation surrounding the selection of the Labour nominee for the role of First Minister of Wales, prior to the first National Assembly elections. Considerable criticsm was directed towards Alun Michael, MP, the UK Labour Party's nominee, because of his strong connections to the central Labour Party machine and to Tony Blair in particular (R. Jones, 2001). He was described as Tony Blair's 'placeman' and 'poodle' (Speed, 2000a: 12), his image being that of a tame politician, 'parachuted' in late in the campaign for the Labour nomination for the role of First Minister (Betts, 2000a: 1). Despite being described as one who 'had the Prime Minister's ear' (Speed, 2000b: 1) – or in other words, one who could influence the decisions made by the Labour Party at the scale of the UK state – the popularly held conception was the opposite – that decisions being made, and policies being implemented, by the Labour administration in Wales were being manipulated by the representatives of the central Labour body in London. Alun Michael, furthermore, received little public or political support when he was subsequently elected as the First Minister for Wales (see Scully et al., 2004). The leadership of the National Assembly for Wales, therefore, became a highly charged and symbolic issue, which chimed with much broader public concerns regarding the Assembly's organisational independence from a Labour-dominated Westminster. It is significant, in this respect, that Rhodri Morgan, Michael's successor to the post of First Secretary in February 2000, declared 'I won't be Blair's puppet' (Betts, 2000b: 1). Morgan clearly sought to distance himself from Michael, and to demonstrate his full commitment to the Assembly and all that it represented.

More positive synergies have also taken place between the leaders of devolved bodies and the organisations that they run. In Scotland, for instance, a change in the leadership of HIE was said to have had a perceptible impact on the effectiveness of the organisation. One individual, who had strong connections with HIE, explained as follows:

> It's basically a culture change. A new Chief Executive, who just perceived things differently, had a different management style, was a much more approachable sort of guy, and embarking on a root and branch, sort of, change process, to make the whole place more efficient, and really changed working practices to simplify and streamline things. So, you can't really compare the two, HIE of three or four years ago, with what it is now, certainly from the point of view of somebody being a part of the system.

The positive impact of leadership had also been felt south of the border. The EMDA's Chair, for instance, was seen to have had a beneficial impact on the evolving ethos and culture of the organisation. The EMDA's operational culture was clearly informed by the Chair's business experience (see also EMDA, 2002). One EMDA employee explained that, in contradistinction to other quangos, EMDA, through its Chair, had instigated a culture of 'get up and do things, take risks, don't worry about it, get on and do things'. Issues of positive leadership, in this context, were seen to have impacted in a beneficial way on the workings of the new organisations of the state. In Chapter 7, too, we show in detail how one minister involved in the promotion of economic development in Northern Ireland was held in esteem within the province by civil servants and the general public alike. Moreover, his qualities and attributes as an individual were seen to have acted as a driving force for the promotion of economic development within the region.

But in addition to the role of leadership in shaping the direction taken by new devolved organisations, more interesting connections and tensions have been played out in far more mundane circumstances. Much was made in the period between 1999 and 2006 of the need to develop a sense of corporate loyalty or an organisational culture within a variety of different organisations involved in the delivery of strategies and policies of economic development in the different UK territories. A key concern in ELWa, the organisation charged with implementing all aspects of post-16 education within Wales in the period between 2001 and April 2006, for instance, was to develop a strong and united organisational culture (see ELWa, 2001a, 2001b, 2002). ELWa's corporate strategy, for instance, stated that 'commitment, innovation, performance focus and teamwork are the essential elements we are working on' (ELWa, 2001c). It is clear that individuals working within ELWa were also well aware of this agenda. One employee argued that 'our success depends on the success of our policies and that means having everyone in the organisation "pulling together"'. It was also believed that the benefits brought by this sense of common purpose could be augmented through the development of a sense of loyalty towards ELWa's activities. One high-level Welsh Assembly politician, for instance, referred to the need to encourage a sense of loyalty towards the organisation amongst its employees, maintaining that 'I think people ought to be proud of who they work for'. He added that 'they don't want to go down the pub and then hear the conversation turn to ELWa and then slink off into a corner'. Rather, ELWa personnel should 'actually want to be able to say "Well actually I work for them" and be proud to do so, kind of thing'. For this individual, therefore, issues of 'corporate identity' were seen to be crucial. The issue of loyalty was also emphasised by an ELWa employee when he argued that 'when you look at yourself shaving in the morning, you don't want to think "Oh God, I'm just going to ... [waste my time]", you actually want to think "I'm going to go to work and my contribution and my time on that particular issue will actually make a difference to someone"'.

Certain organisations, though, faced difficulties in developing a common set of cultures. This problem arose in large measure because the new organisations of economic governance were often formed as amalgams of pre-existing organisations. Regional Development Agencies, for instance, were not wholly new institutions but rather represented a merger of a number of pre-existing bodies (see Tomaney and Mawson, 2002). As a result, fostering a single and unified organisational culture from separate predecessor bodies, and accommodating new recruits into the organisation, was a challenge in some instances. This was certainly the case for EMDA. The process of fostering a new and united organisation culture within EMDA was characterised by some initial difficulties, as a board member explained:

> The management did put in, the senior management, did put in an effort to sort of have an EMDA culture but you can't help for a while that you remember where people came from. The people who found it hardest to fit in were one or two from English Partnerships who felt they were losing something and it wasn't just terms and conditions you know. They were important people in a small organisation in the region with lots of money to spend and a hospitality budget and lots of contacts with important developers. And a few of them did feel their status was at risk and took a bit of settling down.

Similar difficulties were faced by the various Sector Skills Partnerships (SecSPs) formed in the East Midlands. The leader of one SecSP, for instance, referred to the efforts that were made to develop an 'institutional culture' where the various members of the partnership could 'gel together as a group'. Part of the problem lay in the reconciliation of private and public sector modes of administration and operation – a recurring theme in local and regional economic development (Peck, 1998). The leader of the same SecSP argued, for instance, that 'some people are used to working in [a business] style, others are not. Others are used to turning up with a set of papers and they were briefed by officers and you know: "this is what we're going to do".' This quote illustrates the difficulties in bringing together personnel from public and private backgrounds to contribute to SecSPs.

Difficulties were also apparent in Wales but these were based on a different organisational legacy (see AGW, 2003). ELWa-National Council, the body that was for a period concerned with training in a post-devolution in Wales, was formed on the basis of four pre-existing TECs. One high-level ELWa employee explained the problems of developing a 'common culture within the organisation'. The four TECs possessed 'very distinctive styles and distinctive cultures'. Consequently, ELWa was seen to have 'inherited those different cultures, different ways of working. Even though the TECs were working to common objectives set by the Assembly, their internal business processes were very different.' The key point that the interviewee wanted to make, in this respect, was the 'cultural issue about becoming one organisation'.

A further set of issues that state personnel working within new institutions had to accommodate – and one already touched on to a certain extent – revolved around the unequal working conditions of employees who had come from different institutional backgrounds. This theme was highlighted with regard to the East Midlands Learning and Skills Councils (LSCs). These Councils inherited staff from predecessor organisations, which led to difficulties in harmonising staff pay and conditions. According to one interviewee:

> [Staff from LSCs] had some smashing terms and conditions. They were the ones who couldn't understand that their terms and conditions might have to be frozen. Because they were now working with people who had got, who was historically people out of Government Office for instance who came over, who'd never had a company car in their life and didn't know what one looked like.

The legacy of varying working conditions and salaries was also an issue in the context of the transition from the various TECs to the formation of ELWa (ELWa, 2001b: 45). An ELWa employee described the situation as follows:

> There was a tremendous amount of difference between salaries and benefits with TEC staff. North Wales [TEC], very well paid, generally speaking, and the best benefits. Mid-Wales and Swansea [South-West Wales TEC] they were the poor relatives, and then Bedwas [South-East Wales TEC] was probably close to North Wales, but you see the difference with Bedwas being, TEC South-East Wales had already, 12 months prior to merger, had gone through a merger themselves, with Gwent TEC, South Glam TEC and Mid Glam TEC, so they had ... different contracts floating around, so it was a real mess. Very unhappy people, so [you had] two people, one getting 20 days' holiday entitlement and the other getting 30, and one getting £10,000 more than the other, one working flexi-hours the other not.

Further evidence of this problem appeared in a Auditor General's report on ELWa, which drew attention, amongst other things, to the difficulties created by the organisational legacies of predecessor TECs (AGW, 2003). Not surprisingly, attempts to create a set of common working conditions for ELWa employees, although obviously necessary, led to further antagonism within the organisation. One ELWa employee emphasised this point by noting the following: 'you have to be very careful really when you're doing a big structural reorganisation because you don't want to lose that commitment that people have got ... they become cynical and fed up ... there's a lot of trust involved, you've got to trust them [employees] else they won't do their job'.

The process of reorganisation within ELWa was furthered through a twin-pronged strategy of sidelining or making redundant those personnel who were resistant to change, as well as bringing in new staff who were more attuned to the priorities of the new organisation. Certain perils were deemed to arise from the former strategy, as one employee explained:

> I think at the moment, we've got a reputation as a bad employer, because people have seen the redundancy notices and they think we're a bad employer. And we're struggling in terms of the calibre of applicants we get, 'cause I think we pay reasonably well, a nice working environment, but people see the pressure and stress and the bad press and people are not particularly jumping up to come and work for us.

The role of redundancies in undermining any sense of corporate loyalty was further illustrated with the subsequent efforts made in 2003 to streamline the organisation through the shedding of nearly one hundred staff (ELWa, 2003b).

At the same time, there is some evidence that new working cultures were formed within the organisation through the pursuit of a strategy of appointing individuals who possessed little or no institutional 'baggage' from previous organisations. An ELWa employee explained how the appointment of new people was viewed as a process that would help to 'bring an ELWa feeling to the organisation'. It is significant that the benefits of appointing new staff were perceived elsewhere. One EMDA board member, for instance, maintained that 'yes there is [a common culture]. It has gelled now. And I mean that's assisted by the fact the people that came in from the pre-existing organisations – there were never enough people. So there had to be new ones.'

The need for staff to develop new common frames of reference, therefore, was a recurring cause for concern for the various devolved administrations and their numerous agencies (see, for example, HIE, 2001). One interviewee, for instance, spoke of the need for people to 'erase bits of their corporate memory'. In doing so, personnel could be 'de-programmed' and then 're-programmed' into the new mindsets needed to ensure that the new organisations of economic governance delivered on their stated objectives. Although the terminology used here has somewhat sinister undertones, it clearly illustrates the importance ascribed to shaping a new culture and organisational identity within these new bodies. Our argument in this section has been that it was various state personnel, working on the ground as it were, who made sense of the devolution settlement in their day-to-day practice of economic governance. Therein lies the significance of the role of state personnel in reproducing new organisations of economic governance in a devolved UK. It is apparent in this respect that the examples discussed in this section have come from the East Midlands and Wales. The evidence from Northern Ireland, discussed at length in Chapter 6, also points to a series of difficult negotiations between state personnel and the new devolved organisations within which they work. Scotland has been largely noticeable by its absence, having experienced somewhat of a more stable organisational settlement between 1999 and 2006, with fewer new organisations being created. This enabled it to avoid the majority of the problems discussed with regard to the creation of new organisations of economic governance in the other three territories.

State personnel and the reproduction of new state territories

State personnel, as well as helping to shape the organisations within which they work, also played a crucial role in shaping – and being shaped by – the new spaces and territories of economic governance that were formed as a result of devolution. Nowhere was the relationship and tension between state personnel and new territories and scales of economic governance more apparent, we would argue, than in Wales in the context of ELWa-National Council (ELWa, 2001a: 18; see also ELWa, 2002). Significantly, numerous tensions existed between ELWa-National Council personnel and the organisation's territorial and scalar structure, ones which had far-reaching implications for the organisation's long-term viability.

In the period between 2001 and 2005, it is clear that the national, the regional and the local scales all played an important role in structuring ELWa-National Council's activities. The most important scale for the organisation for much of its existence, as we argued in the previous chapter, was the regional scale and we focus primarily on this scale in this section. We noted in Chapters 3 and 4, for instance, that the National Council for a long period did not possess a national headquarters and operated 'as a decentralised organisation with strong emphasis on the regional delivery of [its] programmes' (ELWa, 2001b: 42). Executive staff were, therefore, located across the four established regions of Wales (see Map 5.1).

The reasons for adopting such a devolved structure are manifold and the debate surrounding the emergence of ELWa's regional structure have been captured well by Morgan and Rees (2001; see also Morgan and Mungham, 2000). We want to focus, in particular, here on the upshot of this regional structure on the working practices of ELWa employees. There is no doubt that the official interpretations of the regional structure were very positive, at least at the outset. ELWa's Operational Plan (2001b: 47), for instance, stressed that 'Wales and its many diverse regions have unique needs requiring tailor-made solutions. That is why we have developed a unique organization, which mixes both all-Wales and regional functions.' An ELWa employee echoed this sentiment, noting that the regional structure adopted by the National Council reflected 'the need to make decisions at a local level as much as possible'. Crucially, however, there

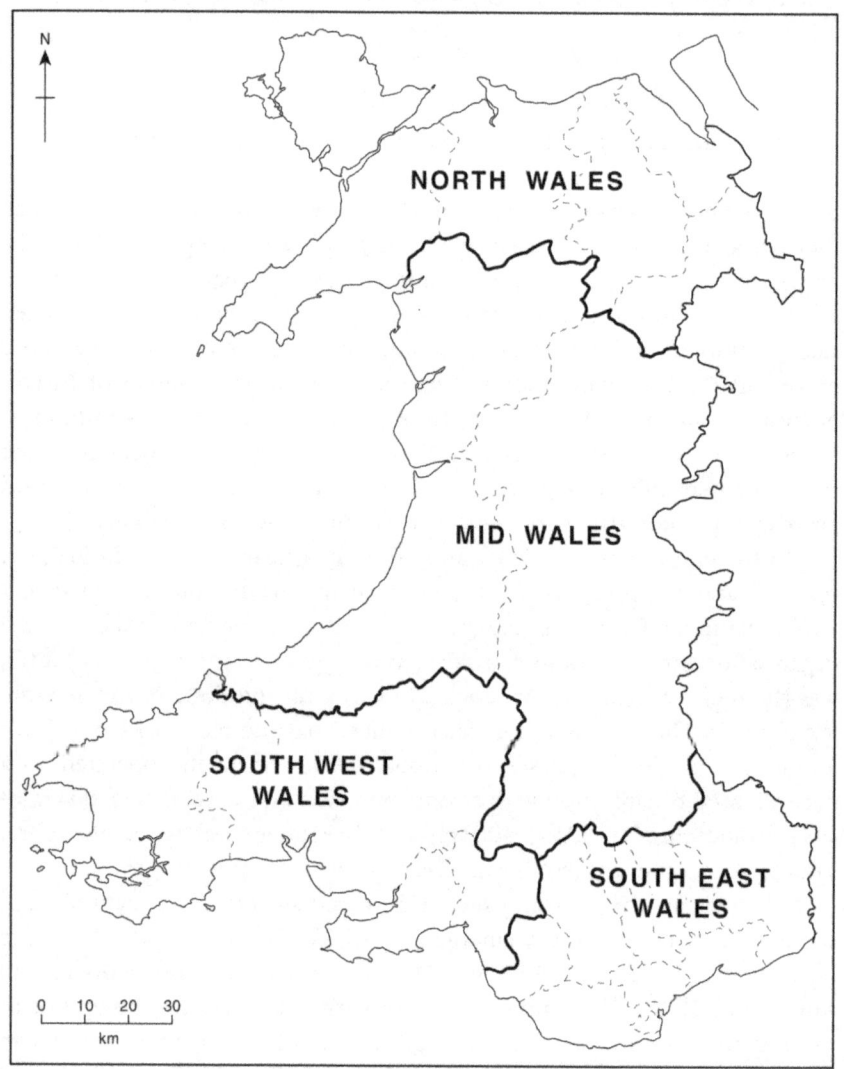

Map 5.1 Wales's four regions in 2005

were a number of tensions associated with the National Council's regional structure, which posed considerable challenges for its personnel. It is in this context that we witness the role of state personnel in both reproducing and contesting the territorial makeup of devolved forms of economic governance. One difficulty lay in the novelty of this regional form of organisational structure. This had implications for the personnel who had to make sense of the National Council as an organisation. One employee noted, for instance, that

> The challenge is that people are not used to it ... We've got different responsibilities in different places but once that's settled down and it becomes a way of working, I do believe it will be very efficient and a very effective model, but it's difficult for people as you would expect in any situation but, it's not an unusual arrangement.

The same respondent added that a particular difficulty revolved around the management of flows of information within such a devolved structure. Great emphasis was placed on the management of information, primarily through the development of ELWa as an 'e.public service organisation', which would 'facilitate internal communications' (ELWa, 2001c: 44). Problems still arose, nonetheless, 'because this place is full of knowledge but we don't know what we don't know'. In addition, the lack of organisational integration afforded by the regional structure was seen as a distinct drawback by some respondents. To a certain extent, part of the problem arose with regard to logistical difficulties:

> We're distributed so within my directorate and within my teams I've people in all the different offices. Team Leaders in our offices, and that obviously means that on a practical level it's much much harder to operate in a very integrated way, because with people around you, you can talk immediately. So a great deal of effort and resources are used travelling around Wales. I think the implications of saying we're an all-Wales body with no headquarters makes communications more difficult.

People who have travelled in Wales may well be aware of the sometimes tortuous character of some journeys. These difficulties in terms of communication had a bearing on the perceived success of ELWa's regional structure. Clearly, in this respect, the relationship between the peopled and the scalar and territorial dynamics of 'filling in' in Wales – at least with regard to ELWa – led to considerable confusion within the organisation. Given these difficulties, it is not surprising that the reorganisation of ELWa-National Council during 2003 reduced the significance of the regional scale. In the 'new-look' organisation, all corporate directors were to be based in the South-East Wales office, with the regional offices concentrating on delivering services to learners in the various regions.

Significantly, part of the reasoning behind this change of emphasis was to 'enable faster decision-making' within the organisation (ELWa, 2003a).

But as well as the problems encountered with the regional structure, ELWa-National Council also faced other difficulties in articulating the relationship between the national and regional scales (ELWa, 2001b: 47; 2001c: 44). During the early period of its existence, a national framework of organisational aims and objectives was promoted by ELWa-National Council, within which regional structures operated. The relationship between national- and regional-level strategies and policies, we argue, was a source of tension for ELWa-National Council. Moreover, this was a challenge that various personnel working within ELWa-National Council's various offices had to deal with. One ELWa employee argued that the 'challenge for us is to balance being within a national framework and having that homogeneous sort of approach to it but at the same time being able to reflect things locally'. It seems, in this regard, that the reorganisation of ELWa in 2003, in which more emphasis was placed on the coordinating role of a national office in the south-east of Wales, signalled a decisive shift in favour of a heavier national coordination of the organisation's various acitivities. Such a shift towards the promotion of a more nationally oriented set of strategies and policies was further emphasised in April 2006 with the incorporation of ELWa-National Council into the National Assembly for Wales.

While we have concentrated in this section on the role of state personnel in reproducing new state territories in Wales, it is apparent that similar tensions have existed in the other regions, especially Scotland. First, the regional jurisdictions of Scottish Enterprise and Highlands and Islands Enterprise testify to the possible existence of 'regional [or local] rhythms' (Jessop, 2001a) of economic development within Scotland. At the regional scale, for instance, HIE (2001: 17) has argued for the need to enhance their relationship with SE in order to ensure a more coherent and 'national' interpretation of economic development needs within Scotland. Second, an interviewee with experience of working within an LEC and LEF in lowland Scotland maintained that similar tensions existed between different localities within Scotland with regard to their conception of economic development:

> I know that the Scottish Executive have kind of considered and are considering how to, what mechanisms and structures, they should create to encourage the Local Economic Forums to work more closely together. And they've had two or three training programmes or awareness sessions where they have had people from the LEFs, the Chairman were invited to attend it and it was, I suppose, an attempt to try and bridge some of these gaps and to kind of

encourage the joint work. But I don't think they are there yet, but some way off from making them work. But it's a recognition I think in the Scottish Executive that whilst it's useful in administrative terms to give something a geography, we need to build in a cross-cutting mechanisms as well to ensure that if someone has a labour market shortage issue that we can share ideas and best practice and look at ways of addressing that.

An argument was made here about the potential for the local focus of LEFs to lead to an overwhelmingly localised attitude towards economic development amongst their members.

Mind the gap: state personnel as agents of joined-up economic governance

In this section, we discuss the importance of state personnel as individuals that can bridge the divide between the different organisations of economic governance that operate with each of the four territories. In academic terms, the need to promote regional coalitions of interests has been emphasised in the writings of so-called new regionalists. A region that can successfully create inter-organisational harmony, according to these authors, is better able to 'pin down' global processes (e.g. Amin, 1999; Amin and Thrift, 1995). This work emphasises the critical importance of inter-organisational norms, networks, trust and social capital in the creation of a 'joined-up' approach to economic governance at the regional scale.

As well as being academic concerns, it is clear that such issues acted as a source of considerable debate in policy and practitioner circles in the immediate aftermath of devolution. The promotion of alternative and joined-up methods of delivering policies, for instance, was a key aspect of New Labour's Third Way. According to Driver and Martell (2000: 149), New Labour's interpretation of the Third Way involved: the promotion of wealth creation and social justice; the promotion of the market and of social and community values; an acknowledgement of the importance of both free enterprise and the state for the delivery of various public goods (see also Lee and Woodward, 2002; Tiesdell and Allmendinger, 2001: 904). A key aspect of the delivery of Third Way principles, according to Ling (2002), was New Labour's advocacy of a more 'joined-up' approach to governance (see Cabinet Office, 1999). The Labour Government's promotion of joined-up government was predicated on 'the perception that services had become fragmented and that this fragmentation was preventing the achievement of important goals of public policy' (Ling, 2002: 616). What was needed, therefore, was an effort to

> coordinate activities across organizational boundaries without removing the boundaries themselves ... To join up, initiatives must align organizations with different cultures, incentives, management systems and aims. (Ling, 2002: 616)

It is noticeable that such sentiments filtered down to the type of politics that were advocated within the devolved administrations. They specifically sought to create an ethos of collaboration between different organisations of economic governance. One Welsh politician, for instance, elaborated on the efforts made to introduce this new mindset, stating that the Welsh Assembly had encouraged different agencies to 'work together' and had cautioned against 'turf wars' (see also WAG, 2002; Storer and Cole, 2002). Inter-organisational coordination was also extended in a more fundamental and formal way. For instance, efforts were made in the East Midlands to identify a common agendum for all agencies of economic governance operating within the region. One important factor in this region, as we discussed in the previous chapter, was the adoption of an Integrated Regional Strategy (IRS) for the region, produced by the East Midlands Regional Assembly in December 2000 (EMRA, 2000; updated in EMRA, 2005; see also Foley, 2002).

In Scotland, the main development with regard to inter-organisational collaboration in the period under study was the creation of Local Economic Forums (LEFs). These were formed in April 2001 to facilitate cohesion and counter the 'congestion' that was said to exist with regard to local economic development prior to devolution (McCarthy and Newlands, 1999; Scottish Executive, 2000a). LEFs were also charged with considering local delivery mechanisms for lifelong learning, improvements to labour market coordination and the formulation of local responses in areas such as trade and tourism. The significance of LEFs was that they would draw together all agencies – and, significantly, we would argue, all *agents* – involved in promoting economic development at the local scale in Scotland. However, the role of LEFs was not without its difficulties. One interviewee in Scotland referred to the existence of vested interests within certain LEFs, which made it more difficult to coordinate their activities:

> You can't get a vested interest in the form of a local authority, a vested interest in the form of an LEC (Local Enterprise Company) and anyone else in the room and say, 'Right, who's going to do what?' They will all defend their corner.

As well as these more formal mechanisms for engendering cooperation between different organisations of economic governance, it is noticeable that other, more informal, relationships were also important in the various territories. One respondent in Wales, for instance, described the higher levels of inter-organisational cooperation that took place in formal governmental contexts as follows:

> You've got an Economic Development Committee and Education and Lifelong Learning Committee and it's very interesting that what we've seen this year is the coming together of those two ministers, where we now have joint meetings involving the two ministers and the two chairs of the WDA and the National Council ELWa and also now bringing in the Chair of the HE council ... We would not have seen that at all in the past so it's bringing these sort of key bits together.

In the East Midlands, too, informal personal relationships were particularly effective as bridging mechanisms, especially at a high level. Two senior Government Office for the East Midlands (GOEM) officials, for instance, maintained that 'informal relationships, informal meetings and discussions' had been crucial. In doing this, there was a feeling that 'one builds up hopefully, a good working relationship, and we can't over-estimate the personal influence'.

Significantly, the development of new policies was viewed as a product and a facilitator of a new collaborative approach at a national scale within Wales. A high-level Assembly politician noted the lack of capacity that departments possessed in order to develop new policies in isolation. A collaborative approach was, therefore, critical to the development of new strategies and policies of economic development within Wales. According to one ELWa-National Council employee, the whole point of devolution was to 'make our own policy', but 'because we don't have the capacity, or we didn't have the capacity or expertise, we have to make policy on a collaborative basis. We have to work with WDA, [the] ASPBs.' In all these examples, we witness the importance of informal relationships – or, as one ELWa-National Council employee put it, of 'sharing a fag over a wall' – in shaping the character of economic governance in the devolved territories.

Informal relationships between staff in different organisations were also particularly useful in delineating spheres of interest and policy responsibilities in situations that were highly uncertain, especially during the early post-devolution period. A GOEM official, for instance, discussed the common spheres of interest between EMDA and EMRA, arguing that the delineation of responsibilities in these cases could be 'tricky'. Informal relationships, however, were considered key to the whole process of organisational demarcation. The interviewee maintained that 'the more we worked on it, the more we decided it wasn't actually going to help anybody until everyone understood more about what was going on in the region'. Significantly, many of these key discussions took place at an informal level.

It is noticeable that physical distance was viewed as a way of overcoming inter-organisational rivalries. This was especially the case with the GOEM, where various departmental interests were represented in close proximity to each other.

Admittedly, some difficulties were experienced in achieving this synergy between organisations. One problem arose in the context of the perceived unequal relationships between different organisations operating within the same territory. In Wales, for instance, even though the relationship between ELWa and the Assembly in the period between 2001 and 2003 was described as a 'two way street' – in which both the parent body and the ASPB influenced the development of policies and strategies – there is no doubt in our mind regarding the role played by the Assembly in structuring the terms of the relationship. The relative authority of the Assembly was witnessed most clearly with respect to the remit letter, the mechanism that was used by the Minister of Education to outline ELWa's objectives for the coming year. Significantly, some concern was raised within the ranks of ELWa regarding the prescriptive nature of the remit letter, along with the broader relationship that existed between the Assembly and ELWa. One respondent noted, for instance, that:

> we're trying to get the Assembly to give us a little bit more freedom in that area actually. We would like to say to them, 'You agreed the corporate strategic and the operational plan with us, but don't manage us against the micro-indicators on that basis.' As I say, one of the things that we're looking at in the planning framework is that remit letter, which sets out the main aspects of strategy determined by the Assembly. As time goes on, hopefully they'll begin to trust us more and give us that little bit more freedom.

The irony was particularly evident, in this respect, when ELWa-National Council was incorporated into the NAfW in April 2006. While such an incorporation, at one level, obviated the need to develop effective inter-organisational linkages between the National Assembly for Wales and ELWa-National Council, as one of its most important ASPBs, it may also be seen as an indication of a relationship between the two organisations that had always been inherently unequal in character.

Other, more structural, difficulties mitigated against the development of stronger collaborative links between different organisations (in an English context see RCU, 2001). One theme that was discussed by some of the interviewees in Wales was the lack of discretion afforded to regional branches of national organisations. One respondent argued that it was difficult to foster strong links at a regional scale between ELWa and the WDA 'because the WDA doesn't quite have the same structures, and the WDA is still more Cardiff-orientated, whereas ELWa doesn't have an HQ'.

The reorganisation of ELWa-National Council in 2003, as well as its subsequent incorporation into the National Assembly for Wales, may well have served to remedy this perceived deficiency. Ironically, some regional WDA personnel were keen to level the same accusation against the regional offices of ELWa, claiming that 'they're having their arms and legs cut off' when compared with the predecessor TECs. In this regard, there seemed to be somewhat of a mismatch between the scalar capacities of these two organisations.

Finally, another major difficulty arose in the context of the time and effort needed to forge collaborative links between organisations at a regional scale. A number of respondents in Scotland, for instance, referred to the commitment that was needed to sustain the work of the various LEFs. In this context, while LEFs were viewed as important bridging mechanisms between different organisations, they also 'took up a lot of time'. Moreover, their success was seen to be dependent, in large measure, on a small number of knowledgable and committed individuals. Such a scenario, according to one interviewee who was involved in an LEF in Highland Scotland, raised issues concerning the LEF's sustainability, particular if he were to be 'struck dead'. Similar concerns were voiced in Wales. One person working at the regional level within ELWa maintained, for example, that there were efforts afoot to try 'to get joined-up thinking with the WDA, local authorities, the planning service, the careers service' but was quick to emphasise that 'it does take an unbelievable amount of energy to get all of that thinking capacity to get the job done'. Another interviewee from one of the ELWa-National Council's regional offices admitted to attempting to reduce the organisation's input into some partnerships, especially those to which it had little to contribute. The respondent maintained that:

> We try to take a mature approach to partnership, I actually say to them, 'Please do not invite us, to sit around your table just to have us around your table. Go away because we haven't the time, or the staff, we're not interested in it. Where you believe that we can genuinely make a contribution, tell us what it is, and we'll say yeah, we think we should be there.' And that's the way that we've tried to operate.

The political pressure to further more joined-up forms of governance – almost at all costs – meant that such an approach was not always appreciated. The same respondent, for example, argued that the approach adopted by their particular regional office 'hasn't been received in that spirit by all organisations because they will sometimes write in and say, "Why aren't your people sitting round the table at X?"'. Obviously, a difficult balancing act existed as regional offices sought to negotiate between collaboration for collaboration's sake and collaboration as a means of developing effective policies at the regional scale. Significantly, it was the people attending these partnership meetings that helped determine their effectiveness and thus facilitated or hindered the broader emphasis on joined-up governance that was such a feature of the early post-devolution period in the UK.

Territorial identities, state personnel and devolution

The final substantive section of this chapter is concerned with the way in which territorial identities – either national or regional – have become intermeshed with the filling in of the state under devolution. An underlying principle common to past calls for devolution to Scotland, Wales and Northern Ireland, and to recent debates surrounding the need to form a democratic tier of regional government in England, has been an assumption concerning the need to take account of sub-national or regional identity groupings or civil societies (Chaney et al., 2001; Osmond, 1977; Tomaney and Mawson, 2002). It is these regional identities that have acted as a justification and a considerable driving force for the whole process of devolution. The normative assumption that has been a major contributory factor to the whole devolution project is that these different identity groupings possess different policy needs. In this respect, new devolved bodies were supposed to represent more effectively the desires and needs of their regions (see R. Jones, 2001; see also Paasi, 1991, 2002). Devolution has been underpinned, therefore, by a normative concern regarding the link between governance and identity or, in other words, that state organisations, strategies and policies should correspond closely to the territorial desires and needs of groups of people located in different regions or territories of the UK. But a consideration of the devolved UK state as a peopled organisation, of necessity opens up a new avenue of enquiry. Attention should be directed to examining the significance of the regional or territorial identities of state personnel and the way in which these impact on the practice of governance in a devolved UK. In other words, we need to explore how the broader territorial identities of state personnel shape, and are shaped by, the practice of governance in the contemporary UK.

State personnel in all four territories were keen to emphasise that devolution had changed the nature of their work, along with their overall commitment to the regions that they represented. One official working in the GOEM, for instance, maintained that he was 'here for the East Midlands' rather than being 'here for the government'. He added that 'because I'm an East Midlander, and I think, you know ... well, hang on a minute, if the government's not about helping people, what is it about?'. State personnel working in Wales, too, argued that their broader sense of territorial identity had influenced their commitment towards the organisations within which they worked. A worker in ELWa, for instance, maintained that devolution had increased his commitment to Wales as a country and to the role of ELWa in improving its economic prospects. For this person, 'there is an intangible feeling of "This is us in Wales trying to do something for Wales"'. Another ELWa official agreed, saying that 'quite a lot of people, particular people have been there a long time, people who are born and bred here and then you know they see no reason to move anywhere else, and they feel "Let's do it for Wales"'. These two quotes illustrate that there was a palpable sense of territorial identity, which, we would argue, translated into a firm commitment to the organisation. Territorial identity, in this fashion, could be viewed as a key motivating factor for state personnel that, in turn, impacted on the effectiveness of regional organisations in positive ways.

Another interesting example of the link between territorial identities and the workings of devolved government has been in Scotland. Research by Mitchell (2003), for instance, has demonstrated how the Scottish civil service showed a positive and proactive attitude towards regional government prior to 1997, more so than their counterparts in Northern Ireland and Wales. Throughout the latter half of the twentieth century, civil servants in Scotland were more likely to emphasise the distinctiveness of Scotland, and of their role in sustaining that distinctiveness, than were civil servants working in the other territories. The executive devolution of power to Scotland, through the creation of the Scottish Parliament, only served to invigorate what has always been an active *Scottish* civil service. Whilst the 'Scottishness' of civil servants in Scotland has been apparent over a number of years, our research has shown that certain territorial divisions still exist within Scotland. It is possible that these may well have qualified the development of a unified Scottish conception of devolution. A number of interviewees stressed that spatial and scalar tensions were evident in the context of the economic governance of Scotland. One interviewee in Dumfries and Galloway in lowland Scotland, for instance, was critical of a perceived lack of sensitivity of national policy-makers and implementers to the distinctive needs of the locality within which he lived and worked:

> We have people who come down regularly from Glasgow, all of the time, from Scottish Enterprise, who have never been down to Dumfries and Galloway, have never been there in their lives, they didn't know what it was like, so we have that.

Similar sentiments appear in the following quote:

> Answer: We [Local Enterprise Company] maintain that they don't really understand what's happening on the ground, and they [SE HQ] maintain that we don't understand what's happening at national level. So there …
>
> Question: Never the twain shall meet?
>
> Answer: Well exactly, you know, but it's that, I mean, I've been in economic development many, many decades, but that's the nature of it. That's what it is all about. And there is always a friction between local economic development and national economic development.

Such statements echo Agnew's (1987, 1996) comments regarding the existence of different scales of identity within Scotland. Although, at one level, state personnel may well have identified with devolution, as a national or territorial project, it is still likely that alternative associations with smaller regions and localities played an important role in shaping their attitudes and practices.

It is clear, therefore, that the main tension that arose in many of the devolved territories revolved around the attempt to reconcile national policy directives with the particular needs of various localities (cf. Jones and MacLeod, 2002). This was certainly the case in Wales. Regional tensions, emanating from regional forms of identity, were most apparent in the context of North Wales (Hollingsworth, 2002). One ELWa employee in the region, for instance, stated that there had always existed a strong commitment towards North Wales within that particular regional office. What helped to sustain this regional commitment was a sense of spatial iniquity. North Wales, according to this individual, was perceived to be 'fighting against the odds', especially when compared with the south-east, located near the centre of political and economic power in Cardiff. The employee expanded on this theme as follows:

> We try to get Rhodri [Morgan, the First Minister] here to speak to the forum at least once every year, we have Sue Essex [the Minister for Finance] about once or twice every year and we try to get Jane Davidson [the Minister for Education] … This is where North Wales is to a disadvantage, of course. I mean our colleagues in South-East Wales in particular are meeting with people in social places etc. and it's so much easier for them to articulate their needs. They can do it at rugby matches, everywhere, so we have a disadvantage.

Regional forms of identity within Wales, therefore, problematised the efforts made to generate a sense of territorial cohesiveness at the Welsh scale. The recent re-statisation of agencies such as ELWa, and the perceived centralisation of decision-making in Cardiff that this has generated, we argue, will have only served to heighten these regional tensions within Wales.

Tensions with regard to territorial identity were equally apparent with regard to the relationship between the devolved territories and the broader British governmental imperatives. Certain conflict arose, for instance, between the central and regional branches of the UK state operating within England, one that was evidenced in the cultures of the staff working in the GOEM. We have already mentioned the arguments made by one interviewee who, because of his upbringing in the East Midlands, felt more committed to working wholeheartedly in support of the regional economic and social agenda that was being promoted there. Other interviewees working in the GOEM, however, displayed a greater degree of ambivalence towards their role as employees of the central state working within the East Midlands region. These individuals had to make more difficult decisions in their efforts to reconcile both national and regional priorities (in a related context, see Lee and Woodward, 2002; Mawson and Spencer, 1997; Musson et al., 2003; RCU, 2001). When asked whether they were a regional actor or a central government actor in the East Midlands region, one GOEM official answered that 'we're both of those, but it depends on what day of the week it is in my case'. The official, who found it difficult to reconcile these two roles, maintained further:

> I guess your loyalty always ends up with the government. Don't think I've ever found myself in a position where I actually was publicly against government policy – but at the end of the day one is a civil servant. That's what I'm employed to do. But, I guess the reason you can reconcile it is because what government wants you to do is to make the region work as effectively as you can.

The party political context of devolution also has a bearing on this issue, as was demonstrated in the earlier discussion of the roles of Donald Dewar and Henry McLeish in Scotland, and of Alun Michael and Rhodri Morgan in Wales. In this respect, the role played by the Labour Party within the devolved territories offers a good illustration of the association between the peopling of government and broader issues relating to group identity. The Labour Party in the UK has always demonstrated somewhat of an ambivalent attitude towards devolution since it is the only 'party with a major presence in the "periphery" which is committed to the maintenance of the British state' (Morgan and Mungham, 2000: 82). The Labour Party, as such, has been an advocate of devolved politics since 1999 at the same time as being a party that is not, by any stretch of the imagination, particularly supportive of it in principle (more broadly, see Lee and Woodward, 2002). For instance, the Welsh Labour Party has since its inception been a centralising one that has favoured a close association with the political organisations, if not the broader culture, of Britain. As an indication of this internal tension within the Labour Party, it is significant that the campaigns for and against devolution in Wales drew heavy support from within its ranks (see Morgan and Mungham, 2000: 97–119). Building on these earlier tensions, there have been continuing concerns regarding the role of Labour Assembly Members (AMs) within the running of the Assembly itself. Morgan and Mungham (2000: 211) have evaluated the composition of the first Labour Cabinet, formed after the Assembly elections in 1999, and they suggest that some of the more competent Labour AMs were not chosen to be a part of this Cabinet because of a belief in their lack of loyalty to the central Labour Party and a related perception that they were overzealous in their commitment to a Welsh devolution project. Tensions with regard to the territorial identities of Welsh AMs were viewed, therefore, as central concerns within the unfolding political dynamics of the National Assembly for Wales during its early years.

Issues of territorial identity have the potential to make an impact on the decisions made by state personnel, on their commitment or otherwise to the organisation, and by implication, to the region within which they work. Territorial identities, therefore, have the potential to influence the trajectories of devolution in the various territories and regions of the UK. State personnel in the various territories have negotiated a difficult series of territorial and organisational commitments – between territory and broader British nation and between devolved administrations and the UK state. These challenges have only been exacerbated, we would argue, with the election of an SNP administration in Scotland and a Labour–Plaid Cymru Coalition Government in Wales. In both these cases, we witness the increased potential for territorial identities to infuse the politics of economic governance in the devolved territories. Furthermore, it is likely that these territorial identities will become increasingly significant in coming years, especially in the light of the promised cuts to public expenditure made by the Conservative–Liberal Democrat Coalition Government in London. It is these tangled and difficult negotiations that will make a study of the link between the territorial identities of state personnel and the unfolding dynamics of state organisations even more necessary in coming years.

Conclusions: state personnel in a devolved UK state

The themes discussed in this chapter illustrate how people permeate the very fabric of state organisations. We have shown how state personnel were involved in promoting and problematising economic governance within each of the devolved territories. Some might question the extent to which the actions and identities of these state personnel actually contributed to the unfolding geographies of economic governance. Is it possible to 'measure' this contribution? Can one compare the contribution made by individuals and groups of people to the 'filling in' of the devolved state to that made by the organisations themselves? How does the contribution of a state manager to the geographies of economic governance compare with that of a key policy document? Questions like these are impossible to answer. The evidence discussed in this chapter has shown, nonetheless, that there was an important belief in, or perception of, the significance of these kinds of issues within each of the devolved territories. State managers in each of the territories patently tried to promote more cohesive cultures within their organisations since this was viewed as a key mechanism of ensuring that organisation's success. At the same time, problems with people were interpreted as things that led to problems for organisations and territories. In this respect, the contribution of state personnel to the geographies of economic governance were seen to matter by the vast majority of those that we interviewed and, as such, assumed the status of crucial factors in the process of 'filling in'.

Taken together, we contend that the everyday practice of governance by various individuals has an enormous bearing on the types and vitality of state organisations, as well as on the territorial form that these organisations take. State organisations do not comprise 'an insulated domain of anonymous policy-makers'; nor do they become manifest in the form of 'authorless policy conventions'. Rather, the state is a 'peopled organization' (Peck, 2001) and, being peopled, is subject to the identities, the subjectivities, the commitments, the loyalties and the prejudices of its personnel. The empirical material discussed in this chapter is significant for another reason since it shows that state managers in the period between 1999 and 2006 were well aware of the significance of the role of people in reproducing new state organisations: considerable efforts were made to create a positive organisational culture for new agencies of economic development and various staff were also encouraged to foster synergistic relationships between different organisations. Of course there was no guarantee that these plans would succeed since state personnel also had the potential to question, to ignore, to resist or to develop alternative ideas and practices. Such was the case, for instance, with regard to the role of state personnel in questioning the territorial and scalar formation adopted by ELWa in the period between 2001 and 2003.

The themes discussed in this chapter also echo recent work on the ethnography or anthropology of the state. The emphasis in this body of work has been on examining the people and the day-to-day practices that have furthered or contested the bio-politics associated with the modern state. Rose (1996), for instance, has stressed the need to explore the various classes of state official – bureaucrats, managers and experts for instance – that have been implicated in the development of state governmentality during the modern and late modern periods. What this means is that 'the modern effect of the state' (Mitchell, 2006: 181) is based not only on the promulgation of laws or the fighting of wars but is also predicated on those more mundane and decentred practices of state officials (and ordinary citizens), which help to give meaning to various state projects and strategies. The state, when thought about in this way, is 'seen' in a variety of different ways by the various actors that inhabit it (Corbridge et al., 2005).

What our work, as well as the broader ethnographic and anthropological studies of the state, shows is that the state – in both organisational and territorial terms – is ultimately plural and fractured in character. If individuals person state organisations, write and implement their policies and strategies – admittedly within certain constraints – then the organisational unity and isomorphism of the state is bound to be, at heart, illusory if not unimportant in character. Similar statements can be made when considering the role of state personnel in reproducing state territorialities. Although there has been an effort during the modern period to coordinate the territorial imaginings of state personnel and the representation of territory of different state organisations, this process has always been incomplete. State territories have never been entirely homogeneous, even when the 'chaotic features' of capitalism and private interests are held constant (Lefebvre, 2003: 86). If we take seriously the fact that the state is a peopled organisation, being dependent on the activities and practices of state personnel for its existence, then state territories are always fractured and fissured, the state's claims to territorial homogeneity notwithstanding (R. Jones, 2007). The process of devolution, we would argue, has served to heighten the influence that various state personnel have had on the filling in of state forms within the UK in organisational and territorial contexts.

6
The political geographies of filling in: the case of Northern Ireland

Introduction

Our aim in the preceding chapters has been to demonstrate the value of the concept of filling in for understanding the variety of contexts within which the contemporary UK state has been reconfigured in recent years. A focus on the economic context of devolution has proved to be particularly apposite as a way of illustrating the contours of this process. New organisations of economic governance have been formed, recalibrated or dissolved in each of the UK territories. In a more geographical context, it is apparent that each of these organisations of economic governance has possessed clear territorial and scalar remits, which has influenced their ability to achieve their stated aims and objectives. The process of filling in, notably, has also taken place in peopled contexts. State personnel have had to make sense of the far-reaching organisational and territorial changes that have occurred in the four UK territories, while also acting, in large measure, as the architects of change. The preceding chapters have examined each of these changes in isolation. Our aim in the final substantive chapter is to explore the relationships between these changes in more depth through a sustained case study of the emerging political geographies of filling in within the territory of Northern Ireland. In doing so, we will examine, among other things, how: the formation of new organisations of economic governance has problematised the territorial and scalar makeup of the state; the established and emerging spaces of economic governance both facilitate and undermine the policies and strategies being promoted by key organisations of economic development; people, both within and, to certain extent, outside the state bureaucracy, have helped to form, reproduce, question and challenge this emerging organisational and territorial settlement. In discussing these themes, we also seek to draw out the implications of the various processes of filling in for notions of collaboration and cooperation within economic governance in Northern Ireland.

We have already alluded to the significant relationships that exist between state organisations, state territories and state personnel in a more conceptual sense in Chapter 2 and, to a limited extent, in Chapter 5. We feel it important, nonetheless, briefly to reaffirm the important connections that exist between these elements since they will provide the conceptual foundation upon which the later empirical discussion will be based.

First, we have conceived of devolved state organisations as the bureaucratic forms of the state existing at geographical scales smaller than that of the national scale but greater than that governed by local authorities. Devolved state organisations comprise state projects – or, in other words, those 'initiatives to endow state institutions with organizational coherence, functional coordination and operational unity' (Brenner, 2004: 88) – and state strategies, namely the 'initiatives to mobilize state institutions in order to promote particular forms of socioeconomic [political, cultural or ecological] intervention' (Brenner, 2004: 88). This does not mean that the devolved state's projects or strategies possess an organisational uniformity or singularity of purpose. The filling in of the state that has taken place in the UK over recent years has led to the formation of sometimes collaborating, at other times competing, state organisations within each of the UK territories (Brenner, 2004; Clark and Dear, 1984; Jessop, 1990). The policies and strategies adopted by devolved state organisation, therefore, may well be contradictory despite the efforts of politicians and civil servants in each of the devolved territories to counter such organisational dissent. In a related context, devolved state organisations, along with their projects and strategies, help to produce state territories. They also have the potential to shape the identities of the various people that person them.

Second, the process of filling in leads to the sedimentation of new and reconfigured state territories and scales. These spatial manifestations of the power of the state are key features of the process of filling in. In the first place, the reconfiguration of organizations of governance that has occurred *in lieu* of devolution, of necessity, has filled in UK state space in territorial and scalar contexts. The territorial and scalar form taken by devolution is, in large part, the product of state projects and strategies. Certain devolved organisations exercise authority over particular territories and spatial scales and this territorial delimiting of their power is further emphasised by the specific strategies and policies that they seek to promote. But state territories are also the product of the activities and discourses of state personnel, who, either individually or in concert with one another, emphasise the importance of certain territories at the expense of others through the promotion of certain policy priorities (more broadly, see Lefebvre, 1991). Significantly, the territorial and scalar forms taken by the devolved state also possess broader implications, both for the state organisations themselves and for the broader society within which they are located. The territorial and scalar forms of devolved organisations may either enable or hinder them to achieve their stated aims. More broadly, the territorial and scalar form of devolved organisations may influence the ability of various actors or groups of actors legitimately to gain access to particular branches of the state (Jessop, 2001a).

Third, the process of filling in is also shaped by active state personnel. Despite the assertions of Weberians and Marxists alike, state personnel possess a variety of different identities, subjectivities and prejudices. These identities may be based on notions of gender, place or region, class, personal vanity and so forth. State personnel have always played an active role in the continual emergence of the state and nowhere is this contribution more evident than in the current process of devolution taking place in the UK. Although all state personnel in each of the devolved territories play a role in shaping the process of filling in, it is clear that different actors possess different capacities to do so. At certain times, the activities of these various types of individual may help to reproduce devolved state organisations. State officials in each of the devolved territories may, however, seek to contest the character of state forms and functions. It is likely, however, that state officials have to negotiate a difficult route between total subservience to, and outright contestation of, state organisations. As Corbridge et al. (2005: 7) maintain, the actual impact of the state on particular socio-spatial processes 'will depend on the manner in which ... [it is] ... interpreted and put into play by lower-level government workers, elected representatives and others'. Considering the state in such a way makes us think of a process of filling in that is heterogeneous, fractured and in a continual state of flux and emergence. At the same time, state organisations and territories contribute to the reproduction and transformation of the identities of state personnel of all kinds.

The modified SRA that we have invoked in this book, we contend, offers the most appropriate and insightful way of bringing together these three elements into a cohernent conceptual framework. The practices of state actors reproduce state structures, while the selfsame structures impinge upon and help shape the practices of state personnel. At the same time, the mutual constitution of state actors and state organisations is inherently spatialised. The territories and scales of the state within the SRA, therefore, reflect 'particular types of state spatial projects and state spatial strategies that are articulated at a variety of scales and differentiated among distinct territorial locations' (Brenner, 2004: 103). We would add here, that these territories and scales also reflect the peopled aspects of state projects and strategies. In a similar vein, the state's territories and scalar manifestations influence its organisational and peopled form.

We aim to explicate the complicated character of this interaction between state organisations, state territories and scales and state personnel – manifest in the process of filling in – through a sustained study of the devolution of economic governance to Northern Ireland. In particular, we focus on the issue of collaboration since this illustrates well the totality of the political geographies of filling in; in organisational, territorial and peopled contexts. We contend that the success or otherwise of the devolution of economic governance revolves around the degree to which new organisations of governance possess an effective capacity to act or, in other words, an ability to respond to the various economic challenges that they face. An effective capacity to act derives in no small measure from the extent to which the various organisations of economic governance within the four territories become entwined and well integrated – with regard to their policies and strategies, their territories and scales, and their broader organisational cultures. In theoretic terms, a close relationship between the organisational, territorial and peopled aspects of filling in speaks of a devolution process that has been managed effectively and may well contribute to an increase in the capacity of organisations of economic governance – and the devolved bodies that govern them – to act in effective ways (cf. Jessop, 2008). Conversely, tensions between the organisational, territorial and peopled aspects of filling in may pose broader questions concerning the ability of organisations of economic governance to achieve their stated goals. We want to propose that one key way in which we can consider the multi-faceted character of the process of filling in is with regard to the issue of collaboration between different organisations of economic governance. Issues to do with collaboration test the degree to which organisations of economic governance are well integrated, one with another, in terms of their organisational formats and goals, their territorial and scalar reach, and their working cultures. A focus on collaboration also highlights the potential tensions between as well as within organisations in each of these different contexts. A focus on this issue, therefore, provides an ideal context within which to examine the multi-faceted character of filling in within a devolved UK.

The following section briefly contextualises the devolution process that has taken place in Northern Ireland over the past few years. Three further substantive sections follow, which examine, in turn, the coordination of economic governance in organisational, territorial/scalar and peopled contexts.

Distinct, not different? Devolution in Northern Ireland

Much has been made, both in academic and more popular literatures, of the distinctiveness of devolution in Northern Ireland. Doing so raises broader issues about whether devolution in Northern Ireland should be considered as a case apart or, in other words, as an instance of devolution from which it is impossible to learn broader lessons (Wilford and Wilson, 2000: 114–15; for a criticism of this perspective, see Munck and Hamilton, 1998: 157). While particular factors illustrate Northern Ireland's distinctiveness as a province – and as an instance of the filling in of the UK state – we believe that there are sufficient similarities between the experiences of Northern Ireland and the remaining UK territories to make a sustained examination of Northern Ireland a valuable comparative case study of the devolution of economic governance within the UK.

In making such a statement, we do not wish to underestimate the particular challenges that face organisations of economic governance in Northern Ireland. The so-called 'Troubles', in particular, have left their imprint as much on the structures of economic governance within the province as they have on its broader society and culture. Some of the impacts of the ethno-religious conflict in Northern Ireland on economic governance within the territory will be discussed at length in a subsequent section but suffice to say at this stage that one of the main consequences of the 'Troubles' was witnessed in the suspension of the Northern Ireland Assembly, which took place between 2002 and 2007. This suspension demonstrates in a quite blatant way how the process of filling in has been wholly subsumed by ethno-religious considerations. While we would not want to gainsay the significance of the suspension of the Northern Ireland Assembly, it is also clear that the business of economic development – in terms of the implementation, if not the formulation, of policies and strategies – continued to operate in the period of suspension.

Interestingly, it has been argued that the distinctive medium-term history of the governance of Northern Ireland has, in many respects, helped to shape the kind of politics that have characterised the devolved administration. It has been argued, in this respect, that Northern Ireland had suffered especially badly from a lack of accountability. A large 'democratic deficit' was said to exist prior to devolution because of direct rule, the use of non-elected bodies, the overbearing influence of civil servants on decision-making and the secrecy that was associated with 'the machinery of consultation established by the British and Irish governments since 1980' (Greer, 1999: 147; Northern Ireland Civil Service, 2002). Devolution offered the prospect of an increasingly accountable and more open form of regional government, something which echoed the hopes of the other UK territories on the eve of devolution. Northern Ireland's actual experience of this attempt to address the accountability gap has been mixed. Some of our interviewees, for instance, maintained that the fact that there was a 'minister up on the hill' who monitored the activities of particular organisations of economic governance had had a positive impact on the effectiveness of those organisations and this is a theme that will be explored in more detail in the following section. At the same time, it is clear that the socio-cultural particularities of Northern Ireland have impacted greatly on the success of the Northern Ireland Assembly in bringing a greater degree of accountability to politics within the province. The main stumbling block, in this respect, has been the suspension of the Assembly itself but other more chronic issues, such as a lack of political trust and a certain reluctance on the part of civil servants to participate wholeheartedly in a new type of open devolved politics (see Wilson and Wilford, 2001b: 99), has meant that the expected democratic dividend associated with devolution has, in large part, failed to materialise.

Northern Ireland has also been marked out by distinct economic features, some of which we discussed in Chapter 3. We noted, for instance, that Northern Ireland has been overly dependent for a number of years on public sector employment. During the 1990s, for instance, Northern Ireland received an annual subsidy of almost four billion pounds from the UK Government (Anderson and Hamilton, 1995). In a related context, Munck and Hamilton (1998: 149) elaborated on some of the key failings of the Northern Ireland economy during the 1990s. In terms of productivity, for instance, Northern Ireland performed as poorly as other peripheral regions within the UK despite the considerably higher levels of public investment within the territory (Birnie and Hitchens, 1999). Similarly, research has shown that manufacturing employment and productivity within the province decreased markedly during the 1980s, at exactly the same time as large sums of money were being spent on industrial assistance (see Considine and O'Leary, 1999: 112–16; Gudgin, 1991). More specifically, the dependence on public subsidies in Northern Ireland (see NIEC, 1999a: 4–7) has led to low rates of entrepreneurship within the province. It is patterns such as these, and the economic problems that they generate, that have been the focus of considerable attention by policy-makers within Northern Ireland (e.g. NIDED, 1990). Even though these challenges are common to all peripheral regions within the UK, there is still a sense in which their manifestation in Northern Ireland is far more extreme than in other similar regions.

Finally, the other key difference with regard to the Northern Ireland economy is its relationship with the Republic of Ireland (RoI). The proposition that Ireland should be considered as an 'island economy' (quoted in Bradley, 1996: 147), made back in 1992, signalled a re-evaluation of the character of the relationship between the economy of the North and that of the Republic. It has been argued that the partition of Ireland has had significant impacts on the economic trajectories taken by the North and the South (New Ireland Forum, 1984) and that one way of facilitating economic growth in the North, in particular, would be to engage more fully with economic partners in the Republic (see Hutton, 1994). Certain key industrial sectors took the lead, in this respect, with considerable North–South collaboration taking place with regard to health technologies, food processing and the software industries (Munck and Hamilton, 1998: 151). There are signs, too, of an institutional response to such developments, with the formation of InterTradeIreland as one of six bodies that were set up under the auspices of the North South Ministerial Council. Its role has been to encourage cross-border trade and develop sources of knowledge to further this (PIU, 1999). As Munck and Hamilton (1998) note, however, the promotion of increased economic interaction between North and South has been the subject of considerable political debate in Northern Ireland, in both popular and academic contexts with so-called Unionist economists, in particular, cautioning against the development of too extensive economic relationships between North and South (e.g. Cadogan Group, 1992; Roche and Birnie, 1995). This is yet another example of how the economic governance of Ireland cannot be divorced from the province's broader ethno-religious context.

Yet despite the existence of these differences between the experience of Northern Ireland and the other UK territories under devolution – a distinction that is maybe unwittingly reinforced by our separate treatment of Northern Ireland in the context of this book – we would argue that many of the economic circumstances found within Northern Ireland, along with the more general processes of filling in, have been not dissimilar to the important changes that have affected the other UK territories over recent years. In this regard, it is important to note that many of the economic problems faced in Northern Ireland are, indeed, similar to those being experienced within the other UK territories; a point that was alluded to above. Furthermore, many of the key aims of ecomomic development within the province have been very similar to those in other territories, as we noted in our discussion of Strategy 2010 in Chapter 3 (Cooke et al., 2002; NIDED, 1999; for a review, see NIEC, 1999a; NIEC, 2001).

Here, therefore, is the broad context for devolution in Northern Ireland. The province has been notable for exhibiting certain economic, political and ethno-cultural distinguishing characteristics, and these have inflected the political geography of filling in within the province. And yet this is what should be expected within the SRA since, as Jessop (1990: 269) has noted, 'the power of the state is the power of the forces acting in and through the state'. At the same time, it is clear that politicians and civil servants in Northern Ireland are still grappling with economic issues that are largely the same as those in the other UK territories. This is what makes a study of economic governance in Northern Ireland – in organisational, territorial/scalar and peopled terms – a valuable contribution to a broader study of the filling in of the UK state as a whole.

The following three sections examine in more detail the complex political geographies of filling in exhibited in Northern Ireland in the period between 1999 and 2006. The first section elaborates on the tensions between the various state and non-state organisations that have been involved in governing the Northern Ireland economy and seeks, in particular, to examine the degree to which their activities have been coordinated. The second section builds on the first by considering the territorial and scalar contexts within which this coordination of organisations has unfolded. The final section draws attention to the way in which peopled interactions have served to integrate the activities of these organisations.

Filling in Northern Ireland: organisations of economic governance

Questions concerning collaboration between different organisations of economic governance are especially salient in Northern Ireland where economic governance has become relatively fragmented as a result of devolution and power sharing. As discussed in Chapter 3, in the period between 1999 and 2006, the remit for political decision-making and policy formulation with respect to economic development resided, in the main, in two ministries and departments: the Department of Enterprise, Trade and Investment (DETINI), and; the Department of Employment and Learning (DEL). DETINI was primarily concerned with business development (DETINI, 2002: 6) while DEL's remit, on the other hand, was focused more on the need to develop the human resources or human capital of the population of Northern Ireland (DEL, 2001: 11). DEL's role as a key driver of economic development in Northern Ireland was made clear by one of its high-level employees:

> Nevertheless, we fundamentally see ourselves being involved in economic development, and the department was created by bringing together the higher and further education parts of the old department of education, and the training and employment agency, together with the employment law side of the old [Department of Economic Development], what is now DETI. So it's a bringing together of education and training in a way that hasn't really been done before in this jurisdiction post-16.

Significantly, these two areas of economic governance experienced different trajectories of filling in after 2001. DETINI's remit for business development was characterised by a considerable de-statisation with the creation of INI as a new single economic development body, which lay at arm's length from the Assembly (NIDED, 1999: 206). The organisation involved in training and human capital in Northern Ireland, conversely, experienced considerable re-statisation with the incorporation of the Training and Employment Agency (T&EA), which was previously an executive agency, into DEL. The reason for this large-scale re-statisation is explained in the following quote:

> The T&EA was a next steps agency, and it was an executive agency before. When devolution came along we moved from the Department of Economic Development and became part of Higher and Further Education Training and Employment, and they shortened the name to DEL. When the department was formed, the T&EA merged with higher and further education, the post-16 stuff. So it was a fusion of higher and further education and training and employment ... and after a head count at that point, the T&EA contained three-quarters of the staff of the department, and accounted for about half the budget. It was decided by the new ministers to bring all these things together, rather than have a small department with a big T&EA, and that's what happened, the agency was subsumed into DEL ... There's been no change in the status of people, but what has happened as a result is better cohesion in terms of policy making, because you've got this post-16 remit together.

There are similarities and differences here with ELWa's experience in Wales. While both DEL and ELWa reflected an original desire to combine all aspects of post-16 education into one body, DEL always existed as a formal department of the NIA, it is only during the 'bonfire of the quangos' in Wales in 2006 that ELWa experienced a process of re-statisation.

The continued separation of DEL and DETINI, and the two key areas of economic governance that they reflect, into discrete areas of intervention, speaks of a set of possible policy tensions that need to be reconciled. It is in this context that an emphasis on collaboration has been most apparent with regard to the economic governance of Northern Ireland. We discuss efforts to promote such collaboration in two contexts in this section. We begin by focusing on the role of the Economic Development Forum (EDF), which was formed in 1999 as a way of bringing together all those organisations and agencies interested in the future competitiveness of Northern Ireland. We follow this with a discussion of the role that has been played by INI as the key agency for leading Northern Ireland's attempts to become a competitive and entrepreneurial province.

Northern Ireland's Economic Development Forum

Northern Ireland's EDF was formed in 1999 'to provide a formal mechanims through which a wide range of key organisations could advise ministers in the Northern Ireland Administration on issues relating to the development and formal competitiveness of the Northern Ireland economy' (EDF, 2002: 4; see also NIDED, 1999: 148). It included representatives from the trades unions, business organisations, DEL, the Department of Regional Development and Invest Northern Ireland, and was chaired by Sir Reg Empey, the Minister for Enterprise, Trade and Investment prior to the suspension of the NIA. The EDF was conceived as a vehicle for producing high-level strategic thinking on economic development. It was highly significant, therefore, as a way of bringing an overarching vision to economic development priorities in Northern Ireland. One individual involved in the EDF explained its significance as follows:

> [The EDF has a] long-term view of what the priority issues are for the Northern Ireland economy. What the objectives should be for the economy ... and at a reasonably high level, [establishes] what the key actions should be on the economy ... So it really is a quite unique achievement, setting a picture, setting a scene, setting a framework for action by a lot of key players in pursuit of specific objectives, on the specific priority areas. It really is ... in some senses a master plan, but it's not an imposed master plan, it's a partnership document which has taken us up to a certain point in time. But the challenge now is trying to translate and building on those identified actions in a considered and achievable way.

A key feature of the EDF was the way in which it stretched understandings of economic development into a variety of different policy areas, including transport and planning. One interviewee within DETINI emphasised the value of such an inclusive and, potentially, coordinated approach:

> We believe EDF has value to us as a department, we're servicing EDF to some degree, and EDF is much wider than this department ... it takes in [the Department of] Regional Development, and the Employment and Learning agenda, and you could even argue that in some cases they're stretching right back into education, and some other aspects ... [like] some planning issues.

Even though the EDF sought to bring together a wide range of actors involved in economic development issues in Northern Ireland, it is clear that one of its main achievements was to instigate and sustain a strategic dialogue between DETINI (and its executive agency INI) and DEL. One individual argued, for instance, that the EDF allowed DEL and DETINI to cooperate on 'quite a broad strategic level'. Another individual working in DEL indicated that the EDF had gained a certain legitimacy within the various partner organisations and had begun to influence DEL's internal strategic agenda:

> The EDF is looking right across the board, and it might well be that will become a coordinating group ... there's regional development, us [DEL] and Sir Reg [Empey] chairs it, those are the main players in economic development. This department looks at EDF with a lot of legitimacy. We've bought into what they have to say about the role of education and training in society and we've signed up to their Medium Term Strategic Priorities.

As well as showing how the EDF was beginning to influence DEL's thinking about skills training in Northern Ireland, the above quote also suggests that the EDF took on a bigger role in coordinating the strategies of all the agencies involved in promoting economic development within the province. One way in which the EDF sought to achieve this aim was through its Medium Term Strategic Priorities (MTSP) document (EDF, 2002), alluded to in the above quote. There was evidence that the MTSP was beginning to inform the strategic actions of partner organisations. One respondent from INI, for instance, maintained that

> the facts of the matter are that when the corporate plan of the Invest Northern Ireland was being developed ... another entity called the Economic Development Forum which ... involves trade unions, local representatives and bodies like ourselves, was developing medium-term strategic economic priorities so ... It would have been daft if those had been developed in isolation, and in fact they weren't developed in isolation ... so I think a pretty good effort was made to achieve compatibility between the various elements of the economic development policy.

The above quotes illustrate how different organisations involved in economic development in Northern Ireland were beginning to be influenced by the broader strategic outlook provided by the EDF. There is no doubt, in this respect, that the EDF possessed the potential to bring a measure of coherence to the process of filling in taking place within Northern Ireland and could act as an important counter to the possible fissile character of economic governance within the territory. The EDF, for instance, provided a strategic outlook of the various challenges and opportunities facing the Northern Ireland economy. As an example of this strategic outlook, we can focus on the issue of knowledge and productivity. The EDF's objective in 2002 was to 'generate wealth by maximising opportunities for, encouraging greater collaboration between, and increasing the capabilities and international competitiveness of, NI companies' (EDF, 2002: 8), but what is interesting was its attempt to map out the key organisational contributors for supporting actions in this area. With regard to attracting inward investment in high-technology or knowledge-based areas, for instance, the EDF specified key contributions from INI, DETINI and DEL. Other strategic aims possessed a further organisational reach. The need to enhance skill levels, particularly those in ICT and other growth areas, was said to fall within the purview of DEL and DETINI once again but also included other actors such as Further Education, Higher Education, Schools, Employers, Training Providers, Industry, as well as the Department of Agriculture and Rural Development, the Department of Education, and the Department for Social Development (EDF, 2002: 8). The value of the EDF, in this respect, lay in its ability to think of economic development issues in a rounded way and to combine the various departments of the Northern Ireland Assembly, along with their respective executive agencies, in a coherent and collaborative 'whole'.

The EDF, therefore, acted as a valuable mechanism for bringing a sense of coherence to the process of filling in economic governance in Northern Ireland, in organisational contexts. The high level of collaboration that emerged within the EDF was supplemented by the work of INI and we turn to examine its contribution in the remaining paragraphs of this section.

Leading the way? INI and the economic development of Northern Ireland

The political geographies of the formation of INI provide a fascinating insight into the complex filling in of economic governance in Northern Ireland in organisational contexts. As mentioned above, INI was formed as a single executive agency or non-departmental public body (NDPB) in April 2002 with the responsibility of implementing DETINI's various policies (Industrial Development Act (Northern Ireland), 2002). The formation of the organisation posed some questions regarding the collaboration between different organisations of economic governance in Northern Ireland: between INI and DETINI, its parent department; between INI and other bodies involved in governing the Northern Ireland economy; and within INI itself.

Determining the nature of the relationship between INI and DETINI has been a source of continual debate. At first glance, the relationship between the parent department and the executive agency should have been straightforward. According to DETINI's first Corporate Plan, published in 2002, INI was described as one of the four agencies (along with the Northern Ireland Tourist Board, the Health and Safety Executive for Northern Ireland and the General Consumer Council for Northern Ireland) that were supposed to 'assist in strategy implementation' (DETINI, 2002: 8). DETINI expanded further on their vision of INI's role by stating that the latter should be primarily concerned with 'service delivery' (DETINI, 2002: 21–3). The implication of the ascription of the title of a 'service provider' or 'service deliverer' on INI, of course, is that DETINI should be considered as the parent department whose responsibility it was to develop policies and strategies. One DETINI employee explained the nature of this relationship in colourful terms:

> It's a cuckoo's nest, you know, this is the cuckoo [INI] and we're [DETINI] going to have to fly back and forward to keep this cuckoo fed, but that doesn't mean that we don't have a role. I think it's important that that role is exercised properly. And if it is exercised properly [DETINI] will be a significant player in economic development. It has to be, it has to be the policy former.

The policy development role of DETINI certainly led to a number of challenges for the department. One series of challenges concerned the department's lack of experience of developing their own policies, something that echoes the issues that were faced by governmental departments involved in economic governance in the other UK territories. Another challenge was posed by the difficulties in defining the line of separation between DETINI and INI with regard to the development and implementation of economic development policy. Many respondents in both DETINI and INI referred to this issue. One DETINI employee, for instance, noted that

> it's not a black and white cut off ... a clear demarcation line with the department going it alone in splendid isolation, and then it sort of says to Invest Northern Ireland 'right get on with that' ... It doesn't work that way, it can't work that way, there has to be a close understanding and working relationships between ourselves and the new agency. And equally, in so far as Invest Northern Ireland is the delivery body ... implementing the policies,

it's important that we are in touch with them about implementation issues.

It was also suggested that INI could have an important advisory role in relation to policy. One INI employee, for instance, argued that 'I think that the actual policy development will not be as segregated, we will be a contributor rather than a policy developer.' This sentiment was echoed by another DETINI employee, who maintained that 'good policy formulation has to be informed by implementation and the experiences on the ground'. In this sense, the difficulty in determining the respective roles of DETINI and INI as policy developers and implementers could be recast as a virtue, with both organisations seeking to develop and implement policies in concert with one another.

As well as facing difficulties in defining the relationship between policy development and policy implementation, other tensions between DETINI and INI revolved around the degree of latitude that should be afforded to INI in order, as one individual put it, 'to get on with the job'. Of course, this is a perennial theme with regard to the relationship between NDPBs and parent departments (see Jones et al., 2005) and it was a noticeable feature of the relationship between DETINI and INI, especially during the early years of the latter agency's existence. Many respondents in both DETINI and INI drew attention to this challenge. One stated, for instance:

> One of the things we need to be very careful about as well is that we've set up Invest Northern Ireland to do a job. And we will monitor them and keep close to them, we'll try not to be a policeman, but we'll have to be a policeman to some extent. When you empower an agency, you give it significant executive responsibility, when the length of the arm is quite long ... you can't keep reining them in ... Invest Northern Ireland could easily go a direction which we haven't actually tasked them to do. But it's up to us to ensure that the policy statement within which they work is drawn sufficiently realistically, tightly, to ensure they do what they're set up to do, and they don't go off doing something else ... or indeed, that we're responsible enough that if they come to us and say, 'Well, we do think we should be going off on a different direction' that we assess it quickly and let them do it if it's reasonable, or address it in another way.

The above quote illustrates an important tension that needed to be resolved with regard to INI's relationship with DETINI. It was suggested that the relationship between the two organisations would evolve over time. One interviewee, an employee of DETINI, elaborated on this idea when he stated that 'I think the relationship's probably still developing [between DETINI and INI]' and went on to state that 'we've probably developed a more interventionist role, and I think that in turn is not something that we would want to do over the longer term'.

But there was also a very real sense in which certain actors within DETINI have begrudged giving INI too much freedom. Issues of political accountability have meant that it has been difficult for politicians within DETINI to contemplate granting too much freedom to INI. One DETINI employee explained that 'there's no sort of ambiguity at all about who will be responsible: Reg Empey will be responsible'. In other words, the political imperatives of a devolved system of government have meant that politicians have been unwilling to give too much autonomy to agencies such as INI. There is also some evidence to suggest that civil servants within DETINI sought to maintain control over INI (more broadly, see Northern Ireland Civil Service, 2002). This desire, it has been suggested, was borne out of an initial sense of dissatisfaction with the creation of INI as an NDPB. One DETINI employee who was close to the debate when INI was first mooted, and subsequently formed, argued as follows:

> The department wasn't happy about the new agency being outside the civil service. They didn't put up big opposition to it. There's ways of dealing with these things, and one of them is 'Ok, that decision is made, but it's the department who hand out the money, manage the money' ... we have a financial memorandum that states, from the department 'Here's what you are able to do with this money, and here's the processes, and here's what you can and can't do', so it's effectively control through the back door.

Such evidence points to the more complex relationships between parent departments and executive agencies that bald terms such as de-statisation and re-statisation can mask. While the formation of INI, at face value, represented a comprehensive process of de-statisation with regard to economic governance in Northern Ireland, it is clear that the exact configuration of the process of filling in the state – in both organisational and inherently peopled ways – led to a far more complicated and nuanced relationship between DETINI and INI. Such themes echo the broader statements that have been made concerning processes of 'meta-governance', which can enable state organisations to maintain control over a variety of seemingly independent agencies (see Whitehead, 2003).

A second related series of relationships with regard to the political geographies of filling in of economic governance in Northern Ireland existed between INI, as the lead agency of economic development in Northern Ireland, and other bodies possessing a remit within the area of economic governance. We want to focus, briefly, here on the relationship between INI and DEL since, as we outlined earlier, both organisations reflected diverging tendencies within the economic governance of Northern Ireland under devolution. Whereas INI represented a de-statisation of economic governance in Northern Ireland (the above comments notwithstanding),

DEL was illustrative of a considerable re-statisation of economic governance within the province. The negotiation of the relationship between these two key organisations provides a fascinating insight into the political geographies of filling in within Northern Ireland. One key way in which the relationship between DEL and INI (as well as with DETI, the parent department) was negotiated was through the EDF and we have already discussed the importance of this forum for bringing a degree of collaboration between different aspects of the economic governance of Northern Ireland. We want to consider in the following paragraphs the more direct interface between INI and DEL.

Despite their different trajectories of governance, employees within DEL and INI were keen to emphasise the way in which devolution had facilitated a degree of collaboration between the two organisations. There was evidence of collaboration between DEL and INI, for instance, at a strategic level. DEL, in this regard, were party to discussions concerning INI's strategy. One DEL employee commented that 'we've had one wider strategy meeting with INI, the blue-sky stuff, that involved our permanent secretary and Leslie Morrison [Chief Executive of INI] and both senior teams, and it was to try to identify what the issues are'. The employee maintained further that 'entrepreneurship came out very strongly' within these discussions and that 'we're trying to get that embedded in our HE and FE courses, but there's still a long way to go'. But as well as taking place in broad strategic contexts, there was also evidence of collaboration between DEL and INI on more specific policies. One good example was provided with reference to the Learn Direct scheme, which sought to promote a more programmed approach to staff training:

> Learn Direct are engaging with Invest Northern Ireland to see how Invest Northern Ireland can help them get these SMEs [Small and Medium Enterprises] to take up this concept of training staff. That wouldn't have happened in the past, you'd have had DEL going out separately, they wouldn't even have come near us ... so I see a change in that there, that whole interconnection with the likes of DEL in terms of employability. They're trying to get better joined-up government, there is a sense that INI wouldn't dare go out and develop an employability initiative, without engaging DEL in the planning process.

At the same time, a number of INI personnel elaborated on the practical difficulties associated with maintaining such links with other partner organisations in Northern Ireland, including DEL. We take up this theme further in a later section of this chapter.

The final set of connections and contradictions that we want to discuss in this section were based on INI's internal structure. As we noted in

Chapter 3, when it was formed INI represented an amalgam of the Industrial Development Board (IDB), the Local Enterprise Development Unit (LEDU), the Industrial Research and Technology Unit (IRTU) and the Training and Employment Agency's (T&EA's) Company Development Programme (CDP). The main reason for creating this new organisation was as follows:

> Bringing all economic services under the direction of one unit would have a number of benefits. It would sharpen the direction and delivery of overall economic development policy, presenting a clearer structure to users and removing the potential for confusion in the market place. It would simplify companies' dealings with the Department [DETI], and help to ensure that a clear and coherent policy message is present to potential investors in Nothern Ireland, whether indigenous or external. In addition, the integration of administrative services should yield worthwhile savings. (NIDED, 1999: 206; see also NIEC, 1999a)

While the creation of INI as a single agency was touted as a facilitator of Northern Ireland's ability to deal with the various socio-economic challenges that it faced, other commentators suggested that it may have actually hampered Northern Ireland's overall competitiveness. At a general level, some disquiet was shown towards the work of the IDB, which has been subsumed into INI. In a report on the effectiveness of the IDB, IRTU and LEDU with regard to the implementation of the *Competing in the 1990s* economic development strategy, the Northern Ireland Economic Council (NIEC) noted that the IDB had failed to fulfil its targets and that 'Strategy 2010's proposed single agency would only be successful if its predominant culture was that of the agencies, such as LEDU, IRTU and T&EA, which had implemented *Competing in the 1990s*' (NIEC, 1999b: 70). The clear implication in such a statement, of course, was that the IDB, given its previous failure to fulfil its aims, should not influence the culture of INI in any major way. The NIEC emphasised these sentiments in a separate report in which it argued that the single agency created as part of Strategy 2010 should not be a 'bolting together of IDB, LEDU, IRTU and the T&EA's CDP. It would have to be structured so that the success of the LEDU, IRTU and the T&EA's CDP were not compromised, but built upon and enhanced' (NIEC, 1999b: 63). Such strong statements allude to the internal tensions that influenced the work of INI during its early years in operation. In large measure, these internal tensions were based on the different working practices of the four predecessor organisations and, as such, will be discussed at greater length in a subsequent section of this chapter.

In this section, we have attempted to demonstrate the difficulties that were faced by politicians, policy-makers and civil servants in trying to coordinate a new organisational landscape in Northern Ireland with respect to economic governance. The Economic Development Forum was viewed as a key mechanism for drawing together different organisations into a common policy agenda but INI's role as the lead organisation of economic development in Northern Ireland was hampered, particularly with respect to its internal structure. In broader terms, the discussion in this section has also highlighted the blurred relationship that exists between organisational collaboration and the more territorial/scalar and (especially) the peopled aspects of collaboration. We turn in the following section to examine the territorial/scalar aspects of filling in in Northern Ireland in more detail.

Creating new territories and scales of economic governance

At first glance, the territories and scales of economic governance in Northern Ireland seem settled and, some might say, relatively uninteresting. Much has been made of the fact that the geography of Northern Ireland makes any discussion about territories and scales of governance within the province straightforward. The relatively small scale of the province has traditionally meant that there has been little need to subdivide it into smaller regions. At the same time, the distant and sometimes uneasy relationship that has existed between Northern Ireland and the Republic of Ireland has meant that Northern Ireland itself has been viewed as a self-contained entity on the island of Ireland. Some of our interviewees drew attention to these issues. An important factor that a number of interviewees stressed was the way in which the scale of government within Northern Ireland enabled a more coherent approach to the development of a unified ethos of economic governance, as well as of specific policies (Birnie and Hitchens, 1998, 2000). One noted, for instance, that 'one of the features of Northern Ireland is that the scale is such that it is not hard to find somebody to engage in these things [economic development]'. An advantage of the relatively small scale of economic governance in Northern Ireland was the way in which many people – representing different organisations – knew each other personally. One individual emphasised the significance of common board membership in ensuring collaboration between DEL and INI:

> You can put structures in place but the informal aspect shouldn't be forgotten. We have an advisory board in this department, called the Learning and Skills Advisory Board, chaired by [name], he's also a member of the board of Invest Northern Ireland, and is also the chair of the Northern Ireland Skills Task Force, so there's a network going on there, and that's actually happening, it's

alive. I think it's because we've got a village approach to life, everyone speaks to each other. You have to look at the link between the people involved in these different organisations.

While the above quote illustrates the significance of inter-personal links within the economic governance of the province, it also alludes to the fact that the governance of Northern Ireland is viewed by many as unproblematic in territorial and scalar senses. It is the 'village approach to life', in which the whole of the province is one homegeneous entity, that makes, at one level, the governance of the province relatively straightforward.

And yet our research also demonstrated different ways in which Northern Ireland's territorial and scalar unity had been increasingly challenged as a result of devolution. We want to focus, in particular, on the way in which the territorial and scalar unity of Northern Ireland was stretched in two directions: upwards and downwards. First, and as mentioned in the Introduction, what makes the economic governance of Northern Ireland interesting from a geographical viewpoint is the way in which it has increasingly had to take heed of its relationship with its southern neighbour. InterTradeIreland (PIU, 1999), for instance, was formed as a government-sponsored organisation, whose responsibility it was to consider the economic development of the island of Ireland and the way in which this goal could be furthered by integrating the economies of Northern Ireland and the Republic of Ireland in more effective ways. InterTradeIreland, in this respect, was viewed as an organisation that was supposed to react to the already-existing economic links between the North and South. In its report on business networks on the island of Ireland, for instance, InterTradeIreland (2005a: 21) identified 110 different networks and, of these, nineteen crossed the border between North and South. At the same time, InterTradeIreland was viewed as an organisation that should support and encourage higher levels of economic interaction between the North and South. Its report on entrepreneurship in Ireland, for instance, sought to reflect on levels of entrepreneurship in Northern Ireland, the Republic of Ireland and Ireland as a whole, as well as thinking about different ways of encouraging higher levels of entrepreneurship within each of these territories (InterTradeIreland, 2005b: 19–23). While the creation of such an organisation clearly reflects the realities of economic life on the island of Ireland, it is evident that some individuals and groups have viewed InterTradeIreland – and the whole ethos of cooperation between North and South that it reflects – as a sign of an unhealthy government support for an island of Ireland (e.g. Cadogan Group, 1992; Roche and Birnie, 1995).

But as well as being stretched upwards, economic governance in

Northern Ireland has been regionalised at scales smaller than that of the province as a whole, as we noted in Chapter 3. Northern Ireland's Department of Regional Development, for instance, maintained that a key element of its strategy was to 'encourage a balanced spread of economic growth to strengthen the network of opportunities and mobilise local resources across the Region' (NIDRD, 2001: 136) and this goal was predicated on the subdivision of Northern Ireland into a series of sub-territorial regions. INI's (2005a: 16) Operational Plan, too, argued that its 'network of regional offices is involved in a wide range of activities which support the development of existing businesses and the establishment of new businesses'. Such regional activity was especially apparent in the context of INI's efforts to revitalise the deprived urban areas of Belfast and the north-west of the province (INI, 2005a: 16). In this way, the regional offices were viewed as key delivery mechanisms for INI.

But it is significant that the existence of these regions, as well as being a potential positive contributory factor to the generation of economic success in Northern Ireland, were also a source of tension. One way in which these regional tensions were manifest was in the context of the relationship between INI's regional offices and its headquarters. The incorporation of LEDU into INI, in particular, had a scalar dimension, since LEDU's regional offices were now part of a much larger organisation. As was intimated earlier in the previous section, issues concerning procedural and culture changes were apparently more profound for ex-LEDU employees, and this tension also took on a territorial and scalar form. The following quote from one former LEDU employee flags up a concern about a diminution of local empowerment (Shuttleworth et al., 2005), and a reduction in responsiveness to local needs at the regional level:

> In the LEDU days, the regional manager was really the king of the castle, the big fish in the small pond. We were empowered to respond to local needs, so if there was one of our major textile companies closing, we could put in a programme straight away to address that ... we no longer have the ability to move quickly to address those local needs. We will have to go through the central departments to get the ok needed to run them. We're not being told we can't do them, but the process of justifying them and spending money will be more bureaucratic.

The same individual expanded on this theme by saying that 'you have to have a system and procedure that still allows you [as a regional manager] to respond and respond quickly'. According to the individual, this meant that 'sometimes you have to empower people to make a decision there and then'. In many respects, the situation had changed from one in which 'we were incredibly flexible, to one where it's a lot more bureaucratic'. The adoption of such a centralised and bureaucratic mode of operation, according to some interviewees, seemed to run contrary to the alleged ethos of INI as a 'client-centred' and 'responsive' agency (e.g. INI, 2005a, 2005b). This is not to suggest that there was nothing to be said in favour of having more central control over the activities of the regional offices. As a representative of one of INI's economic development partners argued, prior to reorganisation, 'the customer at the end of it all was getting a different service in different areas. The LEDU regions were treating us differently.' The same individual went on to maintain that 'one of the benefits for us of the merger is that there is a more consistent approach across Northern Ireland now'. Obviously, there was a need to strike a balance between the need for a coherent and coordinated approach for INI at the scale of the province of Northern Ireland and the desire to create a responsive and client-focused organisation at the regional scale within Northern Ireland.

Another interesting aspect of the process of regionalisation within INI was its efforts to engage with other more regional economic initiatives. Indeed, one main aim of INI's regional structure was to enable the organisation to 'continue to work with District Councils and other partners in areas across Northern Ireland' so that 'other smaller-scale locally-based economic initiatives ... [could] ... be taken forward' (INI, 2005a: 16). The interaction between INI and groups of local authorities could be both productive and problematic. The regional offices of INI encouraged groups of local authorities to coalesce into sub-territorial regions throughout Northern Ireland. INI was keen to deal with regional groupings of district councils, rather than individual councils, since such an approach saved time and resources, and helped to improve coordination (INI, 2005a). Such an approach was not without tensions, as an INI employee commented:

> IDB and LEDU were moving this way, operating in tandem to try and get councils to operate in clusters, and that's really now the policy on economic development issues. Because you've got some very small councils, and say they're trying to run a sector initiative, there's not enough companies, so across five or six councils you may be able to get the required mass to work with, and the councils themselves would recognise that, and be co-operative with that ... the major problem for councils hasn't gone away, if Invest NI is chasing an inward investment project, they expect it to involve their area, whereas getting the project is the most important thing, getting it to the right part of Northern Ireland is a key issue, but the councils are in competition, so it's not an easy thing to reconcile.

In other words, even though local authorities may well have appreciated the benefit of coming together as regional groupings, it was still a challenge for them to adopt a more holistic attitude towards the attraction of inward investment to Northern Ireland as a whole.

An additional impetus for the creation of regional clusters of local authorities came from the so-called Regional Sales Propositions (RSPs), which were formed for FDI purposes. The objective of the RSPs was to give local and regional actors more input into the FDI equation. They were also an attempt to address the fractionalism of FDI efforts, whereby each council would perhaps attempt independently to seek inward investment. The propositions recognised INI's pre-eminence in acquiring FDI. At the same time, the RSPs facilitated district council involvement in order to gain 'buy in' and unify, at least at a regional level, efforts to attract foreign investment into Northern Ireland. The key significance of RSPs for the purposes of the present discussion was that they have contributed to a further process of regionalisation within Northern Ireland. Certain local authorities were deemed to be too small to attract FDI and, thus, the creation of RSPs was viewed as a way of presenting the economic virtues of particular local authorities as part of a larger regional package, as the following quote from an INI employee makes clear:

> Here's the skills they require. 'Now, what have you got in your council area?' Some of the smaller ones, they've got nothing ... So what we're doing is we're working with five regional groupings of councils, to develop regional offerings for FDI.

What was most interesting about the emergence of these regional clusters of local authorities, however, was that they were not necessarily coterminous with INI's regions. It is significant, in this respect, that INI did not view such a territorial discrepancy as a major drawback. Indeed, the following quote shows that INI actually celebrated this bottom-up definition of regions within Northern Ireland:

> In this [the Southern] region, we have the SEED group, South-East Economic Development, a group of six councils in the South-Eastern region ... Basically, the [Southern] Invest Northern Ireland region has five councils in it, and the SEED region has six, so it's Invest Northern Ireland's region, plus one. *As far as we're concerned, it's not for us to draw boundaries. If they want to come together as those six, so be it.* (Emphasis added)

The emergence of what we may term a bottom-up process of regionalisation – or, alternatively, 'regional spaces' – within Northern Ireland had the potential to both complement and sometimes contradict the 'spaces of regionalism' of INI (see Jones and MacLeod, 2004). The individual in the above quote seemed remarkably sanguine concerning the clear territorial mismatch that existed in INI's southern region. The danger, however, is that such mismatches could lead to uncertainty concerning territorial spheres of responsibility between groupings of local authorities and INI regions.

Peopling economic governance in Northern Ireland

In the final substantive section of this chapter, we want to focus on the way in which the identities and practices of people in Northern Ireland have fed into the devolution of economic governance within the province. In general terms, it is clear that notions of territorial or ethno-religious identity have impacted on the economic governance of the province. As well as explaining the suspension of the NIA, the impact of ethno-religious divides, as we noted in Chapter 3, influenced the structure of the Northern Ireland Executive in far-reaching ways through the creation of the two separate ministries concerned with economic development (Laver, 2000; Wilson and Wilford, 2001a: 84; Wilson and Wilford, 2001b). Fortunately, it has been maintained that the ministers responsible for these two departments managed to develop an effective working relationship. Sir Reg Empey, the Minister for Enterprise, Trade and Investment, and Sean Farren, the Minister of Higher and Further Education, Training and Employment, for instance, were described as ministers who sought to 'behave in a co-operative fashion' (Wilson and Wilford, 2001a: 85).

We do not want to spend more time discussing the ethno-religious context for economic governance in Northern Ireland. Rather, we want to explore two other themes in this section. First, we examine in more detail the role played by individuals in enabling connections to be made between different organisations of economic governance. Second, we explore how individuals have also had to make sense of the internal workings and cultures of new organisations of economic governance.

In terms of 'bridging' (Coleman, 1988) the divide between different organisations of economic governance, we should not underestimate the role played by the EDF. Although fora such as these can be characterised by tensions and personal squabbles – and this may be truer of somewhere such as Northern Ireland with its broader ethno-religious context – they are also potentially places where individuals from different organisations can create productive relationships with one another. Although the evidence was limited in this respect, there were some indications that the EDF fulfilled a role of bringing a collaborative coherence to filling in a peopled sense with regard to economic governance in Northern Ireland. One employee from DETINI, for instance, argued as follows:

> It was a case of getting lots of different views that have been accommodated within a common forum, towards a common purpose, and again, that's where EDF sits, if you like, as drawing in partners ... if [Sir Reg Empey] didn't have EDF, there would be at the very least, a need to meet on a fairly regular basis, to talk to these different groupings of people on these type of subjects.

INI, too, was viewed as an organisation that had considerable potential to bring together a range of people working on similar themes in Northern Ireland. The development and execution of INI's Business Birth Rate Strategy, in which the organisation sought to 'stimulate the level of new firm formation by creating more positive attitudes to enterprise and entrepreneurship' (see INI, 2005b: 16) was, significantly, predicated upon the coordinated acitivies of a group of people. The following individual, representing DETINI, drew attention to how interaction had occurred at a number of different levels:

> What we're saying is that it is a Business Birth Rate Strategy for Northern Ireland, so first and foremost you need to go into a number of government departments. Again, in the past we would have worked in silo departments, but there's now this sense that when we launch this strategy, it will be launched by four departments. We will be the lead in terms of strategic development, monitoring and measuring its progress. But it'll need the commitment of the Department for Education, DEL, the Department of Culture Arts and Leisure, and the Department for Agriculture, they're very much involved in rural economic development. And our job is to make sure that all the departments are on board with the Business Birth Rate Strategy.

It is clear that it was the peopling of a cross-departmental or inter-agency working group such as this that facilitated its success. The individual whose words appear in the above quote, for instance, argued that the collaboration between departments and agencies was maintained through an active cooperation between individuals on steering groups and committees. The peopled aspect of these coordinating groups was obvious as respondents repeatedly referred to these working groups, and the collaborative links between different organisations that they fostered, in highly peopled terms: Mike from INI, Bill from DEL, David from DETINI and so on. Once again, such evidence highlights the significance of examining how a process of filling in is influenced by the people that staff devolved organisations of governance.

While the work of individuals in forging and maintaining strong connections between different organisations was appreciated, it was also evident that the effort needed to do so could pose some difficulties. An individual from INI, for instance, noted that:

> We have to work harder at inter-departmental activity and we are, how can I best express this? We are active on that front, although I'm not sure we've got

it absolutely right. I was asking my staff recently how many inter-departmental groups we're involved with and the answer is 45. So I think we have probably overdone it in that sense.

At one level, such a high level of inter-departmental and inter-agency collaboration and partnership placed a strain on the organisations involved but it was also a burden that had to be shouldered by certain individuals who sat on steering groups and partnership meetings. The successful development of a collaborative approach to economic governance in Northern Ireland was clearly an aspect of filling in that was highly dependent on the contribution, commitment and personalities of key state personnel.

But in addition to the role played by state personnel in enabling connections between different orgaisations, there was evidence of their contribution in enabling and/or questioning the internal workings of organisations. We witnessed evidence for such themes especially in the context of INI. As noted in an earlier section, INI was created out of the merger of a series of pre-existing organisations, namely the IDB, IRTU, LEDU and T&EA's CDP. In general terms, it is evident that the bringing together of different people from governmental (IDB and IRTU) and non-governmental (LEDU and T&EA's CDP) backgrounds proved to be difficult. These organisations possessed different working practices and cultures, and often different pay and conditions, and this proved a challenge for the development of a common organisational culture for INI. The main tensions arose in the context of harmonising the working cultures of staff previously employed by LEDU, who were characterised as people who were used to showing initiative and taking risks, and the civil servants of the IDB and IRTU. Former LEDU staff, in particular, found it difficult to adjust to the different 'speed' of working in INI, as the following quote illustrates:

> In terms of flexibility, response times, on a scale of one to ten, LEDU was sitting about six, could do better. In Invest Northern Ireland, you're really coming down to about three, a bigger and slower organisation. Equally so, you've got to understand that those from IDB and IRTU, they were maybe sitting at one or two on the same scale. So they're now thinking 'This is getting a bit fast for me'.

The above quote highlights the concerns being voiced – particularly from ex-LEDU personnel – that INI was far more bureaucratic and unresponsive than its executive agency status would suggest. There were differing views as to why INI possessed such a 'bureaucratic' approach. INI was obviously a larger, more complex organisation than its predecessors, and it was suggested that this went a long way to explaining new working procedures:

> At the moment, the only difference I see, from a LEDU perspective, a lot of people have difficulty with procedures, but we're a lot bigger organisation, which hasn't really bedded down yet. And you need to have more coordination in a bigger organisation, by necessity, and I think people haven't come to terms with that yet.

Others pointed to the tight relationship with the sponsoring department, whilst others suggested that the high proportion of civil service employees was having an impact. In the following quote, a representative of a key partnership agency suggested that more bureaucratic procedures were having detrimental effects on responsiveness, and that this could be partly attributed to having civil service staff within the organisation:

> Things seem to have slowed down. Very basic things like getting payments out of them, have slowed down, getting decisions, definitely slowed down. Decision-making has changed now. People that we would have spoken to who make decisions, don't make them any more ... To be totally honest the IDB people were civil servants and the LEDU people were slightly private sector and it looks like it has gone worse, in terms of response ... it is quite hard to merge in all these staff, and they probably need to get rid of a few of them.

As noted in the above quote, there was a view that decision-making ability was migrating up the organisational hierarchy. While this could be defended as being in the interests of a joined-up approach, preventing an uncoordinated plethora of commitments and programmes, it mitigated against the notion that INI should be a responsive – and, in the words of one politician, 'nimble' – organisation. One individual working for INI even went so far as to suggest that INI employees were, in effect, all civil servants:

> With working practices, the reality is we're part of the civil service, there's no doubt about it, that's a fact. We're not operating in the way we would have operated in LEDU. It's a reining back, even IDB people would say that. They're reining back partly because we've lost a lot of power over decision-making.

Similar sentiments were also apparent in the following quote, which illustrates some of the disillusionment felt by many INI staff, especially those who were previously employed within LEDU:

> What we really have now is a civil service culture, all the civil service terminology, and the reality is that 80 per cent of the people in Invest Northern Ireland are civil servants anyway ... It's right in the heart of government, NDPB, arm's length, or not. It's like a division of the department. If you walk like a duck, talk like a duck, you're a bloody duck – we're civil servants.

Further complications arose from the fact that around 80 per cent of staff working in INI were civil service secondees, who were able to return into the civil service after a period of three years working for INI. The potential problem of a secondee 'mass exodus' back to the civil service made planning for staff problematic. It was remarked by one INI employee that 'a huge barrier to bedding it all down is the fact that you have the civil service staff seconded for a three-year period, so you're never going to be quite sure as to where things sit until the end of that period ... it's a huge difficulty'. Other employees agreed that this secondment arrangement was hindering the development of employee skills necessary for the achievement of corporate goals:

> The changes will happen in three years' time, it'll never really settle until then. You never really know if there's a big block of forty or fifty people just about to walk out, and it's bound to be very hard for [the chief executive]. In any other circumstance, you'd know your goal, you'd focus to it, if the skills don't match, you'd train them, you know, you'd know what you'd got. You could spend a lot of time training a person, and that person leaves.

It was also proposed that secondees, perhaps those who saw their futures within the civil service, were not fully dedicated to the new organisation. One INI employee maintained that 'it's certainly possible that a large number of civil servants will revert to the civil service' and that 'obviously it creates that environment where people aren't necessarily as committed as they might be'. In a similar vein, another individual suggested that the situation was

> far from ideal, as an organisation, having these two groups of staff. There will be people who are not motivated, but the LEDU people, they have no exit route, so I suspect they're more motivated ... But as I say, there's such a high proportion, I'm not sure of the exact figure, but if it is 600 out of 780, it is a very high proportion, with this 'should I, shouldn't I' dilemma going on in their minds. It's far from ideal, there's no way to hide from that ... Let's hope we can convince most of them that the organisation is worth staying in, because if all 600 decided to walk out, you've got a problem [laughs], a mega problem.

However, the matter of secondees potentially returning to the civil service was not simply, as the above quote highlights, a numerical problem. There was an important consideration in terms of the potential loss of high quality staff. Many of the people working in INI, particularly those inherited from the higher echelons of IRTU and IDB, possessed specific knowledge and abilities relevant to the organisation. As the following quote emphasises, such people could not easily be substituted:

> We would be worried if we started to lose a great part of our expertise ... if all that started to bleed quite heavily back towards the department [DETINI]. We would try and be strong, and try not to panic but it would cause us concern because we can recruit staff ... but we can't recruit that type of knowledge ... I think what they [civil service people] are doing is playing a wait and see game ... they are hedging their bets and understandably so.

The commitment of civil servants to INI could in some senses be gauged by their willingness to put themselves forward for internal competitions for promotion. Under the terms of the Industrial Development Act 2002 (Northern Ireland), secondees who gained a new position in the organisation through internal competition would cease to be civil servants, becoming instead Invest Northern Ireland employees, with no special rights of return to the civil service. When asked whether some employees from the legacy agencies possibly lacked commitment to the new organisation, one interviewee commented that

> The only place, to be honest with you, that it is showing at the moment, is in terms of some internal competitions [for employment] that we are running. Ex-civil service people are reluctant to commit to Invest Northern Ireland at this time, and we are getting lower numbers than we had hoped for on some internal competitions.

Once again, such evidence highlights the precariousness of staffing issues within INI. At a broader level, it also alludes to the conceptual uncertainty over the nature of the process of filling in experienced with regard to INI. In policy and organisational terms, it was clearly an NDPB that represented a de-statisation of economic governance in Northern Ireland. A more sustained and detailed interrogation of the peopled aspects of filling in with regard to INI reveal a far more nuanced and complicated picture of the unfolding geographies of devolution within the province.

Conclusions

Our aim in this chapter has been to show how the different elements of the process of filling in – discussed in relative isolation in previous chapters – ultimately need to be addressed as a whole. In theoretic contexts, one needs to consider the unfolding connections between the new organisations, new territories and new peopled relationships and cultures that constitute devolved governmental forms if one is fully to understand the complex dynamics of filling in. State organisations, territories and personnel exist in a triple dialectic in which each element continually reproduces and transforms the other (see Jones, 2007). At the same time, it is clear that any effort to comprehend the actualities of the devolution of economic governance in the UK must be based on a similar understanding of how new state organisations affect, and are affected by, pre-existing and new state territories and personnel. Adopting such a conception of filling in has aided our understanding of the intricacies of filling in in Northern Ireland. The differing trajectories taken by DEL and DETINI under devolution in Northern Ireland are marked when one focuses solely on the organisational context; the former has experienced considerable re-statisation as a result of the incorporation of T&EA into DEL, while the latter has undergone a process of relative de-statisation as a result of the formation of INI. But when a peopled understanding of filling in is allied to this more organisational interpretation, then a more complex picture arises, in which INI's apparent quasi-independent status becomes slightly more questionable. Similarly, one can only understand some of the organisational and peopled tensions that have become apparent in INI – most notably between former semi-private sector LEDU employees and IDB civil servants – when one also considers the territorial makeup of LEDU/INI; numerous tensions have arisen, in this regard, because of the high level of independence granted to LEDU regional offices prior to devolution, and which has been emasculated as a result of the creation of a more centralised organisational and territorial structure within INI.

In more normative contexts, we would want to suggest that a key aim of policy-makers and politicians involved in devolved economic governance must be to align these different elements of the filling in process. The ability of devolved organisations to achieve their stated goals depends, at heart, on their ability to ensure a concord between organisational structures, projects and strategies (Brenner, 2004; Jessop, 2008), the organisations' territorial and scalar forms, and the working cultures and commitments of the personnel working for them. The existence of a disjuncture between any one of these three elements is likely to lead to unproductive tensions within devolved organisations of economic governance and a dissipation of organisational energy, whereas a unity of organisational structure, territories and personnel is more likely to enable an organisation of economic governance to reach its goals. Given the political significance of issues relating to economic development for the whole devolution project, then this should be a key policy aim of devolved politicians in the coming years.

7
Conclusions: devolution in retrospect

Introduction

Our aim in the preceding chapters has been to show the value of adopting a spatially and agency sensitive reading of the SRA as a way of understanding the process of devolution that took place in the UK between approximately 1999 and 2006. We showed how socio-political struggles in each of the four territories of the UK led to a differential devolution settlement with specific reference to organisations of economic governance. These socio-political struggles, significantly, were played out in territorial and scalar contexts as the devolved organisations of economic governance sought to find appropriate solutions for the economic problems faced within their jurisdictions. At the same time, state personnel were at the heart of efforts to negotiate a workable solution to devolution in each of the territories. While we addressed each of these three issues – organisations, territories/scales and people – in three separate chapters, we also attempted to demonstrate the benefits accruing from considering the connections between these three themes in the context of an in-depth study of economic governance in Northern Ireland.

We do not in this chapter seek merely to reaffirm the conclusions of preceding chapters. Rather, the chapter has two main aims. First, we seek to bring up to date the preceding empirical discussion by elaborating on some of the major recent developments (post-2006) that have taken place in each of the four territories. If devolution should be considered a process rather than an event (Davies, 1999), then it is certain that organisations of economic governance in the four territories have not remained static since 2006 but have, instead, been reconfigured in far-reaching ways. Significantly, the economic downturn and the concomitant retrenchment in public spending, while reaffirming the need for organisations of economic governance within each of the four territories, has also served to raise fundamental questions about the ability of the various devolved administrations in the UK to commit large amounts of money to support these selfsame organisations. From May 2010, the Labour Government was replaced by a coalition and we note some of the Conservative–Liberal UK Government's responses to this challenge (see Cabinet Office, 2010). Our second goal is to consider the broader conceptual significance of the themes discussed in the various chapters of this book. In particular, we explore the way in which the empirical discussion in this book can be used to augment the SRA. Rather than seeking to decry the usefulness of the SRA, our aim in this chapter is to refine this conceptual framework so that it maintains its utility as a means of understanding contemporary state restructuring in the UK.

Pressing ahead or making do? The recent geographies of devolution

Major changes to the architectures of economic governance have taken place in each of the four territories over recent years. In England, much debate has taken place concerning the way in which economic development should be restructured within the territory. *A Review of Sub-National Economic Development and Regeneration* in 2007, for instance, still maintained that regions should play a key role in fostering economic development within England. It argued, for instance, that 'there should be a devolved approach, giving local authorities and regions the powers to respond to local challenges and improve economic outcomes' (Treasury, BERR and DCLG, 2007: 7). RDAs, in this respect, were said to be crucial organisations in promoting such economic development. The report recommended that an RDA should take on the responsibility of developing an integrated regional strategy for a region (Treasury, BERR and DCLG, 2007: 9). And yet, the report also alluded to a concern that RDAs had become too focused on organisational and strategic issues and had lost sight somewhat of their main aim; namely to foster economic growth. It was argued, for instance, that RDAs' objectives should be changed, 'replacing their current tasking framework with a simplified outcome and growth-focused framework defined by a single over-arching growth objective' (Treasury, BERR and DCLG, 2007: 9). It is in recommendations such as these that we may be able to witness how a Labour Central Government was, perhaps, becoming a little worried, if not a little impatient, about the lack of progress being made by RDAs in achieving their stated aims.

Such concern and impatience was to a reach a head in the June 2010 Budget Report, in which it was announced that the Coalition Government would abolish RDAs, from March 2012, as part of its push towards 'decentralisation and localism' (a Bill by this name signalling broader changes in socio-economic governance for England). In the light of the fiscal challenges facing the UK state, RDAs were viewed as too much of a governmental extravagance. Accusations had been made by the Taxpayers' Alliance (2009), for instance, that the majority of RDA grants over the past two years had been disbursed to public bodies rather than private businesses. The Budget Report advocated that the economic regeneration role of RDAs should be transferred to city-focused Local Enterprise Partnerships (LEPs), which would bring together elected officials from local government, local business people and chambers of commerce (Treasury, 2010: 31). In many ways, the Coalition Government's support for Local Enterprise Partnerships signals a potential shift towards city-regions as new territories and scales of economic governance in the UK (see Etherington and Jones, 2009; Harrison, 2010). The impact of such a policy decision has already been felt in the East Midlands region, the focus of our empirical enquiry in England. The East Midlands Development Agency, like all RDAs, after suffering a 25 per cent reduction in its budget, is currently managing the transition of its responsibilities for economic development to three LEPs, which will go live from March 2012. The three LEPs, as part of a network of twenty-eight (with thirty-five LEPs eventually replacing the RDAs) are: Lincolnshire; Leicester and Leicestershire; and Nottingham, Nottinghamshire, Derby and Derbyshire.

Regional Assemblies, too, have suffered a somewhat rough ride since our original period of research. In 2004, the Labour Government's plans to create more elected Assemblies in the English regions suffered a major setback as 78 per cent of the inhabitants of the north-east of England voted 'no' in a referendum to create such an Assembly in their region. This vote helped to scupper – at an early date – any further plans for more executive forms of devolution to the English regions. The killer blow to English Regional Assemblies, however, came in March 2010 when they were abolished and replaced with Local Authorities Leaders' Boards. Speaking before the East Midlands Assembly's last meeting, Stuart Young, Chief Executive of the Assembly, praised the organisation's work, particularly in relation to its contribution to improving transport links within the region (BBC, 2010). In many ways, such a shift confirms a re-territorialising or rescaling of economic governance in England as the eight officially designated regions have become replaced by coalitions of local authorities, some of which will be centred on cities.

This 'new-new localism' (Jones and Jessop, 2010: 1143) trend has being reinforced by the further rolling back of regional government in England. In

CONCLUSIONS

July 2010, the Regional Leaders' Boards funding ended, and following the abolition of the Government Office for London, plans were announced to abolish the remaining eight Government Offices. The website of the Government Office for the East Midlands (www.goem.gov.uk, accessed 31 August 2011), stated: 'The 2010 Comprehensive Spending Review confirmed that the Government Offices for the Regions will close at the end of March 2011. Responsibilities for the remit of the Government Offices have transferred to a number of different Government departments. The information is available here ...' Eric Pickles, MP, Secretary of State for Communities and Local Government, outlined this thinking on the apparent transfer of power from central government down to local councils and down further to local communities in the following statement:

> We are making good progress with our programme of radical reforms to reduce the burden of bureaucracy on local authorities and businesses, including removing the inflated local government performance regime and doing away with the unnecessary regional tier. Consequently many of the functions Government Offices undertook are no longer necessary. By announcing our intention in principle now, we will further progress our programme of reform, allow staff, councils and departments to take account of this, and make an earlier start in the Spending Review on securing savings for the public purse. I believe that the original intentions behind the establishment of the Government Offices for the Regions (to join up different departmental teams outside London into a 'one stop shop') have been lost. Such functions are no longer necessary in an internet age and given the Coalition Government's commitment to genuine decentralisation and devolution of power. There are, however, some Government Office functions, such as arrangements for resilience and civil contingencies, which will need to continue. The Spending Review process will be used to test which activities currently carried out by the Government Offices should continue, and to decide the most cost-effective and on-going arrangements. The Spending Review will also consider arrangements for the redeployment or release of Government Office staff, and for sharing as appropriate savings, costs, assets and liabilities arising from the decision. *We should be clear: the Government Offices are not voices of the region Whitehall. They have become agents of Whitehall to intervene and interfere in localities, and are a fundamental part of the 'command and control' apparatus of England's over-centralised state.* (Department for Communities and Local Government, 2010: 1–2, emphasis added)

In all this, we are witnessing an attempt to move away from viewing regions as being additional tiers of the state that have been designated by central goverment to seeing localities as the flexible crucibles for new economic governance coalitions. Here, we witness again how the sedimentation of new organisations and territories of governance occurs as a result of the struggles between different actors located in this state and in civil society.

At this stage in the evolution of sub-national economic development in England, where it is becoming apparent that 'there is no such thing as regions' (Cooper, 2011: 7), we are able to spot shortcomings in this decentralisation and localism approach to economic development. The policy rhetoric points to an opportunity for localities to devise unique policy solutions, supported by private sector backing (phrased 'financial freedoms'), and flexibility with planning (given the context of the parallel rolling back of regional planning in England and the rolling of forward of initiatives such as Enterprise Zones, announced in August 2011). But how will the Local Enterprise Partnerships be coordinated and at what spatial scale? Without some form of strategic economic body to negotiate the 'policy space' (Pugalis, 2011: 9) in between sub-regional groupings of localities and the national level, some LEPs will, no doubt, get dwarfed by ambitious core city-regions (such as Manchester and Birmingham). This also raises the issue of cross-boundary cooperation. Will this happen? Will the management of some programmes, historically governed and coordinated at certain scales and across territories, prove to be unworkable at a lower or higher spatial scale (such as transport and European funding)? And, with our neoliberalism interpretative hat on, is this not just about the scapegoating of individual localities for their economic and social failings, the dimensions of which are largely the influence of multi-scalar forces and their complex interactions, and thus displacing problems down to local communities and civic institutions? Another reading of the situation is that coordinated implementation could be hampered by an inherited inflexibility of the state apparatus, due to the fragmented legacies of individual departments and policy initiatives and their scalar interpenetration and/or interference (Fuller, 2010). How resilient, then, is the new economic governance of England?

Equally fundamental changes have taken place in Wales. Admittedly, major reconfigurations of organisations of economic governance took place during our initial period of research and, as such, have already been discussed in Chapters 3, 4 and 5. We noted, for instance, the many changes that happened to ELWa. Its early regional focus proved problematic and its activities were increasingly centralised. The termination of its independent status was announced in 2004 and took place finally in 2006. That year also marked the incorporation of the WDA into the Welsh Assembly Government. In 2011, WAG became the Welsh Government – a move connected to a 'yes' vote in the referendum on further law-making powers for the Assembly on 3 March 2011, with the Welsh Government's functions now including being able to propose bills to the National Assembly for Wales on subjects within twenty fields of policy. In these

CONCLUSIONS

cases, we witnessed major instances of re-statisation within a devolved Wales, perhaps because responsibility for economic development was viewed as something that was too important to be left in the hands of quangos and Whitehall. Once again, these changes highlight the need to examine the specific configuration of state forms within devolved territories. The contours of filling in take on different hues in different territories as a result of the various coalitions of interest that exist within them.

With respect to economic development and its governance, the other main development to have happened in Wales in recent years has been the adoption of the Wales Spatial Plan (WAG, 2004, 2008). The plan has sought to provide a territorial and scalar framework for sustainable development and planning in Wales over a twenty-year period. As well as reflecting in an overt manner the Welsh Assembly's commitment to sustainable development, the Spatial Plan is significant for its attempt to think differently about the regional makeup of Wales. Rather than sticking with the four regions that had served to define the internal geography of devolved Wales, the Spatial Plan proposed that Wales should be divided into six sub-regions. The regions would not possess hard or fixed boundaries and would reflect more closely the daily patterns of movement and flow of people and goods. And so, of the three regions in South Wales that have been portrayed in the Spatial Plan, two are centred around the travel to work areas of Swansea and Cardiff. Once again, the territories and scales of economic governance in Wales are being configured differently and in ways that seek to reflect the realities of regional economies and everyday life in more effective ways than their fixed and rigid predecessors. We may even begin to view them as attempts by WAG to downplay notions of fixed-state territories in favour of more fluid structures that reflect the relational realities of the contemporary world (see Amin 2004; Amin et al., 2003; Jones, 2009).

The changes to forms of economic governance in the other two territories have not been as far-reaching as those that have taken place in England and Wales. As we noted in Chapters 3 and 4, organisations of economic governance in Scotland were characterised by far more stability in the immediate aftermath of devolution than their counterparts in England, Wales and Northern Ireland and this pattern has continued to a large extent. Economic governance is still structured around the two main agencies of Scottish Enterprise and Highlands and Islands Enterprise. The main shift that has taken place in Scotland has been the dissolution of the LECs and LEFs. As recently as 2007, Scottish Enterprise lauded its role in contributing in large measure to the effectiveness of local partnerships and the business community through the work of its LECs and LEFs (Scottish Enterprise, 2007: 73). And yet, and for reasons that are unclear at present, by late 2008 these organisations had been discontinued. Perhaps there was a feeling that the LEFs' stated role of trying to reduce the duplication of responsibilities at a local level in Scotland had, ironically, served to add to organisational congestion within the territory. Whatever the reasons for the dissolution of the two related organisations, it is clear that the process has led to a centralisation of economic governance within the territory with the migration of decision-making and agenda-setting upwards to the two regions governed by Scottish Enterprise and Highlands and Islands Enterprise. Further evidence for this scalar shift can be found in the fact that the forum for discussing economic development issues now exists at this regional scale, instead of the local scale. Highlands and Islands Enterprise (2009), for instance, has recently announced that it will form a Highland Economic Forum in order to discuss the key economic challenges facing the Highlands region as a whole.

Changes to organisations of economic governance have also been relatively muted in Northern Ireland. INI still exists as the key driver of economic development within the province and is still supported by DETINI and, to a lesser extent, DEL. There has, however, been discussion about the possibility of changing the contours of economic governance within the region in some far-reaching ways. In 2009, an Independent Review of Economic Policy, commissioned jointly by DETINI and INI (2009) and chaired by Professor Richard Barnett, attempted to map out an alternative structure of economic governance for Northern Ireland. In addition to a series of recommendations about INI's and the Northern Ireland Executive's specific policies, the report recommended two significant changes to the contours of economic governance in the province. First, it was recommended that the EDF, the forum that has brought together different organisations of economic governance in Northern Ireland since 1999, should be discontinued. This recommendation came into effect in January 2010 (www.edfni.com, accessed 20 October 2010). Second, an argument was made in favour of creating a 'Department of the Economy', which would unite the activities of DETINI and DEL (DETINI/INI, 2009: 8). These recommendations are highly significant given the discussion in Chapter 6. Creating an all-encompassing 'Department of the Economy' would certainly help INI and the Northern Ireland Executive to approach economic development in a more holistic way than it has done to date. There has, however, been limited movement on this front since the recommendation was made. This is not surprising given the fact that the makeup of departments in the

Northern Ireland Executive is so highly influenced by ethno-religious considerations. And yet the abolition of the EDF would seem to suggest that there is now a pressing need to find an alternative mechanism for bringing about a more cohesive approach to economic governance within Northern Ireland. Once again, we witness here how debates about state structures are predicated upon the social forces that act and operate through them (Jessop, 1990).

In a related context, it is evident that the organisations of economic governance in each of the four territories are still adhering – in broad terms – to the policies and strategies that they adopted at the beginning of the devolution process. They still maintain the need to promote higher levels of skills and entrepreneurship among the indigenous workforce, as well as emphasising the need to attract inward investment into their territory. At the same time, these organisations have also had to reshape their strategies and policies somewhat to deal with the additional threats that have been posed by the financial crisis. In Northern Ireland, for instance, INI's most recent annual report (2010) draws attention to the additional challenges being faced by the Northern Ireland economy as a result of the economic downturn and stresses the difficulties in trying to innovate so that it can help its clients weather their short-term challenges while, at the same time, keeping and eye on its longer-term strategic goals. Similar themes appear in Scotland. In Scottish Enterprise's most recent Business Plan, for instance, its Chairman, Crawford Gillies, states that the organisation's key aims are to 'help boost education and the skills of our workforce; it will help to rebuild communities through new investment; and it will provide jobs and prosperity for individuals' (Scottish Enterprise, 2010: 4). At the same time, the Business Plan concedes that businesses in Scotland currently face a 'thoroughly challenging economic environment' (Scottish Enterprise, 2010: 9). Moreover, it is argued that the budget pressures facing Scottish Enterprise will mean that it will have to ensure that it focuses its efforts on where it can 'have the biggest impact on Scotland's economic performance' (Scottish Enterprise, 2010: 9).

Taken together, therefore, it is clear that there has been some movement in terms of the architectures of economic governance in each of the four territories. There are some striking similarities in the developments that have taken place. In general terms, the early years of devolution witnessed a sustained experimentation in the four territories, with a variety of new organisations either being created or being invigorated in each of the four territories. One can think here of the Regional Assemblies and RDAs in England, ELWa and CCETs in Wales, LEFs in Scotland and INI in Northern Ireland. In another context, it is clear that these organisations also tended to exist at arm's length from the devolved governments. This initial flurry in which new organisations were created has been followed by what could be termed a period of reflection and subsequent retrenchment, partly but not wholly due to the financial exigencies of the contemporary period. RDAs and Regional Assemblies (along with the Government Offices) have recently been abolished in England while ELWa and the WDA were incorporated into WAG in 2006. In Scotland, LECs and LEFs have recently been discontinued and there are ongoing debates about the best way of rationalising economic governance in Scotland. In all of this, we may be witnessing a gradual process in which a devolved state – which had been filled in in extensive ways in the immediate aftermath of the devolution process – is progressively being abandoned. This has led one of us to identify an 'impedimenta state', i.e. a trend for the state to become the medium and outcome of a series of economic development rationalities, which are being implemented through multiple spatial strategies and projects, but their apparent incompatibility and baggage-like polity is reproducing irrationality (Jones, 2010).

In addition, we may also be witnessing two contradictory processes occurring in the four different territories of the UK. On the one hand, there is evidence of a considerable re-statisation of economic governance in places such as Wales, through the incorporation of ELWa and the WDA in the formal structures of WAG. In Scotland, too, the dissolution of LECs and LEFs testifies to a trend towards increasing the influence that devolved states have over economic governance. At the same time, this tendency has also marked a territorial and scalar centralising of power; to the territorial scale in the context of Wales and to the regions governed by Scottish Enterprise and Highlands and Islands Enterprise in Scotland. Other trends are apparent in England, where the formal devolved structures of RDAs and Regional Assemblies are being dismantled in favour of regional economic governance that is centred on local coalitions. While this trend represents an alternative form of re-statisation – one that is focused on the local rather than the national or regional state – it is also a process that maintains a strong role for the private sector in shaping priorities of economic development within the English regions (Pugalis and Townsend, 2010). More interestingly, this new form of regional economic governance being proposed in England appears to be more organic and bottom-up in character than the one based on the officially designated regions of RDAs and Regional Assemblies (albeit centrally orchestrated). We may well be witnessing here a process whereby new spaces of regionalism – centred on English cities – are subverting the old regional spaces put in place by the UK state (Jones and MacLeod, 2004). In terms of resilience of the state and UK plc, we would suggest that exit from the crises of neoliberalism (the fiscal crisis, the urban crisis of August 2011, and beyond) requires adequate responses to the socio-spatial contradictions of the neoliberal model without regenerating the older problems that neoliberal state spatial restructuring (in the form of devolution and constitutional change) was meant to resolve.

The SRA, filling in the state and beyond

We claimed in Chapter 2 that there had been a dearth of useful conceptual frameworks that could be used to understand the contemporary processes of devolution in the UK. While work on the new regionalism, multilevel governance and the politics of scale had some useful insights for understanding aspects of devolution, none of these frameworks provided a comprehensive account of the social and spatial processes that characterise devolution. We maintained that a reworked SRA, in which attention was directed to an uneven process of 'filling in' could provide a detailed and comprehensive framework for explaining the state restructuring that has characterised devolution. Filling in encourages researchers to examine the complex, uneven and contingent ways in which new devolved organisations, possessing particular territorial and scalar dimensions, and reflecting various configurations of state personnel, have been sedimented in each of the UK territories. At the same time, we also suggested in Chapter 2 that work on the SRA had been characterised by a lack of empirical enquiry. A perhaps unstated aim in this book has been to argue that researchers should attend to empirical studies of how the state is being reconfigured in complex ways, rather than merely relying on ever-more complicated assertions about the conceptual and theoretical significance of such changes. We are confident, therefore, that we have been able to bridge a gap in this book by combining a valuable theoretical insight into mechanics of devolution with a detailed empirical enquiry of state restructuring as it has taken place in the specific context of economic governance.

As a way of structuring the book – and indeed the project on which it was based – we chose to examine three themes in greater detail. First, an important aspect of the SRA is the fact that it encourages us to explore the way in which state organisations, along with their specific strategies and projects, reflect the condensation of active political struggle between different groups. Our focus on organisations of economic governance in the four territories of the UK immediately drew attention to the significance of capitalist interests in shaping the trajectories taken by the devolution settlement. It has been noticeable, for instance, that business interests have been, in overt ways, drawn into the new organisations of economic governance in each of the four territories, whether in relation to the EDF in Northern Ireland, Regional Assemblies in England, LEFs in Scotland and ELWa's Regional Committees in Wales. While the influence of capitalist interests in these various devolved fora has been significant, it has not, however, been overwhelming. In this respect, we need to consider the political complexion of the territories that have been filled in through devolution and the impact that this has had on the configuration of organisations of economic governance. ELWa's Regional Committees, for instance, contained representation from trades unions and the voluntary sector. Similar tendencies were apparent in Scotland in the context of LEFs. We perhaps witness here the way in which the socialist tendencies of devolved administrations in Scotland and Wales have led to the emergence of organisations of economic governance in these territories whose goals have been slightly more socially inclusive than would otherwise have been the case. In a similar vein, we should appreciate the way in which the ethno-religious context of Northern Ireland has impinged in far-reaching ways on the organisational makeup of the province with regard to economic governance. In all these instances, we witness the way in which different groups gain access to the state, thus helping to influence the configurations of state organisations and strategies in contrasting ways. While SRA theorists often refer to the possibilities for different groups to access the state apparatus, there is often a sense that they merely pay lip service to this possibility. There is a danger, then, that SRA theorists tend to underplay the alternative configurations of state power that may emerge when a state is influenced by groups of people whose main interests may not necessarily revolve around serving the interests of capitalism. In this respect, the process of devolution, we would argue, has helped to highlight not just the differential access of different groups to the state apparatus but also the way in which different groups have actually accessed and shaped the state in different ways in different parts of the UK. As such, there is a need for SRA theorists to take seriously, perhaps for the first time, the way in which state organisations are an expression of the various *forces* – rather than merely one wholly dominant force of capitalism – acting in and through them.

Second, we examined the way in which a reworked SRA could draw attention to the territorial and scalar characteristics of contemporary state restructuring under devolution. Essentially, the notion of filling in discussed in this book was designed to counter a weakness in accounts of the hollowing out of the state; namely that it tended to overlook the contingent territorial and scalar outcomes of the process of hollowing out. Our empirical discussion has highlighted the significance of focusing on

CONCLUSIONS

filling in by demonstrating the way in which territories and scales of economic governance in the four territories have been continually reworked since 1999. Once again, different trends have characterised each of the four territories and these territorial and scalar trends have come about as a result of active and contingent political struggle. The continual and differential rounds of territorial and scalar restructuring that we have discussed in this book reflect Brenner's (2009b: 127) recent contention that 'processes of rescaling must be understood in terms of the contextually specific political strategies that engendered them'. He maintains further that 'the question, from this point of view, is how and why political strategies are mobilized to transform established formations of state scalar organization and how such rescaling strategies in turn evolve over time'. But despite the conceptual insight afforded by our modified SRA, some might ague that recent developments in geography have made a focus on the territorial and scalar makeup of the state redundant or passé. Work on relational space, for instance, has drawn attention to the fact that the contemporary world is characterised by relational networks that are global in character and which call into question work that concentrates on the alleged static and unchanging territories and scales of the state (e.g. Amin et al., 2003). Amin (2004), in this vein, has called for geographers and others to examine a new politics of connectivity that is predicated on these global networks while, at the same time, decrying an old-fashioned kind of politics that draws its sustenance from spatially defined units. In a similar vein, Marston et al. (2005) have called for geographers to jettison the language of scale in favour of a so-called 'flat ontology'. We would contend that two important themes emerge in the empirical discussion in this book, which counter many of the arguments made by authors promoting networked understandings of territory and scale. First, despite their pretentions to the contrary, it is evident that notions of territory and scale still inform the way in which policies and strategies have been developed in each of the territories of the UK. Moreover, the sedimentation of organisations of economic governance over specific territories and at particular scales has influenced the access that various groups have to these organisations. Our discussion of the creation of ELWa, for instance, explored the way in which the organisation – from the very outset – had been hijacked by business rather than educational interests and this business-led focus was further emphasised through the emerging organisation's emphasis on a regional, as opposed to a local, mode of achieving its objectives. Second, our empirical discussion shows that the territories and scales of the UK state under devolution have been anything but static and unmoving. Indeed, territories and scales of economic governance in the UK have been formed through the strategic and relational practices of a whole host of different groups, including business interests, ethno-religious groups and state personnel to name but a few. In this way, the modified SRA that we have advocated in this book can be viewed as a conceptual framework through which to examine the relational production of state spaces of different kinds.

We maintained, finally, that the modified SRA that we developed in this book could be used as a means of examining how state personnel of different kinds played a key role in articulating the way which state organisations and state territories were articulated. As noted earlier, work to date on the SRA has elaborated on the potential for different groups to gain access to the state and shape it in ways that reflect their own interests. And yet, despite such admissions, it is fair to say that little work has examined in any great detail the potentialities for state personnel to influence the organisational and territorial makeup of the state in such ways. We hope that the preceding chapters, particularly Chapters 5 and 6, have demonstrated the worth of such an endeavour. We witnessed in these chapters how state personnel of different kinds were involved in enabling new state organisations to come into existence. It was these same individuals who had make sense of their place and role within these organisations, and, at certain times, questioned the structures of the organisations within which they worked. At the same time, it was individuals such as these that helped to reproduce and sometimes undermine the territorial and scalar integrity of the organisations for which they worked. In this respect, we hope that this book has helped to encourage adherents to the SRA to take more seriously the active contributions made by state personnel to state forms, as well as examining the way in which state organisations and territories can also impinge on the working practices and identities of state personnel. Doing so would place the SRA at the heart of contemporary efforts to develop more anthropological understandings of the state.

Of course, rather than viewing these three elements in isolation, we contended that the process of filling in can only be fully understood by examining the interaction between devolved state organisations, the territories and scales over which they operate, and the role played by state personnel in facilitating or hindering their activities. The discussion in Chapter 6, we hope, helped to demonstrate the value of such a comprehensive approach. The difficulties of adopting such an approach, however, is that it is challenging conceptually to juggle these three elements – organisations, territories/scales and people – at the same time. It is difficult, for instance, not to hold people constant when examining the connections between organisations and territories/scales or to ignore territories/scales when considering the interrelationship between state personnel and the organisations within which they work (see Jones, 2007). And yet, intuitively, it is evident that it is through adopting such a triple dialectic that the ultility of the SRA in comprehensively understanding contemporary state restructuring can be fully demonstrated. While this book can be viewed as one small, yet we would hope significant, step in this direction, the challenge must be for other researchers to develop the conceptual languages and methodological dexterities necessary to examine this three-fold interaction in more thorough and sustained ways in the future.

Finally, while our main aim in this book has been to illustrate the value of adopting a modified SRA, in which attention is drawn to a complex and contingent process of filling in, as a way of understanding contemporary processes of devolution in the UK, we believe that the goal of future research in this area must surely be to examine more explicitly the interactions between the processes of hollowing out and filling in. In effect, in our attempt to demonstrate the need to comprehend the process of filling in taking place in each of the UK territories, we have, perhaps, been guilty of under-emphasising the multifarious connections between the hollowing out of the central UK state and the changes that have taken place in each of its constituent territories. And yet it is clear that there is a need for social scientists of different hues to attend to these connections, not least as a way of understanding the way in which devolution has impacted on the notion of UK plc. The danger, otherwise, is that the debate about devolution and contemporary state restructuring more generally will become too polarised with the views of interlocutors perhaps being caricatured in unhelpful terms. If our aim in this book has been to question somewhat the thesis of hollowing out by advocating an antithesis of filling in, surely the next step must be to develop a synthetic view of state restructuring that builds on the insights of hollowing out and filling in. While we have perhaps been able to allude to the value of such a synthetic approach in this book, our sincere hope is that others working in this area will be able more fully to develop and explicate the value of such an approach in future years.

References

Adam Smith Institute (1983) *The Omega Report*. London: Adam Smith Institute.
Agnew, J. (1987) *Place and Politics: The Geographical Mediation of State and Society*. London: Allen and Unwin.
Agnew, J. (1994) 'The territorial trap: the geographical assumptions of international relations theory', *Review of International Political Economy* 1: 53–80.
Agnew, J. (1996) 'Liminal travellers: Hebrideans at home and away', *Scotlands* 3: 32–41.
AGW (2003) *National Council for Education and Training for Wales: Accounts for the Period Ending 31 March 2002. Report by the Auditor General for Wales*. Cardiff: Auditor General for Wales.
Allmendinger, P. and Haughton, G. (2010) 'Spatial planning, devolution, and new planning spaces', *Environment and Planning C: Government and Policy* 28: 803–18.
Amin, A. (1999) 'An institutionalist perspective on regional economic development', *International Journal of Urban and Regional Research* 23: 356–78.
Amin, A. (2004) 'Regions unbound: towards a new politics of place', *Geografiska Annaler* 86B: 33–44.
Amin, A. and Thrift, N. (1995) 'Institutional issues for European regions: from markets and plans to socioeconomics and powers of association', *Economy and Society* 24: 41–66.
Amin, A. and Thrift, N. (eds) (1994) *Globalization, Institutions, and Regional Development in Europe*. Oxford: Oxford University Press.
Amin, A., Massey, D. and Thrift, N. (2003) *Decentring the Nation: A Radical Approach to Regional Inequality*. London: Catalyst.
Anderson, J. and Hamilton, D. (1995) 'Why Dublin could afford a union', *Parliamentary Brief – Northern Ireland Special Issue* Spring: 26–7.

REFERENCES

Archer, M. (1995) *Realist Social Theory: The Morphogenetic Approach*. Cambridge: Cambridge University Press.
Audit Commission (1989) *Urban Regeneration and Economic Development: The Local Government Dimension*. London: HMSO.
Audit Scotland (2004) *Local Economic Forums: A Follow-up Report*. Audit Scotland: Edinburgh.
BBC (2010) 'Regional Assembly in last meeting', http://news.bbc.co.uk/1/hi/england/nottinghamshire/8551979.stm, accessed 22 October 2010.
Bertramsen, R.B. (1991) 'From the capitalist state to the political economy', in *State, Economy and Society* (eds) R.B. Bertramsen, J. Peter, F. Thomsen and J. Torfing, pp. 94–145. London: Unwin Hyman.
Betts, C. (2000a) 'Michael out, Morgan in', *The Western Mail*, 10 February: 1.
Betts, C. (2000b) 'I won't be Blair's puppet – Morgan', *The Western Mail*, 12 February: 1.
Birnie, E. and Hitchens, D. (1998) 'An economic agenda for the Northern Ireland Assembly', *Regional Studies* 32: 769–76.
Birnie, E. and Hitchens, D. (1999) *The Northern Ireland Economy: Problems, Policies and Prospects*. Aldershot: Ashgate.
Birnie, E. and Hitchens, D. (2000) 'New economic strategies in Northern Ireland and the Republic of Ireland: Strategy 2010 and Enterprise 2010', *Regional Studies* 34: 788–92.
Blacksell, M. (2000) 'Devolution', in *The Dictionary of Human Geography* (eds) R. Johnston, D. Gregory, G. Pratt and M. Watts, pp. 171–2. Oxford: Blackwell.
Blair, T. (2000) 'Speech on Britishness and the government's agenda of constitutional reform'. London: Labour Party.
Block, F. (1987) *Revising State Theory: Essays in Politics and Postindustrialism*. Philadelphia: Temple University Press.
Bogdanor, V. (1999) *Devolution in the United Kingdom*. Oxford: Oxford University Press.
Bradbury, J. (2006) '*Territory and Power* revisited: theorising territorial politics in the United Kingdom after devolution', *Political Studies* 54: 539–82.
Bradley, J. (1996) *Exploring Long-term Economic and Social Consequences of Peace and Reconciliation in the Island of Ireland*, Research Monograph no. 6. Belfast: Northern Ireland Economic Council.
Bratsis, P. (2006) *Everyday Life and the State*. London: Paradigm Publishers.
Brenner, N. (2004) *New State Spaces: Urban Governance and the Rescaling*

of Statehood. Oxford and New York: Oxford University Press.

Brenner, N. (2009a) 'A thousand leaves: notes on the geographies of uneven spatial development', in *The New Political Economy of Scale* (eds) R. Keil and R. Mahon, pp. 27–49. Vancouver, B.C.: University of British Columbia Press.

Brenner, N. (2009b) 'Open questions on state rescaling', *Cambridge Journal of Regions, Economy and Society* 2: 123–39.

Brenner, N. and Theodore, N. (eds) (2002) *Spaces of Neoliberalism: Urban Restructuring in North America and Western Europe*. Oxford: Blackwell.

Brenner, N., Jessop, B., Jones, M. and MacLeod, G. (2003) 'Introduction: state space in question', in *State/Space: A Reader* (eds) N. Brenner, B. Jessop, M. Jones and G. MacLeod, pp. 1–17. Oxford: Blackwell.

Bulmer S., Burch, M., Carter, C., Hogwood, P. and Scott, A. (2002) *British Devolution and European Policy-making: Transforming Britain into Multi-Level Governance*. London: Palgrave.

Cabinet Office (1999) *Modernising Government*. London: Stationery Office.

Cabinet Office (2010) *The Coalition: Our Programme for Government*. London: Stationery Office.

Caborn, R. (1996) 'A new deal for the English regions'. Labour Party Statement on Regional Economic Policy. London: Labour Party.

Cadogan Group (1992) *Northern Limits: Boundaries of the Attainable in Northern Ireland Politics*. Belfast: The Cadogan Group.

Callinicos, A. (2010) *Bonfire of Illusions: The Twin Crises of the Liberal World*. Cambridge: Polity.

Cambridge Journal of Regions, Economy and Society (2009) 'Rescaling the state', *Cambridge Journal of Regions, Economy and Society* 2: 3–138.

Capie, F., Wood, G. and Sensenbrenner, F. (2003) 'Foreign investment in the UK', mimeograph. London: City University.

Carmichael, P. (2001) 'The Northern Ireland civil service', *Public Money and Management* April–June 21: 33–8.

Chaney, P., Hall, T. and Pithouse, A. (eds) (2001) *New Governance, New Democracy? Post-Devolution Wales*. Cardiff: University of Wales Press.

Clark, G. and Dear, M. (1984) *State Apparatus: Structures and Language of Legitimacy*. London: Allen and Unwin.

Coates, D. (2000) *Models of Capitalism*. Oxford: Polity.

Coleman, J.S. (1988) 'Social capital in the creation of human capital', *American Journal of Sociology* 94: 95–120.

Considine, J. and O'Leary, E. (1999) 'The growth performance of Northern Ireland and the Republic of Ireland: 1960 to 1995', in *Political Issues in Ireland Today* (ed) N. Collins, pp. 106–25.

REFERENCES

Manchester: Manchester University Press.
Cooke, P. and Clifton, N. (2005) 'Visionary, precautionary and constrained "varieties of devolution" in the economic governance of the devolved UK territories', *Regional Studies* 39: 437–51.
Cooke, P. and Morgan, K. (1998) *The Associational Economy*. Oxford: Oxford University Press.
Cooke, P., Roper, S. and Wylie, P. (2002) *Developing a Regional Innovation Strategy for Northern Ireland*. Belfast: Northern Ireland Economic Council.
Cooper, H. (2011) 'Made redundant in the regions', *Guardian*, Society, 30 March: 7.
Corbridge, S., Williams, G., Srivastava, M. and Véron, R. (2005) *Seeing the State: Governance and Governmentality in India*. Cambridge: Cambridge University Press.
Davies, R. (1999) *Devolution: A Process Not an Event*. Cardiff: Institute of Welsh Affairs.
DEL (2001) *Department of Employment and Learning: Annual Report 2000–2001*. Belfast: Department of Education and Learning.
Delaney, D. (2005) *Territory: A Short Introduction*. Oxford: Blackwell.
Department for Communities and Local Government (2010) 'Regional government', *Written Statement by the Rt Hon Eric Pickles MP, Secretary of State for Communities and Local Government*. London: Department for Communities and Local Government.
Department for Enterprise, Innovation and Networks (2006) *Working Together for Wales: Enterprise, Innovation and Networks Business Plan 2006/07*. Cardiff: Welsh Assembly Government.
DETINI (2002) *Department of Enterprise, Trade and Investment: Corporate Plan 2002–2005*. Belfast: Department of Enterprise, Trade and Investment.
DETINI (2005) *Economic Vision for Northern Ireland*. Belfast: Department of Enterprise, Trade and Investment.
DETINI/INI (2009) *Independent Review of Economic Policy*. Belfast: Department of Enterprise, Trade and Investment/Invest Northern Ireland.
DETR (1997) *Building Partnerships for Prosperity: Sustainable Growth, Competitiveness and Employment in the English Regions*. London: Department of the Environment, Transport and the Regions.
DfEE (1999) *Learning to Succeed: The New Framework for Post-16 Learning*. London: Department for Education and Employment.
Dicken, P. (2010) *Global Shift: Mapping the Changing Contours of the World Economy*. London: Sage.

Driver, S. and Martell, L. (2000) 'Left, right and the third way', *Policy and Politics* 28: 147–61.

Driver, S. and Martell, L. (2002) *Blair's Britain*. Cambridge: Polity.

Duncan, S. and Goodwin, M. (1988) *The Local State and Uneven Development*. Cambridge: Polity Press.

EDF (2002) *Working Together for a Stronger Economy*. Belfast: Northern Ireland Economic Development Forum.

Elden, S. (2005) 'Missing the point: globalization, deterritorialization and the space of the world', *Transactions of the Institute of British Geographers* 30: 8–19.

Elliott, R.F., Bell, D., Scott, A., Ma, A. and Roberts, E. (2005) 'Devolved government and public sector pay reform: considerations of equity and efficiency', *Regional Studies* 39: 519–39.

ELWa (2001a) *Education and Learning Wales-National Council Corporate Plan 2002–2005*. Cardiff: Welsh Assembly Government.

ELWa (2001b) *Education and Learning Wales-National Council Operational Plan 2001–2004*. Cardiff: Welsh Assembly Government.

ELWa (2001c) *Education and Learning Wales-National Council Draft Corporate Strategy*. Cardiff: Welsh Assembly Government.

ELWa (2002) *Education and Learning Wales-National Council Corporate Strategy*, Cardiff: Welsh Assembly Government.

ELWa (2003a) 'National Council-ELWa announces new structure to drive forward improvements for learners in Wales', press release. Bedwas: Education and Learning Wales.

ELWa (2003b) 'Lifelong learning body reports good progress on reshaping agenda', press release. Bedwas: Education and Learning Wales.

EMDA (1999) *Prosperity through People: 1st East Midlands Economic Strategy*. Nottingham: East Midlands Development Agency.

EMDA (2002) 'Agency's new look aimed at reflecting local needs'. Press release. Nottingham: East Midlands Development Agency.

EMDA (2003) *Destination 2010: 2nd East Midlands Regional Economic Strategy*. Nottingham: East Midlands Development Agency.

EMRA (2000) *East Midlands Integrated Regional Strategy – Our Sustainable Development Framework*. Nottingham: East Midlands Regional Assembly.

EMRA (2005) *England's East Midlands Intergrated Regional Strategy: Our Sustainable Development Framework*, 2nd edition. Nottingham: East Midlands Regional Assembly.

Environment and Planning A (2001) 'Reflections on the "institutional turn" in local economic development', *Environment and Planning A*

33: 1139–241.

Environment, Transport and Regional Affairs Committee (1997) *Regional Development Agencies: First Report*. London: Environment, Transport and Regional Affairs Committee.

Etherington, D. and Jones, M. (2009) 'City-regions: new geographies of uneven development and inequality', *Regional Studies* 43: 247–65.

Evans, M. (2006) 'Elitism', in *The State: Theories and Issues* (eds) C. Hay, M. Lister and D. Marsh, pp. 39–58. London: Palgrave Macmillan.

Fairley, J. and Lloyd, M.G. (1995) 'Economic development and training in Scotland: the roles of Scottish Enterprise, Highlands and Islands Enterprise and the Local Enterprise Companies', *Scottish Affairs* 12: 52–72.

Foley, M. (2004) 'Presidential attribution as an agency of Prime Ministerial critique in a Parliamentary demcracy: the case of Tony Blair', *British Journal of Politics and International Relations* 6: 292–311.

Foley, P. (2002) 'Regional strategy development in the East Midlands', in *England: The State of the Regions* (eds) J. Tomaney and J. Mawson, pp. 147–58. Bristol: Policy Press.

Foster, C.D. (2001) 'The civil service under stress: the fall in civil service power and authority', *Public Administration* 79: 725–49.

Fuller, C. (2010) 'Crisis and institutional change in urban governance', *Environment and Planning A* 42: 1121–37.

Gamble, A. (2002) 'Divided, different, but not a disaster', *Times Higher Education Supplement*, 4 January: 22.

Gerth, H.H. and Mills, C.W. (1991) 'Introduction: the man and his work', in *From Max Weber: Essays in Sociology* (eds) H.H. Gerth and C.W. Mills, pp. 1–74. London: Routledge.

Giddens, A. (1984) *The Constitution of Society: Outline of the Theory of Structuration*. Cambridge: Polity Press.

Giddens, A. (1985) *A Contemporary Critique of Historical Materialism vol. 2, The Nation-state and Violence*. Cambridge: Polity.

Giddens, A. (1998) *The Third Way: Renewal of Social Democracy*. Cambridge: Polity.

Giddens, A. (2002) *Where Now for New Labour?* Cambridge: Polity.

Gillespie A. and Benneworth, P. (2002) 'Industrial and regional policy in a devolved United Kingdom', in *Devolution in Practice: Public Policy Differences Within the UK* (eds) J. Adams and P. Robinson, pp. 69–85. London: Institute for Public Policy Research.

Goodwin, M. and Painter, J. (1996) 'Local governance, the crises of Fordism and the changing geographies of regulation', *Transactions of the Institute of British Geographers* 21: 635–48.

Goodwin, M., Jones, M. and Jones, R. (2005) 'Devolution, constitutional change and economic development: explaining and understanding the new institutional geographies of the British state', *Regional Studies* 39: 421–36.

Goodwin, M., Jones, M. and Jones, R. (2006a) 'Devolution and economic governance in the UK: rescaling territories and organisations', *European Planning Studies* 14: 979–95.

Goodwin, M., Jones, M. and Jones, R. (2006b) 'The Northern Ireland economy: developing economic development structures', in *Devolution and Constitutional Change in Northern Ireland* (eds) P. Carmichael, C. Knox and R. Osborne, pp. 219–30. Manchester: Manchester University Press.

Goodwin, M., Jones, M. and Jones, R. (2006c) 'The theoretical challenge of devolution and constitutional change in Britain', in *Territory, Identity and Space: Spatial Governance in a Fragmented Nation* (eds) M. Tewdwr-Jones and P. Allmendinger, pp. 35–46. London: Routledge.

Goodwin, M., Jones, M., Jones, R., Pett, K. and Simpson, G. (2002) 'Devolution and economic governance in the UK: uneven geographies, uneven capacities?' *Local Economy* 17: 200–15.

Gray, J. (2004) 'Blair's project in retrospect', *International Affairs* 80: 39–48.

Greer, A. (1999) 'Policy-making', in *Politics in Northern Ireland* (eds) P. Mitchell and R. Wilford, pp. 142–69. Boulder, CO.: Westview Press.

Greer, J. (2001) 'Whither partnership governance in Northern Ireland?', *Environment and Planning C: Government and Policy* 19: 751–70.

Gudgin, G. (1991) 'An uncertain future for the Northern Ireland economy', *Irish Banking Review* Autumn: 3–19.

Hall, P. and Soskice, D. (eds) (2001) *Varieties of Capitalism: The Institutional Foundations of Comparative Advantage*. Oxford: Oxford University Press.

Harrison, J. (2006) 'The political-economy of Blair's "New Regional Policy"', *Geoforum* 37: 932–43.

Harrison, J. (2010) 'Networks of connectivity, territorial fragmentation, uneven development: the new politics of city-regionalism', *Political Geography* 29: 17–27.

Harvey, D. (2010) *The Enigma of Capital*. London: Profile Books.

Haughton, G. and Counsell, D. (2004) *Regions, Spatial Strategies and Sustainable Development*. London: Routledge.

Haughton, G. and Peck, J. (1996) 'Geographies of labour market governance', *Regional Studies* 30: 319–21.

Hay, C. (2006) '(What's Marxist about) Marxist state theory?', in *The*

REFERENCES

State: Theories and Issues (eds) C. Hay, M. Lister and D. Marsh, pp. 58–78. London: Palgrave Macmillan.

Hazell, R. (2000) *The State and the Nations: The First Year of Devolution in the United Kingdom.* Exeter: Imprint Academic.

Hazell, R. (ed) (2006) *The English Question.* Manchester: Manchester University Press.

Healey, P. (1997) *Collaborative Planning.* London: Macmillan.

Heffernan, R. (2005) 'Exploring (and explaining) the British Prime Minister', *British Journal of Politics and International Relations* 7: 605–20.

Hennessy, P. (2000) 'The Blair style and the requirements of twenty-first century premiership', *Political Quarterly* 71: 386–95.

Hennessy, P. (2005) 'Informality and circumscription: the Blair style of government in war and peace', *Political Quarterly* 76: 3–11.

HIE (2001) *Highlands and Islands Enterprise Operating Plan 2001–2005.* Inverness: Highlands and Islands Enterprise.

HIE (2009) 'The Highland Council: Planning, Environment and Development Committee', 21 January 2009. Inverness: Highlands and Islands Enterprise.

HM Treasury, DTI and ODPM (2003) *A Modern Regional Policy for the United Kingdom.* London: HM Treasury, Department of Trade and Industry and the Office of the Deputy Prime Minister.

Hobson, J.M. (1998) 'The historical sociology of the state and the state of historical sociology in international relations', *Review of International Political Economy* 5: 284–320.

Hogwood, B. (1996) *Regional Boundaries, Co-ordination and Government.* Bristol: Policy Press and the Joseph Rowntree Foundation.

Holliday, I. (2000) 'Is the British state hollowing out?', *The Political Quarterly* 71: 167–76.

Hollingsworth, J.R. and Boyer, R. (eds) (1997) *Contemporary Capitalism: The Embeddedness of Institutions.* Cambridge: Cambridge University Press.

Hollingsworth, K. (2002) 'Connecting with wider Wales: the role of Regional Committees', in *Building a Civic Culture: Institutional Change, Policy Development and Political Dynamics in the National Assembly for Wales* (eds) B.J. Jones and J. Osmond, pp. 213–23. Cardiff: Institute of Welsh Affairs.

Hutton, W. (1994) *Britain and Northern Ireland, The State We're In – Failure and Opportunity.* Belfast: Northern Ireland Economic Council.

Industry Department for Scotland (1988) *Scottish Enterprise. A New Approach to Training and Enterprise Creation.* Edinburgh: Scottish Office.

INI (2001) *Invest Northern Ireland: Draft Corporate Plan*. Belfast: Invest Northern Ireland.
INI (2005a) *Invest Northern Ireland Operating Plan 2005–2006*. Belfast: Invest Northern Ireland.
INI (2005b) *Invest Northern Ireland Corporate Plan 2005–2008*. Belfast: Invest Northern Ireland.
INI (2010) *Invest Northern Ireland Annual Report and Accounts, 2009–10*. Belfast: Invest Northern Ireland.
InterTradeIreland (2005a) *Business Networks on the Island of Ireland*. Newry: InterTradeIreland.
InterTradeIreland (2005b) *Entrepreneurship on the Island of Ireland 2004*. Newry: InterTradeIreland.
IWA (2001) *World's Best Practice in Regional Economic Development*. Cardiff: Institute of Welsh Affairs.
Jeffery, C. (2002) 'An introduction to the Devolution and Constitutional Change Programme', in *Devolution and Constitutional Change: A Research Programme of the Economic and Social Research Council* (ed) C. Jeffery, pp. 3–4. Birmingham: ESRC Research Programme.
Jeffery, C. (2007) 'The unfinished business of devolution', *Public Policy and Administration* 22: 92–108.
Jessop, B. (1985) *Nicos Poulantzas: Marxist Theory and Political Strategy*. London: Macmillan.
Jessop, B. (1990) *State Theory: Putting Capitalist States in their Place*. Cambridge: Polity.
Jessop, B. (1993) 'Towards a Schumpeterian workfare state? Preliminary remarks on post-Fordist political economy', *Studies in Political Economy*, 40, 7–39.
Jessop, B. (1994) 'Post-Fordism and the State', in *Post-Fordism: A Reader* (ed) A. Amin. Oxford: Blackwell.
Jessop, B. (1995) 'The future of the nation state: erosion or reorganisation?', Lancaster Regionalism Working Papers (Governance Series) Number 50. Lancaster: Department of Sociology, Lancaster University.
Jessop, B. (1997) 'A neo-Gramscian approach to the regulation of urban regimes', in *Reconstructing Urban Regime Theory: Regulating Urban Politics in a Global Economy* (ed) M. Lauria, pp. 51–73. London: Sage.
Jessop, B. (1998) 'The rise of governance and the risks of failure: the case of economic development', *International Social Science Journal* 155: 29–45.
Jessop, B. (1999) 'Globalisation and the national state', in *Rethinking the*

State: Miliband, Poulantzas and State Theory (eds) S. Aaronowitz and P. Bratsis, pp. 185–219. Minneapolis: University of Minnesota Press.

Jessop, B. (2001a) 'Institutional (re)turns and the strategic-relational approach', *Environment and Planning A* 33: 1213–35.

Jessop, B. (2001b) 'Multi-level governance and multi-level meta-governance', mimeograph. Lancaster: Department of Sociology, Lancaster University.

Jessop, B. (2002) *The Future of the Capitalist State*. Cambridge: Polity.

Jessop, B. (2008) *State Power: A Strategic-Relational Approach*. Cambridge: Polity.

Jessop, B. (2009) 'Avoiding traps, rescaling states, governing Europe', in *The New Political Economy of Scale* (eds) R. Keil and R. Mahon, pp. 87–104. Vancouver, B.C.: University of British Columbia Press.

Jessop, B. (2012) *The State*. Cambridge: Polity.

Jessop, B., Brenner, N. and Jones, M. (2008) 'Theorizing sociospatial relations', *Environment and Planning D: Society and Space* 26: 389–401.

John, P. (2000) 'The Europeanisation of sub-national governance', *Urban Studies* 37: 877–94.

Jones, A. and Clark, J. (2001) *The Modalities of European Union Governance: New Institutionalist Explanations of Agri-Environmental Policy*. Oxford: Oxford University Press.

Jones, M. (1997) 'Spatial selectivity of the state? The regulationist enigma and local struggles over economic governance', *Environment and Planning A* 29: 831–64.

Jones, M. (1999) *New Institutional Spaces: Training and Enterprise Councils and the Remaking of Economic Governance*. London: Routledge.

Jones, M. (2001) 'The rise of the regional state in economic governance: "Partnerships for prosperity" or new scales of state power?', *Environment and Planning A* 33: 1185–211.

Jones, M. (2003) 'Critical realism, critical discourse analysis, concrete research', in *Realism, Discourse and Deconstruction* (eds) J. Roberts and J. Joseph, pp. 43–67. London: Routledge.

Jones, M. (2007) 'Regional initiatives and responses', in *Companion Encyclopaedia to Geography: From Local to Global* (eds) I. Douglas, R. Huggett and C. Perkins, pp. 313–25. London: Routledge.

Jones, M. (2008) 'Recovering a sense of political economy', *Political Geography* 27: 377–99.

Jones, M. (2009) 'Phase space: geography, relational thinking, and beyond', *Progress in Human Geography* 33: 487–506.

Jones, M. (2010) 'Impedimenta state: anatomies of neoliberal penality', *Criminology and Criminal Justice* 10: 393–404.

Jones, M. and Jessop, B. (2010) 'Thinking state/space incompossibly', *Antipode* 42: 1119–49.

Jones, M. and Jones, R. (2004) 'Nation states, ideological power and globalisation: can geographers catch the boat?', *Geoforum* 25: 409–24.

Jones, M. and MacLeod, G. (2002) 'Regional tensions: constructing institutional cohesion?', in *City of Revolution: Restructuring Manchester* (eds) J. Peck and K. Ward, pp. 176–89. Manchester: Manchester University Press.

Jones, M. and MacLeod, G. (2004) 'Regional spaces, spaces of regionalism: territory, insurgent politics and the English question', *Transactions of the Institute of British Geographers* 29: 433–52.

Jones, R. (2001) 'Institutional identities and the shifting scales of state governance in the United Kingdom', *European Urban and Regional Studies* 8: 283–96.

Jones, R. (2007) *People/States/Territories: The Political Geographies of British State Transformation*. Oxford: Blackwell.

Jones, R., Goodwin, M., Jones, M. and Pett, K. (2005) 'Filling in the state: economic governance and the evolution of devolution in Wales', *Environment and Planning C: Government and Policy* 23: 337–60.

Jones, R., Goodwin, M., Jones, M. and Simpson, G. (2004) 'Devolution, state personnel and the production of new territories of governance in the UK', *Environment and Planning A* 36: 89–109.

Keating, M. (1998) *The New Regionalism in Western Europe: Territorial Restructuring and Political Change*. Cheltenham: Edward Elgar.

Keating, M. (2002) 'Devolution and public policy in the United Kingdom: divergence or convergence?', in *Devolution in Practice: Public Policy Difference in the UK* (eds) J. Adams and P. Robinson, pp. 3–21. London: IPPR/ESRC.

Keating, M. (2005) 'Policy convergence and divergence in Scotland under devolution', *Regional Studies* 39: 453–63.

Keating, M., Loughlin, J. and Descouwer, K. (2003) *Culture, Institutions and Economic Development*. Cheltenham: Edward Elgar.

Kiel, R. and Mahan, R. (2009) *The New Political Economy of Scale*. Vancouver, B.C.: University of British Columbia Press.

Kooiman, J. (ed) (2003) *Modern Governance: New Government-Society Interactions*. London: Sage.

Laffin, M. and Thomas, A. (2001) 'New ways of working: political-official relations in the National Assembly for Wales', *Public Money and Management* April–June: 45–51.

Laver, M. (2000) 'Coalitions in Northern Ireland: preliminary thoughts', paper presented at the Democratic Dialogue Round Table in Belfast,

Governing with Consensus? The Programme for Government, 20 September 2000.

Lawson, T. (2003) *Reorienting Economics*. London: Routledge.

Lee, S. and Woodward, R. (2002) 'Implementing the Third Way: the delivery of public services under the Blair government', *Public Money and Management* October–December: 49–56.

Lefebvre, H. (1991) *The Production of Space*. Oxford: Blackwell.

Lefebvre, H. (2003) 'Space and the state', in *State/Space: A Reader* (eds) N. Brenner, B. Jessop, M. Jones and G. MacLeod, pp. 84–100. Oxford: Blackwell.

Ling, T. (2002) 'Delivering joined-up government in the UK: dimension, issues and problems', *Public Administration* 80: 615–42.

Lovering, J. (1999) 'Theory led by policy: The inadequacies of the "new regionalism" (illustrated from the case of Wales)', *International Journal of Urban and Regional Research* 23: 379–95.

Lynch, P. (2001) *Scottish Government and Politics: An Introduction*. Edinburgh: Edinburgh University Press.

MacLeod, G. (1996) 'The cult of enterprise in a networked, learning region? Governing business and skills in lowland Scotland', *Regional Studies* 30: 749–55.

MacLeod, G. (2001a) 'Beyond soft institutionalism: accumulation, regulation, and their geographical fixes', *Environment and Planning A* 33: 1145–67.

MacLeod, G. (2001b) 'New regionalism reconsidered: globalization and the remaking of political economic space', *International Journal of Urban and Regional Research* 25: 804–29.

MacLeod, G. and Goodwin, M. (1999a) 'Space, scale and state strategy: rethinking urban and regional governance', *Progress in Human Geography* 23: 503–27.

MacLeod, G. and Goodwin, M. (1999b) 'Reconstructing an urban and regional political economy: on the state, politics, scale and explanation', *Political Geography* 18: 697–730.

Mann, M. (1984) 'The autonomous power of the state: its origins, mechanisms and results', *European Journal of Sociology* 25: 185–213.

Mann, M. (1986) *The Sources of Social Power vol. 1, From the Beginning to AD 1760*. Cambridge: Cambridge University Press.

Mansfield, B. (2005) 'Beyond rescaling: reintegrating the "national" as a dimension of scalar relations', *Progress in Human Geography* 29: 458–73.

Marks, G. (1996) 'An actor-centred approach to multilevel governance', *Regional and Federal Studies* 6: 20–40.

Marr, A. (2000) *The Day Britain Died*. London: Profile Books.

Marston, S.A., Jones III, J.P. and Woodward, K. (2005) 'Human geography without scale', *Transactions of the Institute of British Geographers* 30: 416–32.

Mawson, J. (1998) 'The English regional debate: towards regional governance or government?', in *British Regionalism and Devolution: The Challenges of State Reform and European Integration* (eds) J. Bradbury and J. Mawson, pp. 180–211. London: Jessica Kingsley.

Mawson, J. and Spencer, K. (1997) 'The government offices for the English regions: towards regional governance?', *Policy and Politics* 25: 71–84.

McCarthy, J. and Newlands, D. (1999) 'An economic and spatial policy agenda for the Scottish Parliament', *Regional Studies* 33: 891–5.

McGregor, P.G. and Swales, K. (2005) 'Economics of devolution/decentralisation in the UK: some questions and answers', *Regional Studies* 39: 477–94.

Miliband, R. (1968) *The State in Capitalist Society*. London: Weidenfeld and Nicolson.

Miliband, R. (1983) 'State power and class interest', *Monthly Review* 138: 37–68.

Mitchell, J. (2001) 'Scotland: maturing devolution', in *The State of the Nations 2001* (ed) A. Trench, pp. 45–76. Exeter: Imprint Academic.

Mitchell, J. (2003) *Governing Scotland: The Invention of Administrative Devolution*. Basingstoke: Macmillan.

Mitchell, T. (2006) 'Society, economy and the state effect', in *The Anthropology of the State: A Reader* (eds) A. Sharma and A. Gupta, pp. 169–86. Oxford: Blackwell.

Morgan, K. (2004) 'Bonfire of the quangos: the missing debate', *Agenda*, November Issue.

Morgan, K. and Mungham, G. (2000) *Redesigning Democracy*. Bridgend: Seren.

Morgan, K. and Rees, G. (2001) 'Learning by doing: devolution and the governance of economic development in Wales', in *New Governance, New Democracy? Post Devolution Wales* (eds) P. Chaney, T. Hall and A. Pithouse, pp. 126–71. Cariff: University of Wales Press.

Munck, R. and Hamilton, D. (1998) 'Politics, the economy and peace in Northern Ireland', in *Rethinking Northern Ireland: Culture, Ideology and Colonialism* (ed) D. Miller, pp. 146–59. London: Longman.

Musson, S., Tickell, A. and John, P. (2003) 'A decentralized state? Power, control and responsibility in English devolution', paper presented to the Association of American Geographers Annual Conference, New Orleans:

copy available from S. Musson, Geography and Environmental Science, University of Reading.
NAfW (2001) *Review of Business Support and Development Services*. Cardiff: National Assembly for Wales.
NAfW (2002) *The National Economic Development Strategy*. Cardiff: National Assembly for Wales.
Nairn, T. (2000) *After Britain: New Labour and the Return of Scotland*. London: Granta Books.
Nairn, T. (2002) *Pariah: The Misfortunes of the British Kingdom*. London: Verso.
Nash, F. (2002) 'Devolution dominoes', *The Times Higher Education Supplement*, 1 February: 30.
Needham, C. (2005) 'Brand leaders: Clinton, Blair and the limitations of the permanent campaign', *Political Studies* 53: 343–61.
New Ireland Forum (1984) *Report*. Dublin: Stationery Office.
New Labour's Regional Policy Commission (1996) *Renewing the Regions: Strategies for Regional Economic Development*. Sheffield: PAVIC Publications, Sheffield Hallam University.
NIA (2001) *New Targeting Social Need Research Paper*. Belfast: Northern Ireland Assembly.
NIDED (1990) *Competing in the 1990s*. Belfast: Northern Ireland Department of Economic Development.
NIDED (1999) *Strategy 2010: Report by the Northern Ireland Economic Development Strategy Review Steering Group*. Belfast: Northern Ireland Department of Economic Development.
NIDRD (2001) *Shaping our Future: Regional Development Strategy for Northern Ireland 2025*. Belfast: Northern Ireland Department for Regional Development.
NIEC (1999a) *A Step-change in Performance: A Response to Strategy 2010*. Belfast: Northern Ireland Economic Council.
NIEC (1999b) *The Implementation of Northern Ireland's Economic Development Strategy in the 1990s: Lessons for the Future*. Belfast: Northern Ireland Economic Council.
NIEC (2001) *Developing a Regional Innovation Strategy for Northern Ireland: A Statement by the Economic Council on Research Conducted by Philip Cooke, Stephen Roper and Peter Wylie*. Belfast: Northern Ireland Economic Council.
Northern Ireland Civil Service (2002) *Review of the Northern Ireland Civil Service Response to Devolution*. Belfast: Northern Ireland Civil Service.
Northern Ireland Executive (2001) *Draft Programme for Government*. Belfast: Northern Ireland Executive.

Northern Ireland Executive (2002) *Second Programme for Government*. Belfast: Northern Ireland Executive.

ODPM (2005) *Realising the Potential of All Our Regions: The Story So Far*. London: Office of the Deputy Prime Minister.

Offe, C. (1974) 'Structural problems of the capitalist state', *German Political Studies* 1: 31–57.

Offe, C. (1984) *The Contradictions of the Welfare State*. London: Hutchinson.

Osmond, J. (1977) *Creative Conflict: The Politics of Welsh Devolution*. Llandysul: Gomer Press.

Osmond, J. (2004) 'Wales Quarterly Report: August 2004', in *Nations and Regions: The Dynamics of Devolution*. London: UCL Constitution Unit.

Paasi, A. (1991) 'Deconstructing regions: notes on the scales of spatial life', *Environment and Planning A* 23: 239–56.

Paasi, A. (2002) 'Bounded space in the mobile world: deconstructing "regional identity"', *Tijdschrift voor Economische en Sociale Geografie* 93: 137–48.

Painter, J. (2006) 'Prosaic geographies of stateness', *Political Geography* 25: 752–74.

Parry, R. (2001) 'The role of central units in the Scottish Executive', *Public Money and Management* April–June: 39–44.

Parry, R. and Jones, A. (2000) 'The transition from the Scottish Office to the Scottish Executive', *Public Policy and Administration* 15: 53–66.

Peck, J. (1998) 'Geographies of governance: TECs and the neo-liberalization of "local interests"', *Space and Polity* 2: 5–31.

Peck, J. (2001) 'Neoliberalizing states: thin policies/hard outcomes', *Progress in Human Geography* 25: 445–55.

Peck, J. and Jones, M. (1995) 'Training and enterprise councils: Schumpeterian workfare state, or what?', *Environment and Planning A* 27: 1361–96.

Pemberton, S. and Goodwin, M. (2010) 'Rethinking the changing structures of rural local government: state power, rural politics and local political strategies?', *Journal of Rural Studies* 26: 272–83.

Pierre, J. and Stoker, G. (2000) 'Towards multi-level governance', in *Developments in British Politics 6* (eds) P. Dunleavy, A. Gamble, I. Holliday and G. Peele, pp. 29–46. London: Macmillan.

Pike, A. and Tomaney, J. (2009) 'The state and uneven development: the governance of economic development in England in the post-devolution UK', *Cambridge Journal of Regions, Economy and Society* 2: 13–34.

PIU (1999) *InterTradeIreland Corporate Plan 2002–2004*. London: HMSO.

Poulantzas, N. (1969) *Political Power and Social Classes*. London: New Left Books.
Poulantzas, N. (1978) *State, Power, Socialism*. London: New Left Books.
Pugalis, L. (2011) 'The regional lacuna: a preliminary map of the transition from regional development agencies to local economic partnerships', *Regions* 281: 6–9.
Pugalis, L. and Townsend, A. (2010) 'Can LEPs fill the strategic void?', *Town and Country Planning* 79: 382–7.
Pyper, R. (1995) *The British Civil Service*. London: Prentice-Hall.
Raco, M. (2003) 'Governmentality, subject-building, and the discourses and practices of devolution in the UK', *Transactions of the Institute of British Geographers* 28: 75–95.
RCU (2001) *Reaching Out: Action Plan*. London: Regional Co-ordination Unit, Cabinet Office.
Rees, G. (2002) 'Devolution and the restructuring of post-16 education and training in the UK', in *Devolution in Practice: Public Policy Differences Within the UK* (eds) J. Adams and P. Robinson, pp. 104–14. London: IPPR.
Regional and Federal Studies (2010) 'Studying regions as "spaces for politics": territory, mobilization and political change', *Regional and Federal Studies* 20: 281–430.
Rentoul, J. (1996) *Tony Blair*. London: Little, Brown and Company.
Rhodes, R.A.W. (1994) 'The hollowing out of the state: the changing nature of public services in Britain', *The Political Quarterly* 65: 138–51.
Rhodes, R.A.W. (1997) *Understanding Governance: Policy Networks, Governance, Reflexivity and Accountability*. Buckingham: Open University Press.
Ridderstråle, J. and Nordström, K. (2003) *Karaoke Capitalism: Management for Mankind*. Stockholm: Bookhouse Publishing.
Robson, B., Peck, J. and Holden, A. (2000) *Regional Agencies and Area-based Regeneration*. Bristol: Policy Press.
Roche, P.J. and Birnie, J. (1995) *An Economics Lesson for Irish Nationalists and Republicans*. Belfast: Ulster Unionist Information Institute.
Rodríguez-Pose, A. and Bwire, A. (2004) 'The economic (in)efficiency of devolution', *Environment and Planning A* 36: 1907–28.
Rodríguez-Pose, A. and Gill, N. (2003) 'The global trend towards devolution and its implications', *Environment and Planning C: Government and Policy* 21: 333–51.
Rodríguez-Pose, A. and Gill, N. (2004) 'Is there a link between regional disparities and devolution?', *Environment and Planning A* 36: 2097–117.

Rodríguez-Pose, A. and Gill, N. (2005) 'On the "economic dividend" of devolution", *Regional Studies* 39: 405–20.

Rose, N. (1996) 'Governing "advanced" liberal democracies', in *Foucault and Political Reason: Liberalism, Neo-liberalism and Rationalities of Government* (eds) A. Barry, T. Osborne and N. Rose, pp. 37–64. London: University College of London Press.

Scharpf, F.W. (1997) 'The problem-solving capacity of multi-level governance', *Journal of European Public Policy* 4: 520–38.

Scharpf, F.W. (1999) *Governing in Europe: Effective and Democratic?* Oxford: Oxford University Press.

Scott, A.J. (ed) (2001) *Global City-Regions: Trends, Theory, Policy*. Oxford: Oxford University Press.

Scott, A.J. and Storper, M. (2003) 'Regions, globalization, development', *Regional Studies* 37: 579–93.

Scottish Enterprise (2007) *Scottish Enterprise Operating Plan 2007–2010*. Glasgow: Scottish Enterprise.

Scottish Enterprise (2010) *Scottish Enterprise Business Plan 2011–14*. Glasgow: Scottish Enterprise.

Scottish Executive (2000a) *Response to the Final Report of the Enterprise and Lifelong Learning Committee Inquiry into the Delivery of Local Economic Development Services in Scotland*. Edinburgh: Enterprise and Lifelong Learning Department, Scottish Executive.

Scottish Executive (2000b) *Enterprise Networks Review: Issues Paper*. Edinburgh: Enterprise and Lifelong Learning Department, Scottish Executive.

Scottish Executive (2000c) *The Way Forward: Framework for Economic Development in Scotland*. Edinburgh: Enterprise and Lifelong Learning Department, Scottish Executive.

Scottish Executive (2001a) *A Smart, Successful Scotland: Ambitions for the Enterprise Networks*. Edinburgh: Enterprise and Lifelong Learning Department, Scottish Executive.

Scottish Executive (2004) *The Way Forward: Framework for Economic Development in Scotland (FEDS) Update*. Edinburgh: Enterprise and Lifelong Learning Department, Scottish Executive.

Scully, R., Jones, R.W. and Trystan, D. (2004) 'Turnout, participation and legitimacy in post-devolution Wales', *British Journal of Political Science* 34: 519–37.

Shaw, K. and MacKinnon, D. (2011) 'Moving on with "filling in"? Some thoughts on state restructuring after devolution', *Area* 43: 23–30.

Shipton, M. (2010) 'Revealed: shocking growth in number of Welsh civil servants', *Western Mail*, 17 July: 1–2.

Shuttleworth, I., Tyler, P. and McKinstry, D. (2005) 'Redundancy, readjustment and employability: what can we learn from the 2000 Harland & Wolff redundancy?', *Environment and Planning A* 37: 1651–68.

Soja, E. (1989) *Postmodern Geographies*. Oxford: Blackwell.

Soja, E. (1996) *Thirdspace*. Oxford: Blackwell.

Speed, N. (2000a) 'Has Plaid well and truly arrived?', *The Western Mail*, 10 February: 12–13.

Speed, N. (2000b) 'Parachute's crash-landing humiliates Blair', *The Western Mail*, 10 February: 1.

Storer, A. and Cole, A. (2002) 'Politics as normal: the Economic Development Committee', in *Building a Civic Culture: Institutional Change, Policy Development and Political Dynamics in the National Assembly for Wales* (eds) J.B. Jones and J. Osmond, pp. 113–24. Cardiff: Institute of Welsh Affairs.

Storper, M. (1997) *The Regional World: Territorial Development in a Global Economy*. New York: Guilford Press.

Storper, M. and Salais, R. (1997) *Worlds of Production: The Action Frameworks of the Economy*. London: Harvard University Press.

Swyngedouw, E. (1996) 'Reconstructing citizenship, the re-scaling of the state and the new authoritarianism: closing the Belgian mines', *Urban Studies* 33: 1499–521.

Swyngedouw, E. (2000) 'Authoritarian governance, power, and the politics of rescaling', *Environment and Planning D: Society and Space* 18: 63–76.

Taxpayers' Alliance (2009) 'The case for abolishing Regional Development Agencies', Structure of Government Report no. 3. London: Taxpayers' Alliance.

Taylor, P. (1993) 'The meaning of the north: England's "foreign country" within?', *Political Geography* 12: 136–55.

Tewdwr-Jones, M. and Allmendinger, P. (eds) (2006) *Territory, Identity and Spatial Planning*. London: Routledge.

Thompson, G., Frances, J., Levačić, R. and Mitchell, J. (eds) (1991) *Markets, Hierarchies and Networks: The Coordination of Social Life*. London: Sage.

Thrift, N. (2005) *Knowing Capitalism*. London: Sage.

Tiesdell, S. and Allmendinger, P. (2001) 'Neighbourhood regeneration and New Labour's third way', *Environment and Planning C: Government and Policy* 19: 903–26.

Tomaney, J. (2002) 'The evolution of English regional governance', *Regional Studies* 36: 721–31.

Tomaney, J. and Mawson, J. (eds) (2002) *England: The State of the Regions*. Bristol: Policy Press.

Townroe, P. and Martin, R. (1992) *Regional Development in the 1990s: The*

British Isles in Transition. London: Jessica Kingsley.
Treasury (2010) *Emergency Budget Report*. London: Treasury.
Treasury, BERR and DCLG (2007) *Review of Sub-national Economic Development and Regeneration*. London: Treasury, Department for Business, Enterprise and Regulatory Reform and the Department for Communities and Local Government.
Uitermark, J. (2002) 'Re-scaling, "scale fragmentation" and the regulation of antagonistic relationships', *Progress in Human Geography* 26: 743–65.
WAG (2002) *A Winning Wales: The National Economic Development Strategy of the Welsh Assembly Government*. Cardiff: Welsh Assembly Government.
WAG (2004) *People, Places, Futures: The Wales Spatial Plan*. Cardiff: Welsh Assembly Government.
WAG (2005) *Wales: A Vibrant Economy*. Cardiff: Welsh Assembly Government.
WAG (2008) *People, Places, Futures: The Wales Spatial Plan 2008 Update*. Cardiff: Welsh Assembly Government.
Walker, D. (2002) *In Praise of Centralism: A Critique of the New Localism*. London: Catalyst.
WDA (2001) *Welsh Development Agency Corporate Plan, 2001–2004*. Cardiff: Welsh Development Agency.
Weber, M. (1947) *The Theory of Economic and Social Organization*. London: Free Press.
While, A., Jonas, A.E.G. and Gibbs, D. (2004) 'The environment and the entrepreneurial city: searching for the urban "sustainability fix" in Manchester and Leeds', *International Journal of Urban and Regional Research* 28: 549–69.
Whitehead, M. (2003) ' "In the shadow of hierarchy": meta-governance, policy reform and urban regeneration in the West Midlands', *Area* 35: 6–14.
Whiteside, N. and Salais, R. (eds) (1998) *Governance, Industry and Labour Markets in Britain and France: The Modernising State in the Mid-Twentieth Century*. London: Routledge.
Wilford, R. and Wilson, R. (2000) 'A "bare-knuckle" ride: Northern Ireland', in *The State and the Nations: The First Year of Devolution in the United Kingdom* (ed) R. Hazell, pp. 79–115. Exeter: Imprint Academic.
Wilson, R. and Wilford, R. (2001a) 'Northern Ireland: Endgame', in *The State of the Nations 2001: The Second Year of Devolution in the United Kingdom* (ed) A. Trench, pp. 77–105. Exeter: Imprint Academic.
Wilson, R. and Wilford, R. (2001b) *A Democratic Design? The Political Style of the Northern Ireland Assembly*. London: Constitution Unit.

Index

A Review of Sub-National Economic Development and Regeneration 149
A Smart Successful Scotland 58–60, 83–6
A Winning Wales (NEDS) 55–7, 69
Act of Union (1707) 26
after-Fordism 15
agency-centred approach 90
Agnew, J. 94, 114
Amin, A. 94, 107
anthropology of the state 89, 118, 160
architectures of economic governance 155–6
Assembly Sponsored Public Body (ASPB) 42
asymetrical devolution 10, 24, 29–30, 60, 68, 148

Birnie, E. 125, 136
Blacksell, M. 65
Blair, T. (Prime Minister UK) 2, 6, 26, 48, 95, 97
Bogdanor, V. 2
bonfire of the quangos 43
boosterism 15
Bradbury, J. 13
Bratsis, P. 89
Brenner, N. 14, 17, 27, 65–7, 120, 122, 147, 159
Brown, G. (Prime Minister UK) 49

Business Birth Rate Strategy 142
Business Connect 42

Callinicos, A. 3
capitalist state 5, 15, 17, 91
  peopled 91–2
city-regions 150, 152
civil service reforms 95
Coalition Government (of Conservative & Liberal Parties) 51, 116, 149–51
Coates, D. 4
collaboration and competition 51, 112, 119, 122, 128–31, 134, 136, 142
collaboration between DEL & INI 134, 143
Community Consortia for Education & Training (CCETs) 72–4
Competing in the 1990s (Economic Development Strategy NI) 135
competitive region 63
Cooke, P. 6, 12, 48
Corbridge, S. 118, 121

Davies, A. (Min. Economic Development) 57
Davies, R. 6, 148
denationalisation 18
Department for Education & Skills (DfES) 49
Department for Education, Lifelong Learning & Skills 43

Department for Enterprise & Regulatory Reform 49
Department for Enterprise, Innovation & Networks 43
Department for Innovation, Universities & Skills (DIUS) 49
Department for Transport, Local Government & the Regions (DTLR) 49
Department for Work & Pensions (DWP) 49
Department for Communities & Local Government (DCLG) 49, 151
Department of Economic Development (DED) 36–7
Department of Employment & Learning (DEL) 37–9, 126–34, 136, 147
Department of Enterprise, Trade & Investment (DETINI) 37–8, 54–5, 126–34, 142, 146–7, 154
Department of Regional Development 138
Department of Trade & Industry (DTI) 49
dependency culture 53, 124
de-statisation 17–19, 92–3
and DETINI/INI 127, 133, 147
Destination 2010 (EMDA RES) 63
Development Board for Rural Wales (DBRW) 33, 42
devolution 4–7, 28–30, 48
and constitutional change 5–7, 30–1
and Constitutional Change Research Programme (ESRC) 3, 5
and decentralisation 4, 81, 156
and economic governance 4–5, 147
and rescaling 67, 158–9
and 'third way' 4, 107–8
as political process 8, 148
asymmetrical 10, 24, 29–30, 60

Referendums 28, 152
devolution in Northern Ireland 123–6
devolution settlement 26–30, 67–9
devolved state organisations 120–1, 160
Dewar, D. (First Minister Scotland) 97
Dicken, P. 15
direct rule 32

East Midlands Development Agency (EMDA) 51, 62–4, 76–81, 98, 102, 150
and state personnel 100, 102
East Midlands Region 76, 108
East Midlands Regional Economic Strategy 62–4
East Midlands Regional Government Association (EMRA) 77–80, 108–9
economic clusters 32
economic development 7, 31, 68, 149, 151, 153
in Northern Ireland 128–30
post-devolution strategies of 52–64
Economic Development Forum (EDF) Northern Ireland 38, 128, 154, 158
dissolution 154–5
economic governance 3–4, 18, 34–88, 153
institutional structures of 34–52
of England 47–52, 152
of Northern Ireland 34–9, 126–38
of Scotland 44–7
of UK 30–64, 149
of Wales 39–44, 153
organisations of 23, 73, 89, 95–103, 108, 119–24, 147–8, 152–9
re-statisation of 44, 47
structures of 31–4, 76, 86
Economic Vision for Northern Ireland 54

INDEX

Education & Learning Wales (ELWa) 8, 40, 42–3, 57, 69–74, 100–11, 152, 158
  and state personnel 99, 101–6
  merger 42–3, 73, 106, 111, 152–3, 156
  National Council 69–71, 100, 103–6
Education & Lifelong Learning Department (ELLD) 44
Education & Training Action Group (ETAG) 40
effective capacity to act 122
Empey, R. (Min. Enterprise, Northern Ireland) 128, 133, 141
England, economic governance structures 47, 60–4, 74–81, 149–52
England, Regional Assemblies 29
England, UK relations pre-devolution 31
Enterprise & Lifelong Learning Committee (ELLC) 44
Enterprise Networks 44–6, 58, 84–6
ESRC 3,5
Essex, S. Min. for Finance 43, 114
European Regional Development Funds (ERDF) 49

Farren, S. (Min. Education, Northern Ireland) 141
filling in 13, 19–21, 24–5, 44, 72, 88–9, 92–3, 120–2, 136–47, 157–60
  of economic governance in NI 130–6
  of peopled state 117, 119, 142
  post-devolution 34–52, 70, 72, 87, 105, 157
First Steps programme 95

Giddens, A. 4, 90
Gillespie, A. 32–3
Globalisation 13, 15, 18
  and rescaling 67, 159
  and the region 47–8, 107

Good Friday Agreement 37
Goodwin, M. 3, 9, 13, 20, 22, 67, 93
Governance 18
  and state personnel 107–12
governance (economic), scales and territories of 49, 51, 67–89, 93, 103, 119, 136–41, 150, 158–60
Government of Wales Act (2006) 29
Government Office for the East Midlands (GOEM) 77–8, 109–15, 151
Government Offices for the Regions 48, 74–8, 151–2
Greater London Assembly (GLA) 26, 29, 48, 68

Haughton, G. 3
Hay, C. 91
Heffernan, R. 88
Highlands & Enterprise (HIE) 32, 44–7, 81–5, 98, 106, 153–4
Highlands & Islands Development Board (HIDB) 32
hollowing out 13, 18–21, 24, 29–30, 92, 158–61
  and devolution 19, 81, 158–9
horizontal integration 80
Hutton, W. 125

impedimenta state 156
Independent Review of Economic Policy (NI) 154
Industrial Development Board (IDB) 135, 143
Industrial Research & Technology Unit (IRTU) 135, 143
informal relationships 108–9
Ingram, A. 36, 38
institutional 3–9, 13, 17, 21
institutions, and collaboration and competition 11, 51, 108
instrumentalism 91–2
Integrated Regional Strategy for East Midlands (IRS) 62, 78–81, 108
internationalisation 18–20

InterTradeIreland 125, 137
Invest Northern Ireland (INI) 8, 37, 127, 130–6, 138–47, 154–5
inward investment 33, 69, 130, 140, 155

Jeffery, C. 5–7, 10, 12–13
Jessop, B. 13, 16–24, 27, 29, 43, 64, 66–7, 73, 92–4, 106, 122, 126, 147, 151
joined-up governance 89, 107–12, 143
Joint Performance Team (JPT) 85–6
Jones, M. 9, 13, 15–16, 23, 51, 66, 93, 114, 141, 146, 150, 153
Jones, R. 9, 13, 15, 51, 89, 91, 112, 118

karaoke capitalism 4
Keating, M 3, 15, 28, 31, 68

Labour Party 2, 26, 95, 97, 149
 in Wales 97–8, 115–16
Land Authority for Wales 42
Learn Direct 134
Learning & Skills Act (2000) 69
Learning & Skills Councils (LSCs) 49–51, 77, 80, 101
Lefebvre, H. 93–4, 118
Local Economic Forums (LEF) 8, 44, 46, 85–6, 108, 111, 153–6
Local Enterprise Companies (LECs) 32, 46–7, 82–7, 106–8, 153–6
Local Enterprise Development Unit (LEDU) 33, 135, 138–9, 143–5, 147
Local Enterprise Partnerships (LEPS) 150–2
localism 150–2
localities 151–2
London 28, 61, 151
London Development Agency 48

MacKinnon, D. 13–14, 20
McLeish, H. (First Minister Scotland) 97
MacLeod, G. 16, 32, 47, 67, 140

Mann, M. 13, 90
Mapp, D. 77
Medium Term Strategic Priorities (MTSP – Northern Ireland) 129
metagovernance 20, 133
Michael, A. (First Minister Wales) 97–8
Milliband, R. 91–2
Mitchell, J. 96–7, 113
Mitchell, T. 118
Morgan, K. 33, 42, 44, 47, 72, 103, 115–16
Morgan, R. (First Minister Wales) 39–40, 43, 57, 98, 114
multilevel governance (MLG) 9, 15–16, 24, 78, 157

Nash, F. 13
National Assembly for Wales (NAfW) 2, 26, 29, 33, 40, 68, 98, 110
 Regional Committees 70–1
neoliberalism 4, 152, 157
neo-Marxist state theory 17, 89, 91, 158
networks 68, 159
networks, scale and territory 159
New Labour 26, 28, 48–9, 74, 76, 107
new localism 150–1
new regionalism 9, 15–16, 107
new state spaces 14, 65–6, 68
new state territories 93–4, 103–7, 118
Non-Departmental Public Body (NDPB) 130–3, 144, 146
norms 16, 90, 107
Northern Ireland 26, 28, 34–9, 52–5, 119–47, 154–5
 economy of 124–5
 UK relations pre-devolution 32–3
Northern Ireland Assembly (NIA) 26, 29, 68, 124, 141, 154
 suspension 29, 33, 36, 123–4
Northern Ireland Economic Council (NIEC) 33, 135

INDEX

Northern Ireland Office 29, 32–3

Offe, C. 22
Office of the Deputy Prime Minister (ODPM) 49, 76
Operational Plan (ELWa) 103
organisational culture 96, 99–100, 102, 143
over-centralised state 151

Paasi, A. 112
path-dependency 27, 33
Peck, J. 20–1, 27, 92–3, 117
peopling economic governance 141–6
peopling of government 115–16
Pickles, E. (Min. for Communities & Local Govt.) 151
Plaid Cymru 116
policy development process 131–2
Poulantzas, N. 20, 91–2
process-oriented analysis 27
Programmes for Government (Northern Ireland) 36
Prosperity through People 62

reflexive capitalism 4
region and globalisation 47, 107
Regional Action Plans (NI) 55
Regional Assemblies (England) 29, 48–9, 150–2, 156
Regional Development Agencies 29, 47–52, 60–4, 68, 74–81, 99, 149–50
 abolition of 51, 149–52, 156
Regional Development Agencies Act (1998) 48, 60
Regional Economic Strategies (RESs) 60–4, 76–7
regional identity 76, 112, 114
regional policy and New Labour 6–7
Regional Policy Commission 74
regional rhythms 73, 106
regional scale 71, 74, 103, 106, 138, 149
regional tensions 51, 72, 105–6, 114–15, 138–9
regional territorialisation 73–4
regionalisation within Northern Ireland 139–40
regionalism 9, 15–16, 140, 156–7
relational space 159–60
remit letter 43, 110
representations of space 93
Republic of Ireland 125, 136
rescaling of economic governance 10, 24, 68, 158–9
rescaling of the state 10, 16, 21, 24, 65–7, 81, 150
research design 8–9
reserved powers 28
re-statisation 44, 47, 114–15, 127, 153, 156
 and DEL/T&EA 127, 133–4, 147
restructuring the state 3, 8–10, 15–17, 20–4, 34, 65–6, 157
reterritorialisation 67, 150
Rhodes, R.A.W. 3, 18

scalar architectures 19, 34, 67, 87, 149, 155
scalar differentiation 70, 122, 159
scalar materiality 73
scalar stretching 137–8, 154
scale 9, 16, 24, 49, 67, 73
 political economies of 15–16
scales of identity 114
Schumpeterian Workfare Post-National Regime (SWPR) 17
Scotland 26, 28, 58–60, 81–6, 96–7, 111, 153
 UK relations pre-devolution 31–2
Scottish Development Agency (SDA) 32, 81
Scottish Development International 47
Scottish Enterprise (SE) 32, 44–7, 81–7, 153–5
Scottish Executive 44, 58, 84–6, 97
Scottish National Party (SNP) 97, 116

Scottish Office 32, 44
Scottish Parliament 26, 29, 68, 97, 113
'*Scottishness*' of civil service 113–14
Sector Skills Partnerships (SecSPs) 100
Shaw, K. 13–14, 20
single regeneration budget 49
Skills & Employment Action Plan 55
Skills for Scotland 58
spaces of representation 93
spatial fetishism 14
spatial practices 93
state as peopled organisation 21, 88, 92, 94, 112, 117–18, 122, 141–5
state governmentality 118
state organisations, territories & personnel 146–7
state personnel 10, 87–9, 92, 96, 119–21, 160
  and devolved governance 95–6, 102–7, 144
  and economic governance 89, 96–103, 107–12, 116–18
  and leadership 97–9
  and regional identities 112–17, 121
  and SRA 10
  as agents of change 88, 102–3, 160
  as bridging mechanism 96, 107, 111, 141
state projects 64, 90, 118, 120–2
state restructuring 9–10, 15, 21, 24, 26, 34, 157
state space 14, 64–6, 93–4, 121, 160
state spatiality 27
state strategies 9, 17, 21–2, 27, 64, 68, 70, 74, 76, 120, 147, 159
state theory 13–25
Storper, M. 3–4, 47
strategic selectivity of the state 22
strategic-relational approach (SRA) 9, 13, 17–24, 26–7, 92–3, 126, 148–9, 159–60

and actors and structure 121–2
strategic-relational state theory 9, 21–4, 43, 158–60
Strategy 2010 (Northern Ireland) 36–8, 52–5, 135
sustainable communities 62–3
sustainable development 48, 61, 78
  and Wales 153
Swyngedouw, E. 16–17, 67

Taxpayers Alliance 150
Taylor, P. 31
territorial identities 89, 112–13
  and devolution 116
  of state personnel 89, 112–16, 141
territorial politics 31
territorial reach 70
territorial trap 94
territorialisation of governance 67–8, 71, 86–7, 158
territoriality and the state 13–14, 49, 66, 94
territory 67, 73
Thatcher, M. 26
the 'Troubles' 123
The Way Forward: Framework for Economic Development in Scotland (FEDS) 58–60
Thrift, N. 4, 107
Tomaney, J. 81, 99, 112
Training & Employment Agency (T&EA) 33, 38, 127, 135, 143
Training & Enterprise Councils (TECs) 31, 33, 51, 70, 100–1
triple dialectic 93, 146, 161

uneven development 14, 66

vertical integration 80–1, 87

Wales 2, 26, 28, 39, 55–57, 69–74, 97–8, 152–3
  UK relations pre-devolution 33–4
Wales Spatial Plan (WSP) 153

Wales Tourist Board (WTB) 43
Wales: A Vibrant Economy (W:AVE) 57
Walker, D. 6
Weber, M. 89–91, 121
welfare state 15
Welsh Assembly Government (WAG) 57, 73–4, 108–10, 152
Welsh Development Agency (WDA) 33, 42–3, 57, 71, 109
  merger 42–4, 73, 152
Welsh Government (WG) 152–3
Welsh Office 33–4, 70
Westminster Parliament 28–9
Westphalian system 14, 66
Whitehall departments 60, 74, 76
wimbledonisation effect 6